First World War
and Army of Occupation
War Diary
France, Belgium and Germany

5 DIVISION
Divisional Troops
27 Brigade Royal Field Artillery
1 January 1916 - 31 March 1919

WO95/1531/2

The Naval & Military Press Ltd
www.nmarchive.com
Published in association with The National Archives

Published by

The Naval & Military Press Ltd

Unit 10 Ridgewood Industrial Park,

Uckfield, East Sussex,

TN22 5QE England

Tel: +44 (0) 1825 749494

www.naval-military-press.com

www.nmarchive.com

This diary has been reprinted in facsimile from the original. Any imperfections are inevitably reproduced and the quality may fall short of modern type and cartographic standards.

© Crown Copyright

Images reproduced by permission of The National Archives, London, England, 2015.

Contents

Document type	Place/Title	Date From	Date To
Heading	WO95/1531/2		
Heading	5th Division 27th Bde R.F.A. Apr 1918 To 1918 June From Italy		
Heading	5th Divisional Artillery 27th Brigade R.F.A. April 1918		
Heading	War Diary For The Month of April 1918		
War Diary	Ronchi De Campanile	01/04/1918	08/04/1918
War Diary	Hem	08/04/1918	11/04/1918
War Diary	Ourton	11/04/1918	12/04/1918
War Diary	Aire	12/04/1918	13/04/1918
War Diary	Forest of Nieppe (Taiennes)	13/04/1918	23/04/1918
War Diary	Forest of Nieppe	23/04/1918	30/04/1918
Operation(al) Order(s)	Operation Order No. 1 by Lieut-Col. J. Berkley. D.S.O. Commanding 27th. Brigade R.F.A.	09/04/1918	09/04/1918
Operation(al) Order(s)	Operation Order No. 2 by Lieut-Col. J. Berkley. D.S.O. Commanding 27th. Brigade R.F.A.	11/04/1918	11/04/1918
Miscellaneous	Reference Operation Order No. 2 Sent To You This Morning		
Operation(al) Order(s)	Operation Order No. 3 by Lieut. Colonel. J. Berkley D.S.O. Commanding 27th Brigade R.F.A.	11/04/1918	11/04/1918
Miscellaneous	Officer Commanding	14/04/1918	14/04/1918
Miscellaneous	Officer Commanding	16/04/1918	16/04/1918
Miscellaneous	Officer Commanding	17/04/1918	17/04/1918
Miscellaneous	27th Bde R.F.A. (For Information)		
Diagram etc			
Operation(al) Order(s)	Operation Order No. 24418 by Lieut. Col. Berkley D.S.O. Commanding 27th. Brigade R.F.A.	25/04/1918	25/04/1918
Operation(al) Order(s)	Operation Order No. 181	24/04/1918	24/04/1918
Miscellaneous	Reference Operation Order No. 24418	25/04/1918	25/04/1918
Diagram etc	1/20000 36 A NE		
Heading	War Diary of 27th Brigade R.F.A. Fro The Month Ending 31st May 1918		
War Diary	Foret De Nieppe	01/05/1918	13/05/1918
Miscellaneous	5th Divisional Artillery No. HBM/29/1	07/05/1918	07/05/1918
Miscellaneous	Dispositions-5th Divisional Artillery Group	10/05/1918	10/05/1918
Miscellaneous	5th Divisional Artillery Intelligence Summary 6 PM 10/5/18 To 6 PM 11/5/18	11/05/1918	11/05/1918
Miscellaneous	5th Divisional Artillery Intelligence Summary 6 PM 9/5/18 To 6 PM 10/5/18	10/05/1918	10/05/1918
Miscellaneous	5th Divisional Artillery Intelligence Summary 6 PM 8/5/18 To 6 PM 9/5/18	09/05/1918	09/05/1918
Miscellaneous	5th Divisional Artillery Intelligence Summary 6 PM 7/5/18 To 6 PM 8/5/18	08/05/1918	08/05/1918
Miscellaneous	5th Divisional Artillery Intelligence Summary 6 PM 6/5/18 To 6 PM 7/5/18	07/05/1918	07/05/1918
Miscellaneous	Summary of Operation, ETC 6PM 5/5/18 To 6PM 6/5/1918	06/05/1918	06/05/1918
Miscellaneous	Summary of Operation, ETC 6PM 4/5/18 To 6PM 5/5/1918	05/05/1918	05/05/1918
Miscellaneous	Summary of Operation, ETC 6P.M. 3.8.18 To 6 P.M. 4.5.18	04/05/1918	04/05/1918

Type	Description	Date 1	Date 2
Miscellaneous	Summary of Operation, ETC., 6PM 2/5/18 To 6PM 3/5/18	03/05/1918	03/05/1918
Miscellaneous	Summary of Operation, ETC., 6PM 1/5/18 To 6PM 2/5/18	02/05/1918	02/05/1918
Miscellaneous	Summary of Operation, ETC., 6PM 30/4/18 To 6PM 1/5/18		
War Diary	Foret De Nieppe	13/05/1918	16/05/1918
War Diary	Croix Fores De Nieppe	16/05/1918	17/05/1918
War Diary	Maraisse	17/05/1918	20/05/1918
Miscellaneous	Officer Commanding	15/05/1918	15/05/1918
Miscellaneous	Officer Commanding	14/05/1918	14/05/1918
Miscellaneous	5th Divisional Artillery No. HBM/29/2	14/05/1918	14/05/1918
Miscellaneous	5th Divisional Artillery No. HBM/29/3	15/05/1918	15/05/1918
Miscellaneous	Officer Commanding	19/05/1918	19/05/1918
Miscellaneous	5th Divisional Artillery Intelligence Summary 6PM 11/5/18 To 6PM 12/5/18	12/05/1918	12/05/1918
Miscellaneous	5th Divisional Artillery Intelligence Summary 6PM 12/5/18 To 6PM 13/5/18	13/05/1918	13/05/1918
Miscellaneous	5th Divisional Artillery Intelligence Summary 6PM 13/5/18 To 6PM 14/5/18	14/05/1918	14/05/1918
Miscellaneous	5th Divisional Artillery Intelligence Summary 6PM 14/5/18 To 6PM 15/5/18	15/05/1918	15/05/1918
Miscellaneous	5th Divisional Artillery Intelligence Summary 6PM 15/5/18 To 6PM 16/5/18	16/05/1918	16/05/1918
Miscellaneous	5th Divisional Artillery Intelligence Summary 6 P.M 16-5-18 To 6 P.M 17-5-18	17/05/1918	17/05/1918
Miscellaneous	5th Divisional Artillery Intelligence Summary 6 P.M 17-5-18 To 6 P.M 18-5-18	18/05/1918	18/05/1918
Miscellaneous	5th Divisional Artillery Intelligence Summary, 6PM 18/5/18 To 6PM 19/5/18	19/05/1918	19/05/1918
Miscellaneous	Hostile Shelling		
Miscellaneous	5th Divisional Artillery Intelligence Summary 6 P.M 19/5/18 To 6.0 P.M. 20/5/16	20/05/1918	20/05/1918
War Diary	Croix Maraisse	20/05/1918	31/05/1918
Miscellaneous	OC 27 Ade 80 Aty	20/05/1918	20/05/1918
Map	Caudescure		
Miscellaneous	5th Divisional Artillery No. B.M.	20/05/1918	20/05/1918
Miscellaneous	Reference Attached 5th D.A. Operation Order No. 175	18/05/1918	18/05/1918
Miscellaneous	Reference Attached Order	18/05/1918	18/05/1918
Operation(al) Order(s)	5th Divisional Artillery Order No. 175 by Brig-Gen. A.H. Hussey, C.B., C.M.G. Commanding 5th Divisional Artillery	18/05/1918	18/05/1918
Miscellaneous	27th Bde. No. BM/203	20/05/1918	20/05/1918
Miscellaneous	Officer Commanding, Battery R.F.A.	22/05/1918	22/05/1918
Miscellaneous	Officer Commanding, Battery R.F.A.	27/05/1918	27/05/1918
Miscellaneous	13th Inf. Bde. S.W.271	28/05/1918	28/05/1918
Operation(al) Order(s)	Officer Commanding Battery RFA	28/05/1918	28/05/1918
Operation(al) Order(s)	Operation Order No. 3 by Lieut-Col. C.Stl. G. Hawkes, D.S.O., R.F.A, Commanding Right Group, 5th Divl, Artillery	28/05/1918	28/05/1918
Miscellaneous	5th Divisional Artillery Intelligence Summary 6 P.M. 20-5-18 To 6 P.M. 21-5-18	21/05/1918	21/05/1918
Miscellaneous	Hostile Fire		
Miscellaneous	5th Divisional Artillery Intelligence Summary 6 P.M. 21/5/18 To 6 P.M. 22/5/18	22/05/1918	22/05/1918

Miscellaneous	5th Divisional Artillery Intelligence Report 6 PM 22/5/18 To 6 PM 23/5/18	23/05/1918	23/05/1918
Miscellaneous			
Miscellaneous	5th Divisional Artillery Intelligence Summary 6.0 P.M. 23/5/18 to 6 P.M. 24/5/18		
Miscellaneous	Hostile Fire		
Miscellaneous	5th Divisional Artillery Intelligence Summary 6 P.M. 24-5-18 To 6 P.M. 25-5-18	25/05/1918	25/05/1918
Miscellaneous	Hostile Fire		
Miscellaneous	5th Divisional Artillery Intelligence Summary 6 A.M. 25-5-18 To 6 A.M. 26-5-18		
Miscellaneous	5th Divisional Artillery Intelligence Summary 6 PM 26/5/18 To 6 PM 27/5/18	27/05/1918	27/05/1918
Miscellaneous	5th Divisional Artillery Intelligence Summary, 6.O P.M. 24/5/18 To 6.O P.M. 28/5/18	28/05/1918	28/05/1918
Miscellaneous	5th Divisional Artillery Intelligence Summary, 6. P.M. 28/5/18 To 6.0 P.M. 29/5/18	29/05/1918	29/05/1918
Miscellaneous	5th Divisional Artillery Intelligence Summary, 6.0 P.M. 29/5/18 To 6.O P.M. 30/5/18	30/05/1918	30/05/1918
Miscellaneous	5th Divisional Artillery Intelligence Summary, 6. P.M. 30-5-18 To 6 P.M. 31-5-18	31/05/1918	31/05/1918
Miscellaneous	Casualties During The Month		
Heading	5/Div Art 27 Bde R.F.A. June 1918		
Heading	Chapter XIII 1915-Vol II (1927 Reserve)		
Heading	War Diary (Original) of 27th Brigadier R.F.A. For The Month Ending 30 June 1918		
War Diary	Cron Maraisse (J 26 C 2/3)	01/06/1918	10/06/1918
Miscellaneous	Officer Commanding Battery RFA	07/06/1918	07/06/1918
War Diary	J 26 C 2/3	10/06/1918	01/07/1918
Miscellaneous	Messages And Signals.		
Miscellaneous	Officer Commanding 27th Brigadier R.F.A.	09/06/1918	09/06/1918
Miscellaneous	Officer Commanding 1204 Battery RFA	02/06/1918	02/06/1918
Heading	5th Division 27th Bde R.F.A. July To December 1918		
Miscellaneous	Message Form		
Miscellaneous	DAG GHQ 3rd Echelon		
Heading	War Diary (Original) of 27th Brigadier R.F.A. For The Month Ending July 1918		
War Diary	Croix Maraisse J 26 6 2/3	01/07/1918	13/07/1918
Miscellaneous	5th Divisional Artillery No. HBM/29/11	02/07/1918	02/07/1918
Miscellaneous	5th Divisional Artillery No. HBM/29/10	15/07/1918	15/07/1918
War Diary	Croix Maraisse	13/07/1918	17/07/1918
War Diary	Pib 3/2 Harte Vent	17/07/1918	18/07/1918
Miscellaneous	Reference Attached A.A./7/30	19/07/1918	19/07/1918
Miscellaneous	Right Group, 5th Div. Artillery No. A.A. 7/30	19/07/1918	19/07/1918
War Diary	Harte Vent	18/07/1918	31/07/1918
Heading	War Diary of 27th Bde RFA In The Month August 1918		
War Diary	St. Venant	01/08/1918	08/08/1918
War Diary	Fontes	08/07/1918	15/07/1918
War Diary	Rebreuviette	15/08/1918	20/08/1918
War Diary	Authies	20/08/1918	21/08/1918
War Diary	Longeast Wood	21/08/1918	22/08/1918
War Diary	Longedm Wood	22/08/1918	24/08/1918
War Diary	Bocquoy	23/08/1918	24/08/1918
War Diary	Bihucourt	24/08/1918	29/08/1918
War Diary	Biefvillers	27/08/1918	31/08/1918

War Diary	Favreuil	31/08/1918	01/09/1918
Miscellaneous	Officer Joined During The Month		
Miscellaneous	Administrative Instruction, ETC.		
Miscellaneous	Administrative Instruction For Entrainment Of 5th Division		
Miscellaneous	Officer Commanding Battery RFA	07/08/1918	07/08/1918
Operation(al) Order(s)	5th Divisional Artillery Operation Order No. 193 by Brig. General. A.H. Hussey. C.B., C.M.G.	07/08/1918	07/08/1918
Operation(al) Order(s)	Operation Order No. 16 by Lt. Col. Berkley, D.S.O. Commanding 27th Brigadier R.F.A.	05/08/1918	05/08/1918
Miscellaneous	Extracts From 5th Divisional Order No. 243	05/08/1918	05/08/1918
Operation(al) Order(s)	Administrative Instructions To Accompany 5th Division Order No. 243. Reference Sheets 36.a. (N.E.) And 36.a (N.W.) 1/20,000	04/08/1918	04/08/1918
Operation(al) Order(s)	5th Divisional Artillery Operation Order 191 by Brig. General A.H. Hussey. C.B., C.M.G.	04/08/1918	04/08/1918
Miscellaneous	Relief Table		
Miscellaneous	Reference 27th Brigade Operation Order No. 16	06/08/1918	06/08/1918
Operation(al) Order(s)	Artillery Order No. 34 by Brigadier General L.J. Hext, C.M.G. Commanding Royal Artillery 74th (Yeomanry) Division	05/08/1918	05/08/1918
Operation(al) Order(s)	5th Divisional Artillery Operation Order No. 192 by Brig. General. A.H. Hussey. C.B., C.M.G.	06/08/1918	06/08/1918
Miscellaneous	March Table		
Heading	War Diary 27th Brigade R.F.A. Volume 5 Part 9 September 1918		
War Diary		23/00/1918	26/00/1918
War Diary	Favreuil	01/09/1918	03/09/1918
War Diary	Valu	04/09/1918	04/09/1918
War Diary	Hermies	05/09/1918	15/09/1918
War Diary	Metz	16/09/1918	16/09/1918
Heading	5th Division War Diary 27th Bde. R.F.A. October 1918		
Heading	War Diary 27 Brigadier R.F.A. October 1918 Vol 51		
War Diary	Foonelien	01/10/1918	02/10/1918
War Diary	La Vacquare	03/10/1918	05/10/1918
War Diary	East of Bantaryelle	06/10/1918	13/10/1918
War Diary	Clemont Chateau	14/08/1918	25/08/1918
War Diary	Beaurain	26/10/1918	26/10/1918
Map	VI Corps.		
Miscellaneous	J 5d 6/0		
Miscellaneous	Officer Commanding Battery RFA	19/10/1918	19/10/1918
Operation(al) Order(s)	Operation Order No. 217 By Brig. General A.H. Hussey. O.B. C.M.G. Commanding 5th Division Artillery	22/10/1918	22/10/1918
Map	VI Corps		
Map	Maps		
Miscellaneous	5th Divisional Artillery Instructions	22/10/1918	22/10/1918
Miscellaneous	Addendum No. 1 To 5th Divisional Artillery Operation Order No. 217	22/10/1918	22/10/1918
Operation(al) Order(s)	37th Divisional Artillery Operation Order No. 191	22/10/1918	22/10/1918
Miscellaneous	Reference Attached Operation Order No. 217	22/10/1918	22/10/1918
Miscellaneous	Wireless Press	24/10/1918	24/10/1918
Miscellaneous	The following Reconnaissance Report Is Forward For Your Information	24/10/1918	24/10/1918
Miscellaneous	Officer Commanding Battery RFA	24/10/1918	24/10/1918

Operation(al) Order(s)	Operation Order No. 3 by Lieut. Colonel M. Crofton, D.S.O., R.F.A., Commanding Group	24/10/1918	24/10/1918
Miscellaneous	Wireless Press	25/10/1918	25/10/1918
Miscellaneous	Report On Prisoners Captured During Recent Operations	25/10/1918	25/10/1918
Miscellaneous	5th Division Summary of Information	25/10/1918	25/10/1918
Heading	War Diary 27th Brigade R.F.A. November 1915		
Map	Maps		
Miscellaneous	General Staff 5th Division		
Miscellaneous	Report On Operation From 1st November To 11th November 1918		
War Diary	Beaurany	01/11/1918	04/11/1918
War Diary	Folimet	05/11/1918	11/11/1918
War Diary	Louvignies	16/11/1918	30/11/1918
Miscellaneous	Honours and Awards For The Month of November		
Heading	War Diary of 27th Brigadier Royal Field Artillery For The Month Of		
War Diary	Louvignies	01/12/1918	22/12/1918
War Diary	Vineinette	23/12/1918	31/12/1918
Miscellaneous	Honours and Awards During November-December, 1918-7-11-1919		
Miscellaneous	Honours and Awards For The Month of Jan		
Heading	War Diary of 27th Brigadier Royal Field Artillery For The Month For February 1919		
War Diary	Golzinne Chateau	01/02/1919	28/02/1919
Heading	War Diary of 27th Brigade Royal Field Artillery For The Month Of January 1919		
War Diary	Vichinette Chateau	01/01/1916	20/01/1916
War Diary	Bossiere	21/01/1916	31/01/1916
Heading	War Diary of the 27th Brigade Royal Field Artillery For The Month Of March 1919		
War Diary	Colzinne Chateau	01/03/1919	02/03/1919
War Diary	In Mazy	03/03/1918	14/03/1918
War Diary	Colzinne Chateau	15/03/1919	15/03/1919
War Diary	Gilly	16/03/1919	21/03/1919
War Diary	Antwerp	22/03/1919	26/03/1919
War Diary	Larraill	27/03/1919	31/03/1919

no 95/1531/2

5th Division

27th Bde R.F.A.

~~January To June~~

~~1918~~

APR 1918 ~ 1918 JUNE

FROM ITALY

5th Division

27th Bde R.F.A.

~~January To June~~

~~1918~~

APR 1918 to 1918 JUNE

FROM ITALY

No 95/1531/2

5th Division

27th Bde R.F.A.

~~January to June~~
^To^
~~1918~~

APR 1918 to 1918 JUNE

FROM ITALY

No 95/1531/2

5th Divisional Artillery.

27th BRIGADE R. F. A.

APRIL 1918.

Registered No. 118
Volume No. 4
Serial No. 5

WAR DIARY

for

the month of APRIL 1918.

1/5/1918.

Berkley Lieut.Col. Commanding
27th. Brigade R.F.A.

5th Divisional Artillery.

27th BRIGADE R. F. A.

APRIL 1918.

Registered No. 118
Volume No. 4
Serial No. 5

WAR DIARY

for

the month of APRIL 1918.

1/5/1918.

Berkley Lieut.Col. Commanding
27th. Brigade R.F.A.

Army Form C. 2118.

WAR DIARY
or
INTELLIGENCE SUMMARY.
(Erase heading not required.)

APRIL 1918.

MAP (Italy) 1/100,000 VENEZIA
                         PADOVA
    " (France) " LENS 70/11
    " (BELGIUM) HAZEBROUCK 70/5

Instructions regarding War Diaries and Intelligence Summaries are contained in F. S. Regs., Part II. and the Staff Manual respectively. Title pages will be prepared in manuscript.

Place	Date	Hour	Summary of Events and Information	Remarks and references to Appendices
Roncati di Campanine.	1st/2nd	8 am to 8 am	W.D: Orders received for entrainment for France	Details attached
	2/3	"	Brigade started entraining at PADOVA (Station Campo di MARTE) 7/pm.	attached
	3/4	"	On rail, via BOLOGNA, ARQUATA, GENOVA, VENTIMIGLIA, NICE, LES ARQUES,	"
	4/5	"	GIVORS CANAL, VERSAILLES, ABANCOURT, AMIENS. detraining	
	5/6	"	station at DOULENS area. (DOULENS, PETIT HOUVAIN,	
	6/7	"	MONDICOURT)	
	7/8	"		
HEM	8/9	"	Brigade concentrated in HEM area:- Bde H.Q., 37 TMS & Batteries in HEM.	
	9/10	"	"A"/120 Batteries in OCCOCHES. "B"/120 T.M.T. JILLING's rejoined 120 Bty from CCS	
	10/11	"	Left HEM at 10.30 am to march to billets in SAULTY in connection with relief of 2nd Canadian Division near WAILLY. While passing through DOULENS, cancelling orders were received, and Brigade returned to billets in HEM.	
OURTON	11/12	"	Marched from HEM at 7.30 am to OURTON (on ST POL - ARRAS Road) arriving 6.15 pm after a march of 28 miles. Roads much congested.	"

2353 Wt. W3544/1454 700,000 5/15 D., D. & L. A.D.S.S./Forms/C. 2118.

WAR DIARY or INTELLIGENCE SUMMARY

Army Form C. 2118.

APRIL 1918. Map HAZEBROUCK 1/100,000 No 5A.
40,000 No 36 A.

Place	Date	Hour	Summary of Events and Information	Remarks and references to Appendices
AIRE	12/13	9am to 6pm	Lieut Overton Y.14 & 12th, and marched to AIRE in which area it was expected to billet, march continued to THIENNES and there men re-going into action awaited till 6.30pm. Bde H.Q. 119 Bty, 121 Section, 37th Battery go into action near RUE des MORTS, J.11.b., in the middle of Forest of THIENNES. Train waggonlines are at STEEN BECQUE. We cover 95th Inf Bde holding a line just east of Bois MOYEN. Remaining guns of 121 Battery come into action in LE PARCQ (J.10.d). One gun of 120 u Battery in action forward at J.14.b.87, 500 yards in rear of our line, to hold the MERVILLE – LA MOTTE Road against attack by tanks or armoured cars. Much firing on Bosch side during the day.	
	13/14	"	Wet day, windy.	
Forest of NIEPPE (THIENNES)	15/16	"	All batteries of Brigade are now in action :— Bde H.Q. at J.11.a. 9/8. 119 th. at D.30.c.7½ (West of LA MOTTE Chateau) with section at J.6.d.8/8. 120 " at J.5.c. 4/1. 121st. at LE PARCQ. (J.10.b.7/1 with section at J.12.a.17/5½.) 37th. at RUE des MORTS. (J.11.b.00/46.)	

WAR DIARY or **INTELLIGENCE SUMMARY**

Army Form C. 2118.

APRIL 1916.

Map. HAZEBROUCK 1/100,000. 70 S.A
1/40,000 20 36.A.

Place	Date	Hour	Summary of Events and Information	Remarks and references to Appendices
Forest of NIEPPE (THIENNES)	16/17	1 pm to 6 am	Quiet day.	
	17/18		Bde H.Q. moved to billet in LE PARCQ. An attack was expected morning 18th. All batteries fire harassing fire on own front from 4 am to 6 am. 60 rds per gun per hour.	
	19/20		Cecd: Lieut J.S. WILLIAMS rejoined 37th Battery from Base. 1st Lieut-Colonel J. BERKLEY to be Brevet-Lieut-Colonel from 1st January 1918. Much hostile shelling of area, overnight during the day.	
	20/21			
	21/22		Bde H.Q. move alongside Negro 15th Infantry Brigade (whilst we are now covering) with tents in the Bois Moyen J.18.a, near the "GROS CHENE". Shelled on arrival and gassed out overnight.	
	22/23		Negro Bde moved into woods in J.9.a near CANAL de la NIEPPE. 119th and 37th Batteries were badly gassed with 77m shell overnight, each having 6 casualties.	

J. Berkley
Lt Col
Cmdg 29th Bde RFA

WAR DIARY or INTELLIGENCE SUMMARY

Army Form C. 2118.

APRIL 1918

m.g.s. HAZEBROUCK 1/100,000. Trs S^A
" " 1/40,000 Trs 36 A.

Place	Date	Hour	Summary of Events and Information	Remarks and references to Appendices
FOREST of NIEPPE	23/24	8am to 8am	No. 29933 Sergt. N.H. HARRIS, 120th Battery, posted as 2/Lieutenant to 11th Divisional Artillery. 2/Lieut E.J. JOHNSON wounded (gas) & 2/Lieut T.V. BISHOP " "	
"	24/25	"	Nothing to report	
"	25/26	"	Fine day. 15th Inf. Bde (Bedford Regt) attack in KORA successful, taking 11 prisoners and 2 Machine Guns. Brigade assisted by two batteries of 160th Bde R.F.A. Gun drawn a barrage from 9.35 pm till 10 pm.	
"	26/27	"	Fine day. Hun A.A. gas shelling round 119th Battery overnight. 2/Lieut A.S. NOTT, 120 Bty, posted to 15th Bde R.F.A.	
"	27/28	"	2/Lieut W.L. SALISBURY from 15th Bde posted to 120 Battery	
"	28/29	"	Quiet day	
"	29/30	"	2/Lieut A. CURIE posted to 119th Battery from D.A.C.	
"	30/31	"	Quiet day.	

Casualties during the month

	Killed	Wounded	Gassed
119 Bty.		2 Offs.	11 O.R.
120 Bty.			2 O.R.
121 Bty.		1 O.R.	1 O.R.
87 Bty.		1 O.R.	4 O.R.

C.W. Rutherford
Capt of D.A. & A
Cmdg. 39 D.A.C

OPERATION ORDER.   NO.1.
By,
LIEUT-COL. J. BERKLEY, D.S.O.
COMMANDING 27th. BRIGADE R.F.A.

1. The 27th.Brigade R.F.A. will march to-morrow the 10th. inst. to SAULTY. Order of march - H.Q., 37th., 121st., 120th., 119th.
The Brigade H.Q. will pass the starting point RISQUETOUT at 11-0 a.m.

2. While in present area the 5th.Divnl. Artillery will be ready to move at 3 hours notice and on reaching SAULTE the 27th.Bde.R.F.A. will be ready to move at 2 hours notice.

3. Refilling points from the 10th. instant inclusive will be WONDICOURT with 13th. Infantry Brigade.

4. After arriving at SAULTY the 27th.Brigade R.F.A. if the situation demands, will be used to re-inforce the Corps Front under orders issued direct through the Brigade by VI Corps R.A.
to
5. The D.A.C. are lending one G.S. Wagon to each battery for the move, no orders have yet been received as to when these G.S. Wagons will report to Batteries.

6. Baggage and Supply Wagons will march with the Brigade, they will report early to-morrow morning to their respective batteries.

7. Until further orders the following special distances will be maintained on the march :-
   (i) 100 yards distance will be kept between batteries and sections D.A.C. and 300 yards between Bdes. and D.A.C.
   (ii) 25 yards will be maintained between each group of 6 vehicles.
the
8. On the 13th. instant Brigade will march from SAULTY to the Wagon Lines of the 6th. Cdn. Brigade.
On the night 13th./14th. two sections per battery will relieve two sections per battery of the 6th. Cdn. Brigade.
Further orders for the above moves will be issued later.
On the 16th. instant H.Q. 5th.Div.Arty relieves H.Q. 2nd.Cdn. Div.Arty.
On the 14th. instant 5th.D.A.C. march from OCCOCHES to SAULTY.
On the 15th. instant 5th.D.A.C. marches to Wagon Line of 2nd. Cdn. D.A.C.

9. Any stores which batteries wish to dump should be left under a man in charge at battery billets and arrangements for collecting these will be made later.

10. ACKNOWLEDGE.

Capt.R.F.A.

9-4-18.   Adjutant 27th. Brigade R.F.A.

OPERATION ORDER.   NO. 2.
BY,
LIEUT-COL. J. BERKLEY, D.S.O.
COMMANDING 27TH. BRIGADE R.F.A.

11-4-18.

1. 5th. D.A. and No.1 Coy. Train will march to billets in the DIEVAL Area ~~to-morrow-April 12th.~~ to-day

2. Order of March - H.Q., 37th., 121st. 12th. 119th. Headquarters will pass through RISQUETOUT at 7-45 a.m.

3. Route - IVERGNY - BEAUDRICOURT - ETRE WAMIN - MAIZIERS BAILLEUL aux CORNAILLES - MONCHY BRETON - DIEVAL.

4. Each battery will send on one officer and 2 O.R. to report to the Staff Captain, 5th .D.A. at the Town Major's Office, DIEVAL, at 12 noon April 11th.

5. Bicyclists are not to be allowed to straggle but must march with their Units.

6. Baggage and Supply Wagons will be collected by No.1 Coy Train and will march with that Unit.

7. Units must arrange for guides to meet Baggage and Supply Wagons on the march and guide them to new billets.

8. Maps recently issued, except LENS 1/100,000 will be returned by bearer.

9. Distances to be maintained on the march will be -
   Between Bdes and D.A.C.   300 yards.
   "   Batteries and Sections D.A.C. 100 yards.
   "   every 6 vehicles   25 yards.

10. The column will halt from 10 minutes before every clock hour until the clock hour and from 10 minutes to 12 noon to 12-30 p.m.

11. Supply Wagons will march full. There will be no refill on April 11th.

12. G.S. Wagons loaned to Units yesterday will be returned to their respective Sections D.A.C. at once.

13. ACKNOWLEDGE.

Capt. R.F.A.
Adjutant 27th. Brigade R.F.A.

20 9.15
400

O.C.
119th Bty, RFA
120th   "   "

Reference Operation Order No 2 sent to you this morning.

The 120th and 119th Btys will not march by RISQUETOUT but will march direct to the Cross Roads at BOUQUEMAISON, the head of the 120th Bty to arrive there at 9.20 AM. Brigade HQ will pass this point at 9.15 AM marching from the direction of DOULLENS

OPERATION ORDER No. 3.
by
Lieut.Colonel J.BERKLEY D.S.O.
Commanding 27th Brigade R.F.A.

1. The march will be continued tomorrow April 12th to AIRE.

2. The whole column will halt from 10 minutes before each clock hour until each clock hour and from 11.50 a.m. to 12.30 p.m.
No other halts are to be made.

3. Billetting parties of 1 Officer and 2 other Ranks will meet the Staff Captain at Town Major's Office, AIRE at 10.0 a.m.

4. Distances to be maintained on the march will be -
between Brigades and Brigade Groups 300 yards
between other units 100 yards.

5. All Supply Wagons will report to No 1 Company Train at starting point at 10.50 A.M. and will march with and at the head of that unit.

6. 5th. Divl. Artillery Order of March
   15th Brigade R F A
   27th Brigade R.F.A.
   H.Q. 5th D.A.
   5th D.A.C.
   No. 1 Coy. Train.

7. Brigade Order of March
   H.Q., 37th, 119th, 120th, 121st.
   H.Q. will leave present billets at 7.50 A.M.

8. The 5th Divisional Artillery starting point is Cross Roads between CAMBLAIN CHATELAIN and CAMONNE RICOUART, which place the head of the Brigade will pass at 9.0 A.M.

9. Route - CAUCHY - a-la- TOUR - FERFAY - ST. HILAIRE
   AIRE.

10. ACKNOWLEDGE.

Captain R.F.A.

11-4-18.   Adjutant 27th. Bde. R.F.A

Officer Commanding
119/121/?
............Battery RFA.

S.O.S. Lines are now as follows :-

119th Bty. RFA. - K.16.c 30/00 to K.21.c 50/30.

121st "   "   - K.16.c 30/00 to K.21.c 50/30.
(4 guns)

121st Bty. RFA. - K.21.b 75/45 to K.22.d 15/65.
(2 guns)

37th "   "   - K.11.d 8/9
                  K.17.b 10/75
                  K.18.b 5/1
                  K.18.d 60/15
                  K.22.a 1/3
                  K.22.d 1/7

Cancelled 8.30 PM 14/4/18

The above come into force at once.

                                    [signature]
                                    Captain R.F.A.

14-4-18.   Adjutant 27th. Bde. R.F.A.

119. 121. 37

Officer Commanding

..........Battery RFA.   27th. Bde. No. B.M./31.

The Brigade Zone and S.O.S. Lines are now as follows :-

Brigade Zone.

    N. Boundary :- E. and W. Line through K.10.c 0/0
    S. Boundary :- E. and W. Line through K.16.c 0/0

S.O.S. Lines.

    119th Bty. - K.10.d 4/0 to K.16.a 2/4 to K.16.a 2/1

    121st Bty. - K.16.a 2/1 to K.16.c 2/0
    (4 guns)

    121st Bty. - K.21.b 7/5 to K.22.d 1/7
    (2 guns)

    37th. Bty. - K.17.b 10/75 — altered to K22a 80/60.
                K.16.b 5/1
                K.16.d 00/75 —   16/4/18
                K.16.d 00/15 —
                K.22.a 1/3 —
                K.22.d 1/7 — altered to K22a 40/45

                                          Captain R.F.A.

14-4-1918.   Adjutant 27th. Bde. R.F.A.

Cancelled 4PM 16/4/18.

Officer Commanding

........Battery RFA.   27th. Bde. No. BM/42

The Brigade Zone and S.O.S. Lines are now as follows :-

Brigade Zone.

    N. Boundary - E. and W. Line through K.19.c 0/0
    S. Boundary - E. and W. Line through K.16.c 0/0

S.O.S. Lines.

    119th. Bty. - K.10.d 4/0 to K.16.a 2/4 to K.16.a 2/1
    121st Bty. - K.16.a 2/1 to K.16.c 2/0
    (four guns)
    121st. Bty. - K.21.b 7/5 to K.22.d 1/7
    (two guns)
    120th. Bty. - K.16.a 2/1 to K.16.c 2/0 to K.21.c 6/5
    (five guns)
    37th. Bty. - K.16.b 5/1
                K.16.d 00/75
                K.16.d 60/15
                K.22.a 1/3
                K.22.a 80/60
                K.22.a 45/45 05/95

                                                Captain R.F.A.

4 oPM
15-4-18.   Adjutant 27th. Bde. R.F.A.

Copies 119, 120, 121 3)
     BM 95
     BM SU DA

Officer Commanding

..........Battery   27th. Bde. No. BM/50.

The Brigade Zone and S.O.S. Lines are now as follows :-

Brigade Zone.

    N. Boundary - E. and W. Line through K.10.c 0/0

    S. Boundary - E. and W. Line through K.16.c 0/0

S.O.S. Lines.

    119th. Bty. RFA. - K.10.c 4/0 to K.15.b 9/5 to K.15.d 9/5

    121st. Bty. RFA. - K.15.d 9/5 to K.15.d 85/25 to K.21.b 30/60
    (four guns)

    121st. Bty. RFA. - K.21.b 30/70 to K.22.d 1/7
    (two guns)

    120th. Bty. RFA. - K.10.c 4/0 to K.15.b 9/5 to
                    K.15.d 85/25 to K.21.b 30/60

    37th. Bty. RFA. - K.16.b 5/1
                    K.16.d 00/75
                    K.16.d 60/15
                    K.22.a 1/3
                    K.22.a 80/60
                    K.22.a 05/95

Since the most Southerly point of the 160th Brigade RFA S.O.S. Line is at K.10.d 15/00 the 120th Battery RFA will keep one gun at K.10.c 8/0 to fill the gap.

The 120th Battery RFA will not keep a gun laid on K.21.b 3/6 as this point is already covered by 121st Battery RFA.

17-4-1918.

Captain R.F.A.

Adjutant 27th. Bde. R.F.A.

SECRET

TO: ~~X Bde H.A.~~
27th Bde R.F.A. (for information)

Sender's Number: BM 185
Day of Month: 24

Reference O 181 para 7 attached targets for Hows are redistributed as under

4.5" How
- K 21 a 60.05 — 2 Hows:
- K 21 a 95.05 — 1 How:
- K 21 b 45.60 — 1 How:
- K 21 b 90.80 — 2 Hows:

4 Hows will search road running N.E. & S.W. through K 21 central
2 Hows will search area about K 21 b 5.3

6" Hows
- 1 How — K 21 d 4.2
- 1 How — K 21 b 5.3
- 1 How — K 22 a 1.3
- 1 How — K 16 c 5.1

These targets may be registered or bombarded before Zero

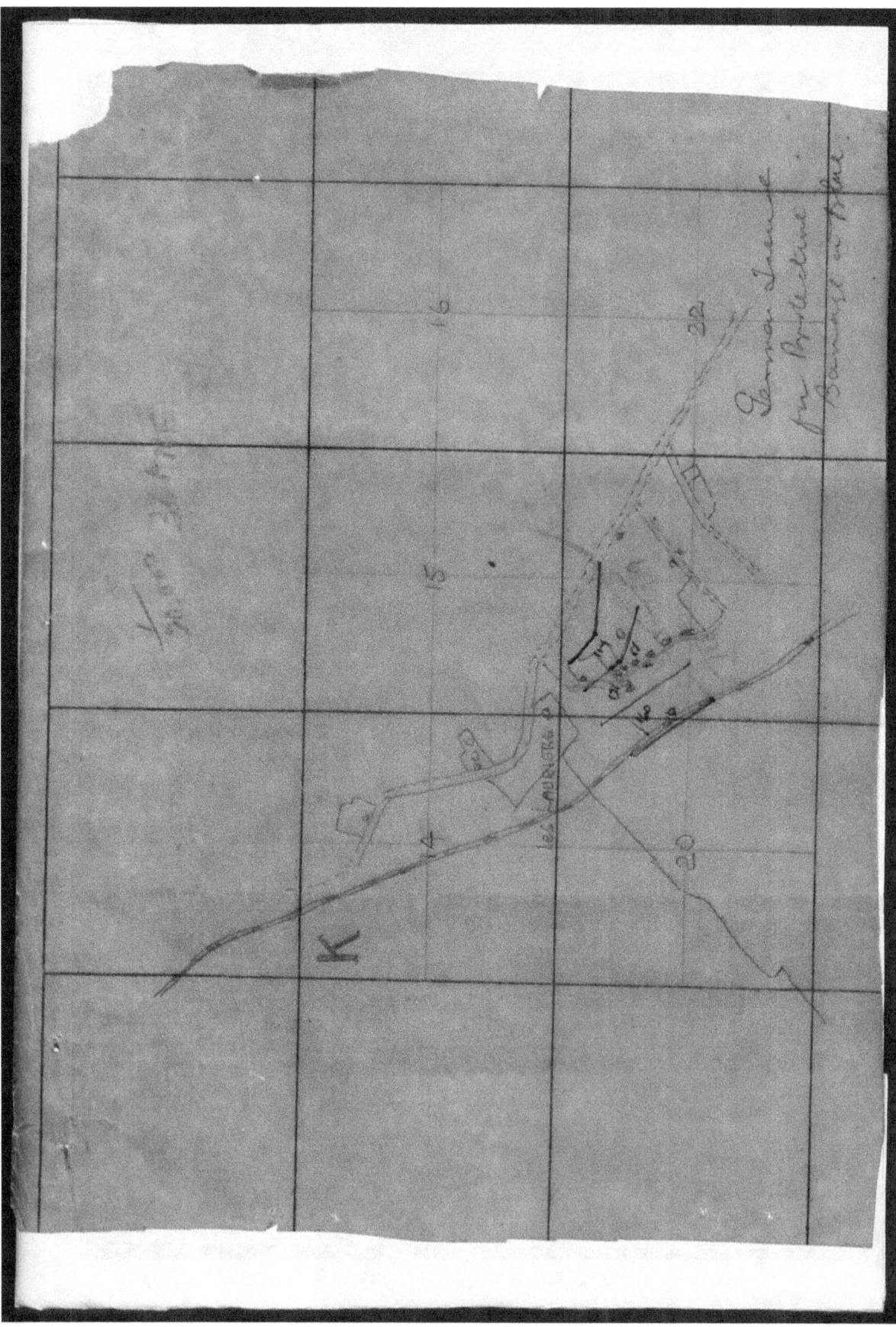

Operation Order No. 244|8

by

Lieut. Col. BERKLEY D.S.O.

Commanding 27th. Brigade R.F.A.
....

Reference Map 1/20,000 36a N.E.

Reference 15th Infantry Brigade O.O. No. 181 (Copy attached) para. 3.

1. The Creeping Barrage will be put down by the following batteries :-
     119th Battery RFA.
     120th Battery RFA.
     121st Battery RFA.
     /160 Bde. RFA.

 Battery boundaries will be as follows :-
119th Bty.   - Left Boundary K.21.a 40/95, K.21.a 60/75, K.21.b 15/75
119th "   - Right " } K.21.a 20/80, K.21.a 40/65, K.21.a 85/40
121st "   - Left " }) K.21.a 85/40.

121st Bty   - Right Boundary - K.20.b 95/65, K.21.a 45/00.

120th Bty   - Superimposed
    Left Boundary - As for 119th Battery
    Right Boundary - As for 121st Battery.

/160 Bde. RFA Left Boundary   - K.20.b 95/65, K.21.a 45/00

/160 Bde. RFA Right "   - K.20.b 75/45, K.21.c 20/80.

 The protective barrage will be along the line running through the last named points of each battery boundary.

 Lifts will be of 100 yards at the rate of 1½ minutes until the protective barrage on German trench is reached.

 All shrapnel to be used for creeping barrage ; protective barrage 50% Shrapnel 50% H.E. ; fuzes and propellants to be carefully sorted, up to 60 rounds per gun.

 Rates of fire :-
 Zero to Zero plus 6   - 4 rounds per gun per minute.
 Zero plus 6 to Zero plus 10 - 3 Rounds per gun per minute.
 Zero plus 10 onwards - Normal.

2. 4.5" Hows. will fire on the undermentioned points from Zero onwards.
37th Battery RFA   - K.21.a 65/05 (2 Hows.)
        K.21.a 95/05
        K.21.b 4/6 (2 Hows.)
        K.21.b 9/8 .
D/160 Brigade RFA - 4 Hows. sweeping the road from K.21.b 70/50 to
        K.21.c 85/75
       2 Hows. searching enclosed area about K.21.b 55/10

Contd.

2. Rate of fire:-
Zero to Zero plus 6 :- 3 rounds per gun per minute.
Zero plus 6 to Zero plus 10 :- 2 rounds per gun per minute.
Zero plus 10 onwards :- 1½ rounds per gun per minute.

3. Zero hour will be notified later.

4. An orderly will be sent with a watch to these gods. at 3.0 p.m.

5. ACKNOWLEDGE

2 -4-1918.

1SL ML Me
5L D/A
154 RFA
119
120
121
3)

[signature]

Captain 4.F.A.

Adjutant 27th Gun. R.F.A.

SECRET.   Copy No. 2
                                                            24-4-18.

                    Operation Order No. 181.

                    Reference Map 1/20,000 36a N.E.

                    1. The 1st Bedford Regiment will advance it's line from LES
                    LAURIER from K.21.a 05/65 to K.21.a 80/95 (Road) taking in the
                    Farm about K.21.a 4/6. This Farm will be known as BEDFORD
12/Glosters   Fm. The 95th Inf. Bde. will conform on our right as far as
                    VERTBOIS.

1/Bedfords.   2. Troops to be employed one Coy. and one Platoon 1/Bedfords.

                    3. Artillery will form a creeping barrage from K.20.b 75/45
5th Div. Arty.   to K.21.a 40/95. About 1 gun to 20 yards. Rate of
34th   "   "   advance 1½ minutes for the three first 100 yards. The
1 How. Bty.   barrage will stop on the line of new enemy trench from about
15th L.T.M.   K.21.b 1/8 to K.21.c 1/7 4.5" How. and 6" How. will co-
    Bty.   operate on certain selected points.
                    1 NEWTON will fire on certain targets.
                    4 L.T.M's will be disposed about LES LAURIERS and co-operate
                    with artillery in the barrage.
                    4.   The attacking troops will consolidate along the line of
                    the hedge and put out at least 2 posts towards the MERVILLE
                    Road to join up with the post at K.15.c 8/1. 2 Posts will
                    be dug about K.21.a 2/5 and K.21.a 05/15 to join up to
                    Railway. A strong supporting platoon will be moved from
                    Bedford Support Coy. to LES LAURIERS.
                    In order to allow of artillery registration the posts at
                    K.15.c 10/05 to K.15.c 4/1 will be withdrawn at dawn on the
                    25th for the whole day.
                    5.   Assembly will take place square to the objective 200
                    yards from the Northern edge of BEDFORD Fm. about K.15.c 15/25.
                    6.   Machine Guns ....
                    1 M.G. will fire ......
                    7.   Howitzer Targets ......
                    8.   Watches will be synchronised at Brigade H.Q. and an
                    orderly sent with a good watch at 2.30 p.m. By telephone at
                    7.0 p.m. on 25th April.

                    9.   Zero hour will be about 9.0 p.m. on 25th April exact
                    hour will be notified later to all concerned.
                    10. Brigade H.Q. will remain at J.16.a 5/7.
                    ACKNOWLEDGE.

                                                        J. ANDERSON Captain,
24-4-18.   Brigade Major 15th Inf. Bde.

Officer Commanding

..............Battery RFA.   27th Bde. No. BM/81

Reference Operation Order No. 24418.

1. The 100 yard lifts will be at the rate of 2½ minutes instead of 1½ minutes, in consequence of this whenever " Zero plus 6 " occurs read " Zero plus 10 " and for " Zero plus 10 " read " Zero plus 14 ".

2. 80 rounds per gun should now be sorted out by fuzes and propellants.

[signature]
Captain R.F.A.

25-4-1918.   Adjutant 27th. Bde. R.F.A.

119.120.14.))
A/160, D/160, 160 Rd

Officer Commanding

.............Battery RFA.

27th Bde. No. BM/78

Reference Operation Order No. 24418.

1. At Zero plus 30 batteries will cease fire unless otherwise ordered.

2. After Zero plus 30 119th and 120th Batteries will remain for the night on the protective barrage line, for purposes of S.O.S. and the 121st Battery will return to their normal S.O.S. Line, boundaries as under.

119th Bty. — K.21.b 15/75 to K.21.a 85/40
120th Bty — K.21.a 85/40 to K.21.a 60/10
121st Bty. — K.16.c 00/55 to K.16.c 05/25 to K.21.b 3/6
(4 guns)
121st Bty. — K.21.b 30/70 to K.22.d 1/7
(2 guns)

   37th Bty. on the following points :-

       K.21.a 65/05
       K.21.a 95/05
       K.21.b 4/6
       K.21.b 9/8
       K.22.a 85/60
   K.16.d 60/20 .

Captain R.F.A.
Adjutant 27th. Bde. R.F.A.

25-4-1918.

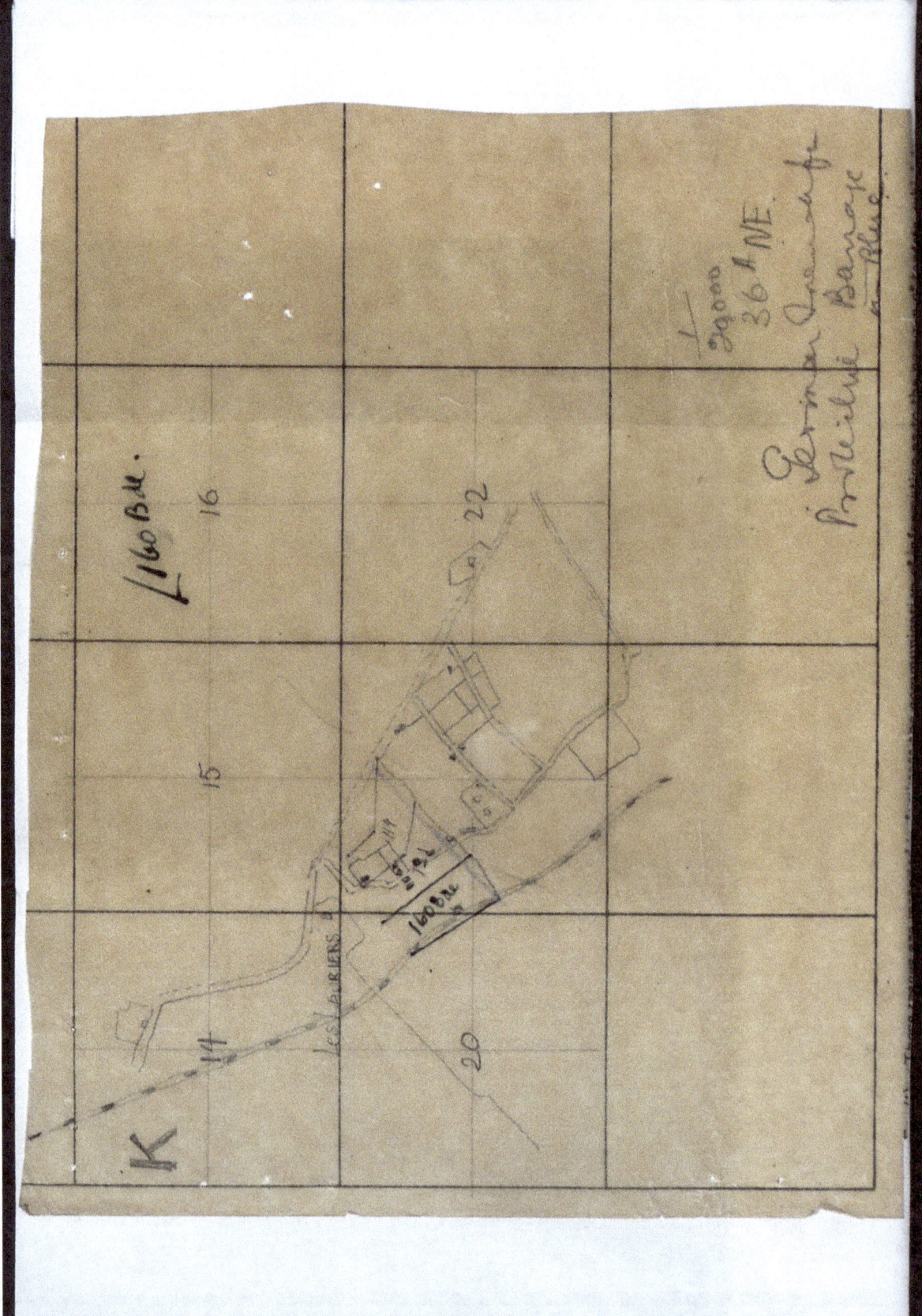

Register No.
Part. No.
Volume No.

WAR DIARY

of

27th Brigade R.F.A.

for the month ending 31st MAY 1918.

1/6/1918.

.... Markley, Lieut-Colonel
Commanding
27th Brigade R.F.A.

Army Form C. 2118.

MAY 1918.   Map 36A 1/40,000

Instructions regarding War Diaries and Intelligence
Summaries are contained in F. S. Regs., Part II.
and the Staff Manual respectively. Title pages
will be prepared in manuscript.

WAR DIARY
or
INTELLIGENCE SUMMARY.
(Erase heading not required.)

Place	Date	Hour	Summary of Events and Information	Remarks and references to Appendices
Forêt de NIEPPE	1st/2nd	8am to 8am	Disposition of Brigade: H.Q. in Wood J.9.d.7/5; 119Bty D.30.c.9/3; 120Bty J.5.c.4/0; 131Bty J.10.b.6/1; 373Bty J.11.c.9/5.	
"	2/3	"	Fine day. Nothing to report.	
"	3/4	"	" "	
"	5/6	"	Wet day.	
"	6/7	"	Fine.	
"	7/8	"	Very wet – Much trouble is being experienced in Batteries owing to short-shooting. Probably defective ammunition. Special tests are being made daily.	
"	8/9	"	Fine day.	
"	9/10	"	" "	
"	10/11	"	Very wet day; overnight much gas-shelling by enemy. Lieut T.H.B. KELLY & 2/Lt C.J. JILLINGS, both K.c.C.S (gassed)	
"	11/12	"	Quiet night day. 2/Lieut H. JOHNSON from B.A.C. attached to 120 Battery. Major M.H. ABELL to C.C.S (gassed). The following awards are notified: No 327119 Corpoal F. LODGE 120Bty. No 124969 Bomb. H. PRIOR 120 Battery } Military Medals	Signature to cover Cmd: M. Burch...
"	12/13	"	Wet day. 2/Lieut R.N. LOCHHEAD from B.A.C. attached to 120 Battery.	

SECRET.   5th Divisional Artillery No. HBM/

1. From 9.0 P.M. on May 8th, 160th Brigade R.F.A. will form a Sub-group under Lieut. Colonel BERKELEY. D.S.O. Commanding 27th Brigade R.F.A.

2. From 9.0 P.M. May 8th, the Field Artillery covering the 5th Division front will be grouped as follows :-

   RIGHT GROUP.   - Lieut. Col. HAWKES. D.S.O.
   H.Q. J.26.a   15th Brigade R.F.A.
        6/0.   84th Army Brigade RFA.

   LEFT GROUP.   - Lieut. Col. BERKELEY. D.S.O.
   H.Q. J.9.d   27th Brigade R.F.A.
        8/4.   160th Brigade R.F.A.

3. On withdrawal to Wagon Lines, 152nd Brigade R.F.A. will be prepared to come into action to cover the Left Inf. Brigade 5th Division, and will be kept in readiness to move at 2 hours notice.

4. Acknowledge.

Headquarters.
R.A. 5 Divn.   Major R.A.
7th May, 1918.   Brigade Major Royal Artillery 5th Division.

        Copies to :- 34th Divnl Art'y.
                     160th Brigade RFA.
                     27th   "   "
                     15th   "   "
                     84th   "   "

5th Divisional Artillery No. HBM/7/8.   SECRET.

DISPOSITIONS - 5TH DIVISIONAL ARTILLERY GROUP.

10th May, 1918.

Divisional Artillery H.Q.   THIENNES.

15th Brigade RFA. H.Q. .. ..   J.26.a 6/1.
52nd Battery.   .. ..   J.28.a 2/2 (5) J.36.b 8/8 (1).
80th   ---"---   .. ..   J.28.b 25/55(2) J.22.c 3/5 (4).
A/15   ---"---   .. ..   J.33.b 6/3.
D/15   ---"---   .. ..   J.27.c 6/8(4) J.28.c 6/0(2).
Wagon Lines.   .. ..   I.22.a.

27th Brigade RFA. H.Q. .. ..   J.9.d 8/5.
119th Battery.   .. ..   D.30.c 2/2.
120th ---"---   .. ..   J.5.c 3/0 (5) K.14.b 3/7 (1).
121st ---"---   .. ..   J.10.b 6/0(4) J.12.a 3/7 (2).
37th   ---"---   .. ..   J.11.c 0/5.
Wagon Lines.   .. ..   I.5.d.

84th Army Brigade RFA. H.Q. .. ..   J.26.b 45/50.
A/84 Brigade.   .. ..   J.33.c 9/8.
B/84   ---"---   .. ..   P.5.b 3/8.
C/84   ---"---   .. ..   J.29.c 6/8.
D/84   ---"---   .. ..   J.10.c 9/4(4) J.15.d 6/6(2).
B.A.C.   .. ..   H.30.a 8/7.

34th Divisional Artillery H.Q.   D.25.c 3/4.

160th Brigade R.F.A. H.Q. .. .. ..   D.22.c 1/9.
A/160 Brigade.   .. ..   J.5.a 66/29.
B/160 ---"---   .. ..   J.5.a 90/49.
C/160 ---"---   .. ..   D.28.b 45/32.
D/160 ---"---   .. ..   D.23.d 51/11.
Wagon Lines.   .. ..   MORBECQUE.

Headquarters,
R.A. 5 Divn.   R.A.
10th May, 1918.   for Major R.A.
                            Brigade Major Royal Art'y 5th Division.

COPIES TO :-   5th Division 'G'.
               XI Corps R.A.
               ---"--- H.A.
               C.B.S.O. XI Corps R.A.
               15th Brigade RFA.
               27th ---"---
               84th ---"---
               160th ---"---
               42nd Squadron R.A.F.
               34th Divnl Art'y.

SECRET

5TH DIVISIONAL ARTILLERY INTELLIGENCE SUMMARY 6PM – 10/5/18 to 6PM 11/5/18.

1. SITUATION. In conjunction with an operation carried out by the Division on our right, we carried out a raid at 2.0 a.m. with one platoon and one L.G. Section on houses at K.31.b 6/1. Very little opposition encountered. 6 prisoners (1 wounded) 2 Light M.G's captured and 4 Germans killed. Our casualties 3 wounded of whom 2 are at duty. Division on our right carried out a successful raid but no prisoners were captured.

2. OUR ARTILLERY. Right Group barraged in support of the raid mentioned above. Increased harassing fire, on bridges and tracks, was continued during the night. Concentrations fired during the afternoon on suspected enemy forward batteries, in K.33.b., 33.a., and 22.c. Today, beside harassing fire and calibration, 37th Bty shelled Les PURESBECQUES and Cross Roads in K.16.b., 121st Bty, B/ and C/84 answered NF K.29.d 25/25 at 3.40 p.m., and 120th shelled T.M.E.at K.22.a 3/9 and silenced an active T.M.
   Trench Mortars. X/5 Battery fired 55 rds on cross roads K.26.c 8/0 in cooperation with raid at 2.0 a.m. Y/5 registered successfully from a new position.

3. ENEMY ARTILLERY. Much quieter night and day. There was practically no retaliation during the raid last night. Early this morning there were some 5.9's on J.28.central, and later some 4.2's on CANDESCURE, and ARREWAGE, 5.9's on J.33.d., and HAVERSKERQUE – ST VENANT road, and during the afternoon some 4.2's on Les Lauriers. At 12.30 p.m. and 2.45 p.m. intense bursts, lasting 3 minutes, on support line from K.31. to K.20 - about 300 rounds of all calibres - possibly anger at the success of the raid during the night.

4. INTELLIGENCE.
   Batteries. K.29.d 25/25 NF Call.
   Aerial. 2.45 p.m. 1 E.A. flew high over Canal to J.35. Driven back by A.A. fire.
   M.G's. Reported active at K.21.b 0/8, K.21.a 6/1, K.21.c 7/5, K.26.c 55/60 (AARON) K.26.d 4/6 and K.32.a 1/2. Also (from Div. Summary) from K.15.b 45/05, K.15.d 80/35, K.15.b 20/05, K.10.c 7/8, K.10.c 80/85 and K.10.c 65/80.
   T.M's. K.32.a 8/7 (ELSIE) and K.15.b 5/0 (L.T.M.).
   Movement etc. Considerable in trench K.15.b 9/9 - K.15.b 6/8, and during night, silhouetted by flames of burning house at K.32.a 7/6. Posts found by patrols at K.10.c 6/4, K.10.c 45/20 and K.10.c 55/60.
   Defences. New thick barbed wire visible at K.15.b 5/0 and K.15.b 55/20. Sleepers have been stacked on railway at K.21.c 4/3 where two loopholes are visible.
   Miscellaneous. Enemy put up GOLDEN RAIN rockets at the commencement of the raid this morning - no enemy barrage materialized. At the same time a string of green lights and two single green rockets were put up some distance behind.

Sd. R.F. MASON. Lieut. R.A.
11th May, 1918.   Intelligence Officer 5th Divnl Arty.

SECRET.

5TH DIVISIONAL ARTILLERY INTELLIGENCE SUMMARY 6PM 9/5/18 TO 6PM 10/5/18.

1. SITUATION. Unchanged.

2. OUR ARTILLERY. Increased harassing fire during the night. Gas concentrations by 4.5" Hows. at 9.30, 9.55 and 10.20 p.m., 37th Battery engaging H.B's reported in K.17.b and D/15 & D/84 another H.B. in K.22.c. After a restless night, today batteries only calibrated, registered and checked lines in addition to the usual harassing fire.

   Trench Mortars. "DICK" put a few rounds into GABY, and houses in vicinity (K.26.b 9/3). HARRY shot at houses and roads around K.21.central during the afternoon.

3. ENEMY ARTILLERY. A lot of gas shelling between 11.30 p.m. and 3.0 a.m., mainly on the BOIS CLOBERT to LE PARC Area, and partly on the Eastern half of BOIS MOYEN - 4.2's and 77mm mustard gas. HAVERSKERQUE lightly shelled with 5.9's at 4.45 a.m. During the day there were some 4.2's near BARQUE, S. of CORBIE - and some 5.9's and 77 mm on LE PARC, BOIS MOYEN, LA MOTTE and PONT TOURNANT. At 11.10 a.m. a sharp burst of about 300 rounds 4.2's and 77mm on Right Battalion Right Brigade front line.

4. INTELLIGENCE.
   Batteries. L.O. Right Battalion Left Brigade reports flashes T.B. 85 degs. from K.15.a 05/40 - 4 77mm guns firing 8 - 10 rounds per minute from 2.30 a.m. to 4.0 a.m. 9/5/18. Also two guns firing from same direction and another battery TSB 84 degs. from K.8.c 40/07 between 11.45 p.m. and 1.30 a.m. last night and another TSB 114 degs. from K.8.c 40/07 between 2.30 a.m. and 4 a.m. (these batteries doing the gas shelling previously reported). It appears that these guns are run forward to do this gas shooting - thought to be in K.16.b and d along the road and in K.22.a and b. Photos show two open 4-gun battery positions at K.17.b 5/5 and 7/7 and the works at K.22.c 8/1, though previously considered not to be a battery position, is now reported to contain a battery. 8.0 p.m. - 9.0 p.m. 4.2's shelling RUE des MORTS in salvoes of 3 and 4 TSB 109 from J.5.c 4/1.

   During night batteries gas-shelling J.5.c TSB 85 degs from J.5.c 4/1. 12.10 p.m. 77mm shelling K.14.a TSB 94 degs from K.15.a 1/4. 1.40 p.m. 5.9" shelling K.9.c TSB 120 degs. from K.15.a 1/4 (during the shelling 121st Bty searched K.16.a and b. A battery in this direction ceased fire, and a small dump was put up.)

   T.B. 125 degs. taken from groove of a 5.9" dud at D.28.b 4/5.

   Aerial. E.A. inactive today. Some over our lines between 7. p.m. and 8.30 p.m. yesterday.

   Balloons. None up today. 7.30 p.m. 9th one up T.B. 118 degs. from K.15.a 1/4.

   M.G's. (From Div. Summary). Active at night from K.26.c 6/6, K.21.a 5/4 and K.15.b 6/8.

   Movement. Very little seen - bad visibility. No unusual movement.

   Fires. A large number seen in the enemy's lines during the night and one 9.15 p.m. - 1.30 a.m. T.B. 110 degs from K.34.a 4/4. Another at 9.0 a.m. this morning T.B. 110 degs. from K.15.a 05/40.

   Miscellaneous. Loophole visible in hedge at K.21.d 0/1.

   3.55 p.m. 9th a pigeon flew towards enemy's lines from over K.14.

   News. French carried out successful minor operation yesterday evening, cleared GRIVESNES PARK and took two hundred prisoners.

   sd. R.F. MASON, Lieut.R.A.
10th May, 1918.   Intelligence Officer 5th Div.Art'y.

5TH DIVISIONAL ARTILLERY INTELLIGENCE SUMMARY 6PM 8/5/18 to 6 PM 9/5/18.

1. **SITUATION.** Unchanged.

2. **OUR ARTILLERY.** Increased harassing fire during the night - the usual during the day. Some gas shell fired during night by 4.5" Hows. on selected areas. Today besides harassing fire, registration and calibration, House at K.16.a 1/1 was shelled with 4.5's, - also H.B. suspected at K.22.c 9/1. D/160 fired a successful aeroplane shoot at L'EPINETTE (K.11.a.) 61 ranging rounds, all shells fell within Y and Z circles - damage caused to buildings and small fire started. 84th Brigade batteries retaliated on K.22.c. and 26.b. at mid-night at Infantry request, and 15th Brigade batteries paid special attention to wiring parties during the night. 84th Brigade responded to NF call at 5.5 p.m. K.36.c 9/5. D/84 carried out several retaliatory shoots on houses and on suspected H.B. K.22.c 9/1. Also shot at and dispersed movement in trench K.21.d 5/8 yesterday.

3. **ENEMY ARTILLERY.** Rather heavier. Right Battalion Right Brigade shelled with 5.9's at 11.30 p.m. - we retaliated. About 60 5.9's on J.34.a and b. and J.28.d. between 10.0 p.m. and 2.0 a.m. Another heavy but short burst of fire of all calibres on the forest front at 3.30 a.m. D.23.a and d. rather heavily shelled between midnight and 4.0 a.m. with gas, 4.2's and 77mm. Today, some 4.2's on Canal Bank K.32. at 8.0 a.m. One 77mm shell hit the house at J.36.a 3/6. Only round fired - thought to be checking lines. About 35 8" on J.4.a between 5 and 6 p.m. Some 4.2's on J.34.d and D.30 during the afternoon; and LA MOTTE and LE PARC intermittently shelled during the day.

4. **INTELLIGENCE.**
   Batteries.) An 18-Pdr fuze set at 19.9 (which with an average corrector of 156 puts the range at 6025) was picked up in ST. VENANT at a spot which had previously been shelled by a suspected 18-Pdr Bty. L.O. Left Battn Right Bde also reported that the enemy seems to have several 18-Pdrs in use on this front.
   Infantry report gun flash 5.10 a.m. TB 86degs from K.26.b 2/7.
   Aerial. E.A. much more active. Bombs have been dropped promiscuously in the forest during the day. E.A. over our line at 6, 7.30, 10.35, and 11.30 a.m. and 12.15, 2, and 3.5 p.m. 5.30 a.m. one bomb dropped near cross roads in HAVERSKERQUE.
   Balloons. 3.45 p.m. T.B. 120 degs. from J.5.a 7/5.
   ? T.B. 68 " " J.36.d 0/4.
   M.G's. Known to be in house at K.21.b 35/60. Others reported at K.21.d 05/35 and (Div. Summary) K.26.b 90/95. (A.A.) at K.26.b 7/3, K.31.b 7/7 and K.26.c 8/7.
   T.M's. Reported still in action at K.26.b 90/35 (GABY) and K.26.d 35/60 (NELLY).
   Movement. etc. Washing hanging out in garden at K.21.c 8/8. Men seen at houses K.5.d 3/5 and K.21.d 5/9. There is a post camouflaged with branches on road at K.11.b 4/9.
   Defences. 20 yards of thick wire at K.32.a 2/6 - breastwork at K.21.d 1/4 - wiring and digging in progress about K.26.b 7/5. Wiring parties seen by patrols at K.10.a 90/02 and K.10.c 7/8. Hedge running E. from K.10.c 6/7 is being wired. A sap from K.10.c 7/8 towards our line is being dug.
   Miscellaneous. Some houses in LE SART on fire at 4A.M.

sd. R.F. MASON. Lieut. R.A.
9th May, 1918. Intelligence Officer 5th Divisional Arty.

SECRET.

5TH DIVISIONAL ARTILLERY INTELLIGENCE SUMMARY 6PM 7/5/18 TO 6PM 8/5/18.

1. SITUATION. Unchanged.

2. OUR ARTILLERY. Harassing fire continued day and night. Some VN fired during the night by 4.5" Hows. on selected targets. Retaliation was called for and given by 18-Pdr batteries covering Right Brigade for T.M. fire from K.26.b 9/4 at 1.45 a.m. Today 37th Battery carried out a destructive shoot of suspected O.P., house at K.16.a 18/10. 160 Brigade obtained 9 direct hits on enemy front line trench in K.10.c - also fired at house K.12.a 15/70. D/84 registered known T.M. and M.G. Emplacements in K.26.b and K.27.b. Other registration and calibration continued.

3. ENEMY ARTILLERY. The usual intermittent night fire was augmented by a light shrapnel barrage from 1.30 a.m. - 1.35 a.m. on the Right Brigade front, and some T.M. fire strong enough to warrant retaliation at 1.45 a.m. Another feature was the sniping of the CROIX MARAISSE area with a 5.9" H.V. gun between 9.30 a.m. and 10.30 a.m. Otherwise no unusual shelling. The LE PARC, PONT des FENDRES, K.14 and K.15 areas were harassed at intervals during the day. J.28.d. was harassed by 77mm at 6.0 a.m. this morning and again this evening - a change from the usual 5.9" and 4.2".

4. INTELLIGENCE.
Batteries. Bearings from grooves of two 5.9" H.V. shells were taken T.B. 78 degs. from J.21.b 9/3 and T.B. 76 degs. from J.22.c 1/5.

Angle of descent in both cases 15 degs. 20 mins.
    11.30 a.m. 77mm shelling K.9.d TSB 57 degs. from K.15.b 0/4.
    12.30 p.m. 77mm shelling K.14.b TSB 92 degs. from K.15.b 0/4.
    2.20 p.m. 77mm TSB 87 degs. from K.15.a 1/4.
    4.55 p.m. one flash seen at K.23.a 4/3 (Approx.)
Aerial. 2 E.A. over K.20 and K.14 at 3000 ft at 6.20 p.m. and 7.0 p.m. engaged by M.G's. One small bomb dropped at K.20.c 3/9. E.A. over our lines at 7.40, 8.45, 10.30 a.m. and 1.10 p.m. Some bombs dropped in BOIS MOYEN this morning.
M.G's. AARON (K.26.c 6/6) active last night - silenced by artillery fire. M.G's seen firing from K.26.c 8/7.
JOSEPH fired from K.26.b 8/7. Another M.G. from K.21.c 1/8.
Movement. etc. Men seen in post at about K.21.a 9/6 - also at K.27.b 7/5 and at house K.21.b 3/6.
Defences. Hedge from K.21.c 6/9 to K.21.a 9/1 is wired. No enemy wire up opposite LE VERTBOIS. New wire from K.32.a 1/4 to 32.a 4/7. Shell-holes are being linked up at K.26.b 8/6 and 27.b 7/5.
Balloons. 6.30 a.m. - 8.15 a.m. T.B. 89 and 95 degs. from K.15.a 0/4.
Miscellaneous. SALOME Dump was blown up by a bomb from one of our planes at 5.25 p.m. today.

Of the 206 German Divisions on the Western front, 148 have already been engaged in the battle since March 21st, 18 are of poor quality, 26 are in line and have not yet been drawn into the battle, and 14 are fresh and in reserve. 44 Divisions having been withdrawn are being refitted.

                sd. R.F. MASON. Lieut. R.A.
8th May, 1918.   Intelligence Officer 5th Divnl Artillery.

SECRET.

5TH DIVISIONAL ARTILLERY INTELLIGENCE SUMMARY 6PM 6/5/18 to 6PM 7/5/18.

1. SITUATION. Unchanged on our front. From prisoner's information it is gathered that the German Division in the PACAUT WOOD Sector on our right is on the defensive for the time being.

2. OUR ARTILLERY. 119 Bty shelled a working party at K.16.c 1/9 during the evening, at Infantry request. D/84 demolished 2 houses (K.27.a and 26.b.). These were set on fire by C/84 at 7.15 p.m., and bursts of fire were put down around them at intervals until mid-night. Harassing fire as usual during the night and day, on targets obtained from aeroplane photos. Today 37th Bty engaged a H.B. at K.23.d 55/85 - D/15 carried out a destructive shoot on houses in K.32.a and 33.a - several direct hits. B/84 silenced a T.M. at K.26.b 9/4. 12 1st Bty engaged a H.B. K.B.80 at 8.55 p.m. (6th.) and set fire to house at K.15.b 8/4 (Approx.)

3. ENEMY ARTILLERY. Harassing fire with 5.9's, 4.2's or 77mm on K.1., K.7., K.25., the HAVERSKERQUE - ST. VENANT Road, the CORBIE - LA MOTTE BAUDET road, ST. VENANT and LE PARC during the night - decreasing from midnight onwards. Quiet, early this morning. D.28, D.30.c, Left Brigade front and support lines, and ST. VENANT lightly shelled at intervals today. Quiet day.

4. INTELLIGENCE. Batteries.
8.45pm 4.2" shelling K.1.c. TSB 103 degs. from K.14.a 65/95.
                    TSB 115 --"------- D.30.c 2/2.
                          (probably K.B.80).
8.0pm 5.9" shelling K.25. From various times taken the Bty was about 8,400 yards from K.34.a 4/4 and at TSB between 80 and 100 degs from there. (Perhaps K.D.60 or K.D.90).
   M.G's. (From Div. Summary). Reported at K.21.a 9/9, K.4.b 9/0, K.10.d 85/85, K.16.a 7/9 and K.26.b 70/25. (Last named a fresh location). M.G. at K.26.c 7/6 was silenced by our Lewis Guns.
   T.M's. Active about mid-night from K.27.a 0/4.
   Aerial. 7 p.m. one low-flying E.A. dropped 3 bombs in wood in K.19. One E.A. high over Canal at 3.20 p.m. as far as J.35. Driven back by A.A. fire. (LA MOTTE - MERVILLE Road at K.14.d 7/3 badly smashed in a bomb.)
   Defences. Enemy is reported to be digging in front of hedge at K.32.a 4/9. (No late photos available). New wire reported in front of house at K.26.c 8/6. There appear to be enemy posts at K.26.c 8/1, K.32.a 3/7 and K.31.b 8/6 (tracks are visible to these points, on photos.) Div. Summary reports digging in progress at K.32.a 4/9. New wire in front of house at K.26.c 6/6. Concertina wire round house at K.10.c 8/9 - wiring party seen and dispersed by patrols at K.10.d 95/95.

                                              sd. R.F. MASON. Lt. R.A.
7th May, 1918.   Intelligence Officer 5th Divisional Art'y

SECRET.

SUMMARY OF OPERATIONS, ETC., 6PM 5/5/18 to 6PM 6/5/1918.

1. SITUATION. Unchanged. Division on our left captured a man of 39th Division who states that men of the 35th Division (which attacked us on Apr. 14th) told him that owing to their failure on the 14th, the 35th Division was no longer classed as an Assault Division. They are now being drilled night and day in order to make them capable of offensive operations.

2. OUR ARTILLERY. Harassing fire as usual on tracks, roads, copses, etc., during the 24 hours. 160th Brigade barraged in support of a raid by Division on our left (on BEAULIEU Farm, which they found empty). Also fired on NEUF BERQUIN in conjunction with Corps H.A. Today registration, calibration, line and ammunition testing - no more defective rounds found. A/84 and C/84 shelled K.27.b at 12 Noon. 27th Brigade fired concentrations on L.7 and L.13 at 4.40 a.m. and 5.20 a.m. 37th Battery fired 80 WN on LES PURESBECQUES during the night.

3. ENEMY ARTILLERY. About 100 4.2" and 40 Gas (Phosgene) shells on RUE des MORTS between 5.15 a.m. and 5.40 a.m. this morning. Bursts of fire on ST. FLORIS during the night. J.28.a shelled with 5.9's between midnight and dawn. HAVERSKERQUE and K.25.a shelled at intervals during the night. Occasional rounds 5.9" on Cross Roads in K.9.a., a few shrapnel on J.10.a and a few 4.2's West of LES LAURIERS during the day. Comparatively quiet day.

4. INTELLIGENCE. Batteries. Enemy battery fires on HAVERS- -KERQUE each night T.B. 109 degs. 30 mins. from J.27.c 5/9. 5.9" shelling cross roads K.9.a TSB 100 degs. from K.15.a 1/4.
   M.G's. 1.50pm (5th) directs hits were obtained on M.G. Post at K.26.c 2/1 from which Germans crawled. Div. reports M.G.'s firing from K.21.a 90/95 (behind sleepers and mounds on railway) K.23.b 7/7, K.31.b 7/1, K.15.b 6/3, K.16.a 0/7 and K.10.c 8/9.
   T.M's. Active at K.21.b 2/2 and K.15.b 9/1.
   Defences. Shell holes at K.27.a 2/7 have been linked up. Thick wire barricade at K.15.b 5/1. Trench running from K.15.b 5/5 to 8/3 has four strands of wire in front of it. Considerable amount of fresh work reported on trenches and wire between K.15.b 6/3 and K.15.b 9/4. Five strands of wire visible - also some concertina wire.
   Aerial. Several E.A. over our lines between 8 a.m. and 10 a.m. 5 p.m. 1 E.A. dropped 4 bombs S. of HAVERSKERQUE. 5.45 p.m. this E.A. was brought down by 4 of ours, and landed up-side down in I.36 (approx.)
   Balloons. Up at 6.30 a.m. T.B. 126, 117, 125, 135 and 116 degs. from K.15.a 1/4.
   Occupied Localities. Germans ran out of house at K.32.a 7/7 when it was shelled on the morning of the 5th. Trench at K.26.c 8/7 occupied - also at K.15.b 5/4. Houses at K.15.b 5/2 and K.21.d 05/40. Houses at K.21.b 2/2 contain at least one T.M. and several Machine Guns, which are a nuisance to our Infantry. During the last week a lot of digging has been done at and around K.15.b 80/25. It probably still continues and would make a good night target.
   Miscellaneous. 6 a.m. house on fire in K.22.a. 6.45 p.m. another in K.16.d. Good observation over MERVILLE and LE SART is possible from K.25.a 7/2. (Lt. McGOWAN, A/15 Bty).

6/5/18.   sd. R. F. MASON. Lieut. R.A. I.O. 5 D.A.

SECRET.

SUMMARY OF OPERATIONS, ETC. 6PM 4/5/18 to 6PM 5/5/18.

1. **SITUATION.** Unchanged on our front. Prisoners taken by Division on our left state that the German Division there have commenced wiring their line.

2. **OUR ARTILLERY.** Harassing fire on roads, tracks and selected targets continued during the 24 hours. A/15 set fire to LE SART yesterday evening. The church started burning, but it is reported today that the spire is still standing. D/15 obtained 30 direct hits on house at K.26.c 85/05 today. Mist and rain have made observed shooting impossible most of the day. 160th Brigade did a little registration and calibration. Ammunition was again tested and not found defective.

   Heavy Artillery set fire to houses at K.23.d 35/50 at 3.30 p.m. Several heavy explosions as of ammunition dumps there between 3.30 p.m. and 4.15 p.m.

3. **ENEMY ARTILLERY.** Areas K.31.d, 25.b, c and d. were shelled at intervals through the night with 77mm and 4.2's. Some 4.2's and 5.9's also on J.28.c and 33.a at 4.0 a.m. this morning. The Canal Bank between HAVERSKERQUE and ST. VENANT was harassed during the night. Today has on the whole been much quieter - possibility owing to bad visibility. D.30.c., K.1., and J.11.a and b were occasionally harassed with 5.9's and 4.2's. Some shrapnel and 5.9's on forward trenches. Very quiet on back areas of Right Brigade. No heavy shelling during the period.

4. **INTELLIGENCE.**
   Batteries. No information available.
   M.G's. L.O. with 1st Cheshire Regt. reports M.G's. at K.26.b 8/7 and 26.b 8/3 active last night. L.O. Right Brigade reports that enemy machine gunning was much less than usual last night and was well kept down by our rifle and M.G. fire. Div. Summary reports M.G's active at K.21.a 5/3, K.21.a 9/8, K.26.c 6/6, K.15.b 6/3, K.16.a 0/7, K.10.d 1/1 and K.10.c 8/9.
   T.M's. Reported active at K.26.b 9/4, K.27.d 0/3 and K.21.b 2/2, - (M.G. in this house also). The last two were not firing last night.
   Defences. Enemy wire is reported along the front of the hedge from K.21.a 7/0 to K.21.b 3/6. Patrols found a large working party - apparently wiring - along the front of the house at K.26.c 6/6 ("MOATED GRANGE"). Another patrol reports wiring in progress from K.15.b 5/3 to b 7/5. Other wiring parties at K.15.d 7/5 and K.10.b 5/5 approx. No wire along hedge K.15.b 05/18 - K.15.b 5/0.
   Occupied Localities. Shell holes at K.21.c 8/8, K.21.c 7/3, K.21.c 8/4 and houses K.26.c 6/6 and K.21.a 9/0.
   Balloons. Seen from J.34.d 4/4.
   3.20pm-4.15pm T.B. 103½ degs.   3.20pm-4pm T.B. 68½ degs.
   3.25pm-3.55pm -"-   70½ -"-   3.55pm-4.25pm T.B. 93½ degs.
   4.0pm-4.25pm -"-   92½ -"-   4.15pm-4.35pm -"- 86 degs.
   4.30pm-4.45pm -"- 100 -"-
   Work. 27th Bde reports a trench has been dug from K.15.b 8/3 to K.15.b 85/50.
   Miscellaneous. Lieut. WINTERTON, 52nd Battery R.F.A., reports that there is a brick-kiln amongst the houses at K.26.d 3/6. It has had one direct hit on it but seems none the worse. It appears very strong, it is loop-holed and probably fortified. The bunch of buildings here commands all the ground sloping away in K.26.d and K.27.c.
   No good enfilade view of our front is possible from S. of the Canal at about K.31.central owing to the number of trees in the way.
   A civilian interviewed by Right Brigade reports cellars in the following houses. K.21.d 3/9, 8/9. K.32.c 3/9. K.26.d 35/60 (good). K.33.a 86/94, K.27.c 86/10. K.27.c 95/05 and K.27.d 07/05 (good).

   sd. R.F. MASON. Lieut. R.A.
5th May, 1918. Intelligence Officer 5th Divnl Art'y.

SECRET.

SUMMARY OF OPERATIONS ETC FROM 6 P.M. 3.5.18 to 6 P.M. 4.5.18.

1. SITUATION.   Unchanged.

2. OUR ARTILLERY.   Harassing fire maintained on tracks, roads and copses during the 24 hours.   To-day A/15 Battery fired incendiary shells into a house at K.33.a.4/0 and set fire to it. (Later they shot at and set fire to LE SART about 7 p.m.)   12 noon 37th Howitzer Battery fired 150 VN into a H.B. seen firing in K.23.d. - observed shoot with good results.   The H.B. had been shelling RUE des MORTS.   160 Brigade carried out shoots on houses etc. - Cross Roads K.17.b 6/7, house K.12.a 1/1, houses K.10.d 05/60 and suspected H.B's in K.18.a and K.6.b. A/84 fired bursts of fire on E.A. reported crashed in K.32.b at 6.30 p.m. last night, and on movement in K.28.c today. Registration, calibration and ammunition-testing continued.   No more ammunition found defective as yet.

3. ENEMY ARTILLERY.   LE VERTBOIS was shelled at frequent intervals with 5.9's both by day and night.   Between 4.0 a.m. and 6.0 a.m. some 5.9's on roads round PAPOTE and on J.28.b., 4.2"s on J.28.d. and J.29.c.   Also heavy shelling by 4.2's and shrapnel of ST. FLORIS 5.30 a.m. to 6.0 a.m. Between 11.0 a.m. and 12.30 p.m. J.11 and 12 (Rue des Morts) was treated to a heavy apparently counter battery, area shoot with 4.2's and gas.   11.30 a.m. - 11.50 a.m. hurricane fire about 200 4.2's - 11.40 a.m. - 12.50 p.m. Gas Shells 3 or 4 a minute.   Damage done - small house at J.5.c 6/1, set on fire.   One aiming post at 121 section position damaged.   Counter Batteries did all they could to stop it, and Field Guns retaliated.   70 5.9's on ST. VENANT and BOIS des VACHES during the afternoon - also a few 4.2's and 77mm on D.16.a.

4. INTELLIGENCE.   Batteries.   During shoot on Rue des Morts battery seen firing 115 degs. T.B. from K.15.a 1/4 - placed at K.23.d 55/85 to 40/90.   TSB's of 120 degs. from J.5.c 36/07 and 110 approx. from J.11.c 1/6 taken on batteries engaged in the shoot.
    M.G's. A rather troublesome M.G. is located at K.26.c 6/3 inside the edge of the grove near the southern house.   L.O. Battalion of Right Brigade reports M.G's - 2 at K.26.b 6/0, 2 in hedge at K.26.b 8/3 and 1 in house at K.26.b 7/8. Div. Summary states - M.G. very active all night from K.26.c 7/4
    Movement, etc. Transport heard on road in K.32.a at 12.45 a.m.   And 8.30 p.m. to 9.30 p.m. on VIERHOEK - CORNET PERDU road.
    Miscellaneous. 160th Brigade reports house at K.10.d 6/0 unoccupied.
    8.20 p.m. 2 houses were set on fire, by 15th Brigade 18-pdr incendiary shells, at T.B. 95 degs. and 96 degs. from J.34.a 4/4, and burned all night.
    4.30 p.m. several green balloons or parachutes fell near CORBIE at J.36.central.
    The enemy barrage is reported to be nowadays from LES LAURIERS along the edge of the wood to K.25.a 6/1 thence S. to K.31.a 5/0.   Most of his retaliatory shooting is done on the edge of the wood and at LE VERTBOIS, with 77mm and 5.9's respectively.   Most of the shelling comes from the direction of MERVILLE AND S.E. of LE SART.
    From a tube containing what is thought to be Thirmite, picked up in J.28.b., this morning, it is thought that the enemy is firing a few 4.2" incendiary shell there.

                                    sd/- R.F.MASON, Lieut.R.A.
4-5-18.   Intelligence Officer, 5th Divisional Artillery.

SECRET.

SUMMARY OF OPERATIONS, ETC., 6PM 2/5/18 to 6PM 3/5/18.

1. SITUATION. Unchanged on our front. Division on our right carried out a small raid in Q.2.b. last night, destroyed M.G's and captured three prisoners of 15th Res. Division which relieved the 16th Division on night May1st/2nd.

2. OUR ARTILLERY. Continued harassing enemy communications and roads during the 24 hours. 37th Bty fired 30 rounds VN into each of K.22.d 1/7, K.23.d 4/6, K.23.c 5/9 and K.16.d 6/6. 52nd Battery fired incendiary shells at houses behind the enemy's lines. Today registration and calibration by most batteries. 160th Brigade carried out shoots on houses in K.10.c., 11.d., 16.b., and 17.a. D/84 engaged a T.M. at K.21.b 6/6 (yesterday evening). D/160 fired 100 rounds at H.B. at K.11.central this morning.

3. ENEMY ARTILLERY. J.28.b again worried by 5.9's during the night. Some 4.2's and 5.9's also on LE PARC, the edge of the Wood in K.25.a and K.20.c., ST. VENANT, and 4 bursts of 77 mm fire on J.15. during the night. Today ST VENANT, LE PARC, and ST. FLORIS were intermittently shelled with 4.2's, K.20.a, K.9.b and c., K.14.b, D.23 were shelled at intervals with 5.9's and K.14.b and J.3.c with 77mm.

The enemy appears to test Meteor at about 9 a.m. every morning on ST VENANT Church, with a 4.1" H.V. Gun. This has occurred the last 4 mornings with high H.E. bursts.

4. INTELLIGENCE. Batteries. 2.30 p.m. 4.2's shelling K.14.b TSB 110 degs. from K.15.a 1/4.
Aerial. 5 E.A. seen over our lines (high) during the day. One is reported brought down by three of ours in K.32.b at 6.30 p.m. E.A. dropped a few bombs on K.20.c at 3.0 p.m. May 2nd.
Balloons. NIL.
M.G's. (From Div. Summary). New M.G. position located in house at K.15.d 70/25. Others active from K.16.a 7/8, K.15.b 5/3, K.15.d 90/25 and K.15.b 7/2.
T.M's. Reported firing at 9.20 p.m. from K.21.b 6/6 - engaged and silenced by D/84.
Movement, etc. 6.20 p.m. car seen on road K.16.d 7/2 to K.22.b 6/8. Wiring party seen at K.21.b 4/7 - wiring in progress from K.15.b 7/6 to K.15.b 3/8. Men seen drawing tools from Camouflaged Dump at K.10.d 5/5. New earth seen at K.10.d 5/5.
Miscellaneous. A red light was fired when the enemy obtained a direct hit on our trenches in K.9.d, the firing then ceased.
Houses burning 10.30 p.m. - midnight T.B. 112 degs. from J.34.a 4/4 and 2.10 a.m. T.B. 87 degs. from same place.

sd. R.F. MASON. Lieut. R.A.
Intelligence Officer,
5th Divisional Artillery.

3rd May, 1918.

SECRET.

SUMMARY OF OPERATIONS, ETC., 6 PM 1/5/18 to 6 PM 2/5/18.

1. **SITUATION.** Unchanged.

2. **OUR ARTILLERY.** Harassing fire as usual on Farms, roads, and other occupied areas, during the 24 hours. D/15 Battery retaliated on LE SART this morning, 120th Battery engaged T.M's at K.15.d 8/3 and K.16.c 6/2 and 18-Pdr batteries of 160 Brigade shelled K.6.c 1/6 — all at Infantry request this morning. 37th Battery fired a few gas shell at 1 a.m. into NEUF BERQUIN and shelled K.22.b 8/8 this afternoon. 119th Battery twice engaged K.D.21 battery. 160 Brigade batteries shelled K.17.b 65/60, and houses K.10.d 0/5 and d 0/6 (suspected M.G.E's.) Registration, calibration, and Ammunition-testing was continued today. D/84 set on fire the house at K.21.b 2/2.

3. **ENEMY ARTILLERY.** HAVERSKERQUE and J.28.b were shelled with 4.2's between 3.0 a.m. and 4.30 a.m. Some 5.9's on J.11.b about mid-night and on LA MOTTE intermittently throughout the night. Today occasional rounds 4.2" on roads in LE PARC, J.29.c.&J.9.LE VERTBOIS was shelled intermittently with 5.9's and 77mm all day.
A 4.1" H.V. is reported shelling K.9.b and c. during the early afternoon. A few 4.2's on K.1., and some 77mm on CAUDESCURE, houses K.3.d 5/2., and K.2.d 8/4 comprised the rest of the day's shelling on this front. About 200 4.2's on the West edge of ST VENANT reported during the day.

4. **INTELLIGENCE.** Batteries. During the day. 4.1" H.V. shell-ing K.9.b and c. TSB 58 degs. from K.15.a 1/4. 4.30pm. 4.2" (4-gun Bty) shelling K.9.c TSB 96 degs. from K.15.a 1/4. During early morning. 4.2" shelling HAVERSKERQUE & J.28 TSB 105 degs. from J.27.c 4/9. (This battery is a nuisance to our batteries in the neighbourhood and is active every morning commencing about 3.0 a.m.).
Aerial. Fewer E.A. and more of ours seen.
M.G's. Reported at K.16.a 65/90 and K.16.a 80/85 (By Inf.)
(From Div.Summary) M.G's active last night at K.16.a 3/8 - K.16.a 50/85 (K.16.a seems to be a hot-bed of M.G's) K.10.c 75/80 - K.10.d 0/7 and K.15.b 5/8.
T.M's. H.T.M. reported at K.21.b 6/4. Others at K.26.d 35/65 and K.15.d 7/4.
Movement. Considerable at K.27.b 3/5. Men seen entering house at K.16.c 0/0 (houses at K.10.a 7/2 and K.10.c 8/9 found, by patrols, unoccupied). At 8 p.m. transport was heard on the road from K.16.b 5/1 to MERVILLE and going N.E. along road at about K.10.d 8/9.
Defences. Patrols report an enemy's front line trench from K.10.c 65/70 to K.10.b 3/1.
LATER. During day D/15 Battery put 60 rounds athouses at K.33.5 5/1 and K.33.a 5/1 obtaining several direct hits. 1 shell must have opened up a dugout as the timber can plainly be seen sticking up.
Hostile Batteries. Rough bearing of a 4.2" shell-groove at J.30.d 41/57 is 100½ degs. true.
The shelling of LE VERTBOIS today came from TSB 115 degs. from K.26.a 1/3 and time from report to burst 15 secs.
Aerial. 12.45 p.m. E.A. flew low over J.25 and 29. 3 p.m. one E.A. flew very high over Canal to J.32.a.
Miscellaneous. 10 p.m.(1st) Glare of a fire seen T.B. 122 degs from J.34.a 5/4. 12.5 - 1.30 a.m. dump burning in enemy's lines T.B. 107 degs. from J.34.a 5/4.
The Canal bank from the brickfields to house K.33.a 5/0 now seems deserted and is very much knocked about.

          sd. R.F. MASON, Lieut. R.A.
2nd May, 1918. Intelligence Officer 5th Divisional Arty.

SUMMARY OF OPERATIONS, ETC., 6PM 30/4/18 to 6PM 1/5/18.

1. **SITUATION.** Unchanged.

2. **OUR ARTILLERY.** Harassing fire was continued during night and day, on communications, troublesome houses, etc. Owing to bad weather and consequent lack of aeroplane photos, tracks used by the enemy are mostly unknown and cannot yet be harassed. Today 18-Pounders of 160 Bde shelled PONT RONDIN, and D/84 engaged a Tank gun at K.22.d 15/80 and T.M. Position at K.21.b 2/2 obtaining several hits on the latter. 120 Battery shelled house at K.15.b 5/1 at Infantry request. B/ and C/84 answered a N.F. call in K.29.v at 11.4.a.m. In addition to this and harassing fire, batteries registered and checked lines and tested ammunition - and found one lot defective.

3. **ENEMY ARTILLERY.** The LE FORET - LE CORBIE Road was again sniped with 4.2's throughout the night. J.28 was harassed with 5.9's and 4.2's especially around a 6" How. position there. Today CHAPEL BOOM was worried again with 5.9's, LE PARC and ST VENANT with 4.2's and LES LAURIERS, ST FLORIS and LA MOTTE BAUDET with 77mm. Also a few 5.9's on J.3.d and J.14.a during the morning. Hostile fire, on the whole, lighter.

4. **INTELLIGENCE.** Batteries, TSB 110 degs. from J.26.a 60/05 was taken on 4.2" sniping LE FORET - LE CORBIE Road last night - bearing will be verified or contradicted tonight.
5.9's shelling CHAPEL BOOM during day TSB 76 degs. from K.15.a 1/4 and 77 mm. on LE PARC TSB 110 degs. from J.5.c 3/0.
Infantry report H.B. active at about K.6.c 1/6.
(From Div. Summary). M.G's. Reported at K.15.b 5/8 - K.10.d 0/6 - behind hedge at K.10.c 75/80 and K.15.b 65/95.
L.T.M(s. Located at K.26.c 7/3 (approx.)
Movement. Considerable between house at K.28.c 2/3 and trench just in front of it. Houses in K.26.b are still believed occupied.
Defences. Through K.21.b and d. the enemy's line appears to run parallel with ours and about 400 yards distant.
A new trench is visible at K.10.a 2/0. New earth has been observed in front house at K.5.d 65/40 and in front of hedge at K.10.c 65/80 (latter thought a M.G.E.). Continuous but unoccupied trench found by patrols from K.15.b 7/5 to K.15.b 5/4.

5. **MISCELLANEOUS.** The square sandbagged work at about J.36.b 0/5 makes a passable O.P. for the brickfields and N. of them.

sd. R.F. MASON. Lieut. R.A.
1st May, 1918. Intelligence Officer 5th Divnl Art'y.

LATER. 5.0 p.m. - hostile battery observed from K.8.c 7/0 on G.B. 70 degs. 45 mins. firing on area of LA MOTTE aaa - Periscope suspected in chimney of house K.16.b 45/10.

Army Form C. 2118.

WAR DIARY
or
INTELLIGENCE SUMMARY.

(Erase heading not required.)

MAY 1918.

Instructions regarding War Diaries and Intelligence Summaries are contained in F.S. Regs., Part II. and the Staff Manual respectively. Title pages will be prepared in manuscript.

W.A.L. 10,000. 36A.

Place	Date	Hour	Summary of Events and Information	Remarks and references to Appendices
FORÊT DE NIEPPE.	13/14	8am to 8am	Wet day very quiet.	
"	14/15	"	Fine. Relief commenced preparatory to a side slip to south by the brigade. Two guns per battery of 182nd Brigade for not relieve 37th Brigade Batteries, in turn relieving 8th Bde. Brigade RFA.	
"	15/16	"	Relief completed. Dispositions are now as follows:— H.Q. at J 26 b 45/30 on the CROIX MARAISSE — TANNAY Road.	
			119 Bty at J 33 e 9/6. on the CANAL D'AIRE.	
			120 " J 35 d 4/6 "	
			121 " J 29 c 4/8 "	
			37 " J 15 d 6/6 in Bois D'AMONT.	
			During relief 120 & 121 Batteries heavily shelled Yperite. 11 casualties. Nothing to report.	
CROIX MARAISSE	16/17	"		
	17/18	"	120th Battery heavily gas shelled overnight. 5 casualties (wounded).	
	18/19	"	Fine day.	
	19/20	"	quiet.	

J. Berthier
for Lieut. Col.
Cmdg. 77 Brigade

Officer Commanding

27th Bde. No. BM/170.

............Battery RFA.

Reference 5th D.A. BM/29/2 and this Office No. BM/166.

1. Batteries on relief will take over the zones and S.O.S. Lines of the batteries they relieve.

2. The 120th Battery are finding the Battalion Liaison Officer from 6.0 p.m. tonight; an Officer of 121st Battery RFA will relieve him at 6.0 p.m. on the 17th inst.

3. Batteries will take over the roster of day and night firing at present in use by the 84th Brigade Batteries.

4. The 120th Battery will hand over the 15-pdr. B.L.C. at present in their wagon lines to B/152 Battery RFA.

5. Batteries will report tonight by phone when the relief is complete, that is, when their guns are in action and laid on their S.O.S. Lines.

Captain R.F.A.

15-5-18.

Adjutant 27th. Bde. R.F.A.

Officer Commanding

............Battery RFA.

119
180
181
37

27th Bde. No. BM/166.

Reference attached BBM/29/2.

1. The guns of the 152nd Brigade Batteries are being taken to 27th Brigade Wagon Lines and should arrive about 8.0 p.m. tonight. 27th Brigade teams will take these guns up to their present battery positions, hook into their own guns and take them over to relieve the guns of the 84th Brigade. After relieving 84th Brigade the 27th Brigade teams will take back the 84th Brigade guns to the 84th Brigade Wagon Lines, Guides being found by the 84th Brigade Batteries.

2. The 84th Brigade have arranged tonight for guides from A/84 B/84, C/84 batteries to be at the Cross Roads in J.21.d from 10.30 p.m.

3. Batteries will report to this office by telephone when their section has been relieved by the section of 152nd Brigade.

4. Batteries will report to this office total ammunition handed over and taken over on completion of relief.

Captain R.F.A.

14-5-18.

Adjutant 27th. Bde. R.F.A.

SECRET.   5th Divisional Artillery No.HBM/29/2.

. . . .

1. 84th Army Brigade R.F.A. will be withdrawn to Wagon Lines :-
        152nd Brigade, R.F.A. will relieve 27th Brigade R.F.A.
        27th.Brigade, R.F.A. will relieve 84th. Army Bde. R.F.A.

2. Reliefs will take place on the nights 14th/15th. May and 15th/16th.
   May, one section per battery being relieved on the first night and
   two sections per battery on the 2nd. night. On each night sections
   of 27th. Brigade will not move to relieve sections 84th. Brigade
   until they have been relieved by sections 152nd. Brigade. Reliefs
   by 152nd. Brigade batteries will be completed not later than 10-30p.m.

3. Reliefs will be as follows -
        A/152. relieves 119th.   119th. relieves A/84.
        B/152.   "   120th.   120th.   "   B/84.
        C/152.   "   121st.   121st.   "   C/84.
        D/152.   "   37th.   37th.   "   D/84.
        Hqrs. 152 Bde. relieves Hqrs. 27th. Bde.
        Hqrs. 27th. Bde. relieves Hqrs. 84th. Bde.

4. On completion of relief the artillery covering the 5th. Division Front
   will be grouped as follows -
   RIGHT GROUP.   Lieut-Col. HAWKES, D.S.O., 15th. Brigade R.F.A.
                   15th. Brigade R.F.A.
                   27th. Brigade R.F.A.
   LEFT GROUP.   Lieut-Col. ALLCARD, D.S.O., 152nd. Brigade R.F.A.
                   152nd. Brigade R.F.A.
                   160th. Brigade R.F.A.

5. Command of battery positions will pass on completion of reliefs.
   Command of LEFT Group will pass to Lieut-Col. ALLCARD at 6 p.m. May
   15th.

6. All photographs, intelligence maps, artillery boards, ammunition, back
   positions etc. will be handed over to relieving units.

7. Positions at present are -
        27th. Brigade R.F.A.   Hqrs.   J.9.d.8/5.
                                    119th.Bty. D.30.c.2/2.
                                    120th Bty. J.5.c.3/0.
                                    121st Bty, J.10.b.6/0.   (4 guns)
                                               J.12.a.3/7.   (2 guns)
                                    37th. Bty. J.11.c.0/5.

        84th Army Bde.R.F.A.   Hqrs.   J.26.b.45/50.
                                    A/84 Bty. J.33.c.9/8.
                                    B/84 Bty. P.5.b.3/8.
                                    C/84 Bty. J.29.c.6/8.
                                    D/84 Bty. J.15.d.6/6.   (4 Hows.)
                                               J.10.c.9/4.   (2 Hows.)

                                                   J Wallace
                                                       Major, R.A.
14th May, 1918.   Brigade Major, 5th Divisional Artillery.

Copies to:-   34th Divisional Artillery   (8 copies)
               27th Brigade, R.F.A.   (5 ---"---)
               84th Army Bde.R.F.A.   (5 ---"---)
               15th Brigade, R.F.A.   (1 copy)

5th Divisional Artillery No. HBM/29/3.

SECRET.

1. 84th Army Brigade R.F.A. will march from present Wagon Lines at 9.0 A.M. May 16th, under Orders of O.C. 84th Army Brigade, to the Rest Billets vacated by 152nd Brigade R.F.A. at WITTES.

2. 152nd Brigade R.F.A. Wagon Lines will move to 27th Brigade R.F.A. present Wagon Lines at 9.0 A.M. May 16th., under Orders of O.C. 152nd Brigade R.F.A.

3. 27th Brigade R.F.A. Wagon Lines will move to 84th Army Brigade R.F.A. Wagon Lines at 9.0 A.M. May 16th., under Orders of O.C. 27th Brigade R.F.A.

4. Acknowledge.

Headquarters.
R.A. 5 Divn.
15th May, '18.

Major R.A.
Brigade Major R.A. 5th Division.

Copies to :- 84th Army Brigade RFA.
27th Brigade RFA.
152nd Brigade RFA (Left Group).
34th Div. Arty.
5th Division 'G'.
    "   'Q'.
XI Corps R.A.
15th Brigade RFA.

Officer Commanding

............Battery RFA   37   27th Bde. No. BM/198.

The O.P. in the Chateau at F.5 b 3/8 will be used as the Brigade O.P.

This O.P. will be manned both night and day; while the principal object is to report enemy shelling and to look out for S.O.S. rockets during the night, every opportunity will be taken for reporting gun flashes, movement and any general information.

Each Officer will take up with him a reliable N.C.O. who can assist him in keeping the front under observation.

The 120th Battery RFA. will please arrange to erect as soon as possible a rocket board showing the Battalion Sectors.

Tour of duty 24 hours ; hour of relief 10.0 a.m.

20th May	...	121st Bty.
21st "	...	119th "
22nd "	...	37th "
23rd "	...	120th "
24th "	...	121st "
25th "	...	119th "
26th "	...	37th "
27th "	...	120th "
28th "	...	121st "
29th "	...	119th "
30th "	...	37th "

Captain R.F.A.

19-5-18.   Adjutant 27th. Bde. R.F.A.

SECRET.

5TH DIVISIONAL ARTILLERY INTELLIGENCE SUMMARY 6PM 11/5/18 to 6PM 12/5/18.

1. SITUATION. Unchanged.

2. OUR ARTILLERY. The usual increased harassing fire on tracks, bridges, etc., during the night. 27th Brigade batteries fired a concentration on H.B. suspected at K.16.d 6/1 - gas shell. Today harassing fire, calibration and registration continued. No special shoots.
   Trench Mortars. Registered on house and cross roads K.22.a 0/9 and K.26.c 8/0 and fired a few rounds at GABY.

3. ENEMY ARTILLERY. Quieter generally. Sharp 3-minute burst on Right Brigade front at 12.15 a.m. - all calibres. Some 4.2's and 5.9's on HAVERSKERQUE in the early morning. LES LAURIERS was shelled with 5.9's twice during the day otherwise only scattered harassing fire.

4. INTELLIGENCE.
   Batteries. Grid bearing from scoop of a dud 5.9" 97 degs from J.25.c 55/08. Infantry verify the presence of a 5.9" battery in K.30.c and report time of flight as 12 secs. - this 5.9" shells the front and support lines in K.20.b and 21.a.
   Aerial. 5 E.A. flew over K.13. and 19 at 3.45 p.m. - driven back by A.A. fire. 2 E.A. dropped small bombs near CAUDESCURE and in the forest early this morning. E.A. active over our lines at 6.30 p.m. yesterday and again this afternoon.
   Balloons. 10 up between 4.30 p.m. and 5.30 p.m. T.B's varying from 108 degs. true to 64 degs. true from J.34.a 4/4.
   M.G's. Firing from K.26.a 7/1, K.21.a 6/1 (troublesome) K.10.c 80/85 and 65/80, K.16.a 3/7 to 7/9, K.15.b 45/05, K.15.b 6/8 and K.15.b 30/05. 4.5" Hows. reported to have knocked out M.G. at K.21.b 3/6 during the afternoon - direct hit.
   T.M's. Fired a few rounds from K.21.b 2/2, K.15.b 5/2 and K.15.b 5/0 (last two possibly the same).
   Movement, etc. 121 Bty drove a man out of trench at K.15.b 7/4 and hit him in the open. Men seen at houses at K.15.b 6/2 and 45/05, in trench at K.15.b 60/45 and in post at K.15.b 70/75 (loopholes visible here). Sentry post reported at K.15.b 85/80. Smoke seen at suspected H.Q. at K.26.c 7/0.
   Defences. Fresh earth at K.26.c 7/8. Wire is being put up at K.26.b 2/5 and that in front of hedge K.21.c 6/9 to 21.a 9/1 has been thickened. New wire reported at K.15.b 4/1 and kniferests on road at K.15.d 4/9 and K.15.b 90/25. Fresh wire also at K.15.b 90/85 (all from Div. Summary).
   A new trench is visible along front of hedge K.32.a 3/8 to K.26.c 4/0.
   Miscellaneous. The heavies obtained 4 direct hits on MERVILLE Church this afternoon.

                        sd. R.F. MASON, Lieut, RA
12th May, '18.   Intelligence Officer 5th Divnl Art'y.

SECRET.

5TH DIVISIONAL ARTILLERY INTELLIGENCE SUMMARY 6PM 12/5/18 TO 6PM 13/5/18.

1. SITUATION. Unchanged.

2. OUR ARTILLERY. Continued harassing fire on tracks, and occupied localities during the day and night. A/84 fired at K.22.a.61/05 at 11.50 p.m. at Infantry request. D/84, 120th and 37th Batteries answered N.F.call K.22.a.6/3 (?) at 6.55 p.m. To-day D/15 Battery obtained 3 direct hits on house at K.26.c.75/10 and 52nd Battery 8 on house at K.26.c.0/0 besides harassing fire and ammunition checking. No special shoots.
   Trench Mortars. Y/5 again engaged GABY, otherwise quiet.

3. ENEMY FIRE. The usual 5.9"s and 4.2"s on J.34.b. and 28.b., and HAVERSKERQUE between 4 a.m. and 5 a.m. 3 bursts/of about 30 rounds shrapnel along Canal Bank in K.31. and J.36.a. between 7.30 a.m. and 8.30 a.m. - probably to stop early morning shoots, observed from that neighbourhood. A few 4.2"s on J.5.c., some 4.2"s and 5.9"s on LES LAURIERS and some 5.9"s on J.29.c. during the day - the rest negligible.

4. INTELLIGENCE.
   Batteries. J.22.a 6/1 N.F. Call.
   Aerial. E.A. active during the night bombing ST OMER, AIRE, HAVERSKERQUE and ST. VENANT amongst other places. No E.A. up today. At 6.30 p.m. yesterday one flew over K.31 remaining about there about 15 minutes. On returning, it dropped a balloon-message in the enemy's lines T.B. 81 degs. from J.34.a 4/4.
   Balloons. 10 were up between 5.0 a.m. and 9.0 a.m. today T.B. 61, 64, 64½, 73, 74, 75, 76½, 78, 83½ and 103 degs from J.34.a 4/4. Between 6 and 7.30 p.m. yesterday three up T.B's 85, 95 and 97 degs from same O.P.
   At 7.0 p.m. yesterday an enemy balloon, fired at by shrapnel, was pulled slowly down, turning up on end on its way down. Occupants descended by parachute, and balloon collapsed just before disappearing from view.
   M.G's. Active at K.15.b 45/05, K.15.d 80/35, K.21.a 95/90, K.26.b 7/7, K.26.c 6/3, K.26.c 25/10, K.26.c 30/25, K.26.c 2/2 and K.26.a 75/10 (From Div. Summary).
   Movement. etc. Infantry report that most Germans opposite this front are wearing new uniforms and new tin hats. Working parties seen at K.32.a 15/85 and K.31.b 5/5.
   Defences. etc. Much work - apparently a dugout - has been done on S. side of house at K.26.c 4/0 (shewn on map at K.26.c 4/1)
   Miscellaneous. 10.7 p.m. searchlight T.B. 87 degs. from J.34.a 4/4.
   7.40 p.m. dump blew up T.B. 87 degs. from J.34.a 4/4.
   MERVILLE Church is reported to be on the verge of a nervous breakdown.
   LATER. C/84 knocked LE SART Church spire down this evening.

   sd. R.F. MASON, Lt. R.A.
13th May, '18.   Intelligence Officer 5th Divnl Art'y.

SECRET.

5TH DIVISIONAL ARTILLERY INTELLIGENCE SUMMARY.
6PM 13/5/18 to 6PM 14/5/18.

1. **SITUATION.** Unchanged.

2. **OUR ARTILLERY.** Scheme of harassing all approaches carried out last night. C/ and D/84 engaged M.G's at 10.30 p.m. and A/84 engaged T.M's at K.33(2?).a 1/1, K.32.a 7/7 and K.26.d 9/4 at 4.30 a.m. Today's fire, was chiefly harassing and testing ammunition. 37 Bty engaged M.G's at K.15.b 9/3 at Infantry request and 84th Brigade responded to NF Call K.34.d 9/2 at 5.30 p.m. 52nd Bty shelled and burnt down the house at K.26.c 4/0. 160th Brigade shelled L'EPINETTE and drove 15 men out of one of the houses there and silenced M.G. at K.10.c 82/85 (BOVER) put bursts of fire on M.G's at K.10.d 25/65 (MUD) and K.10.d 90/88 (ANCHOR).
   Trench Mortars. X/5 fired 24 rounds during the afternoon and evening registering. Y/5 registered on suspected T.M.E. at K.15.d 65/40, fired 13 rounds at M.G.E's at K.26.b 8/7 and K.21.b 2/8 at 10.30 p.m. in conjunction with Field Guns.

3. **ENEMY ARTILLERY.** Fairly quiet night till 4.0 a.m. From then to 6.0 a.m. 35 4.2's on J.34.a and b, 15 5.9's on J.28.c., 20 4.2's round house J.28.a 7/1, intermittent 77mm and 4.2" fire on Canal bank in K.31 and J.36, and some 5.9's on J.11.d 3/7. T.M's were active on K.25.d at 4.0 a.m., and on Les Lauriers at 3.0 p.m. Some 4.2's on wood in K.25.a and the halt in the morning and a few 5.9's LE PARC during day.

4. **INTELLIGENCE.**
   Batteries. 5.30 p.m. K.34.d 9/2 NF Call.
   4.15 a.m. 4.2" shelling J.34.a and b TSB 76 degs from J.34.a 4/4.
   7.0 p.m., 14th. flashes 10 mins. left of L'EPINETTE (K.11.a 35/55) from K.14.a 75/75.
   Aerial. One E.A. low over our lines at 5.45 a.m. and another over BOIS DES VACHES at 9.40 a.m. 3 E.A. over our lines at 5.30 p.m.
   Balloons. 16 up again, at one p.m. T.B's from J.22.c 4/6, 72, 72½ (2), 74(2), 79, 79½, 81, 83½, 88½, 104, 105, 106½, 109, 116 and 119½ degs. 4 up at 4.15 p.m. T.B's 78, 86, 104, and 105 from J.28.a 3/0.
   M.G's. Reported at K.26.c 6/6 (light is seen in cellar of this house each night), K.26.c 2/2 (troublesome) and (from Div. Summary) at K.15.b 45/05 and 6/8, K.21.a 95/90 and 6/4, K.26.c 25/20 and 26.b 7/4.
   T.M's. Suspected at K.15.d 6/5. Pineapple bomb throwers active from K.21.a 70/05 and K.21.b 4/6.
   Movement. etc. Continual movement about new wooden house at K.15.b 60/25. Several small parties seen on tracks at K.16.a 50/35, and K.16.a 00/25. Men seen in trenches at K.15.b 6/4, K.10.c 8/0, and K.16.a 0/9 to K.15.b 7/8.
   Defences. Wire seen at K.26.c 7/3, from K.26.c 5/5 to 2/1 and at K.26.d 2/6. Large wiring parties seen at K.26.b 8/5 (approx.). Infantry patrols report new wire has been put out in front of the greater part of the enemy's line - also round a post at K.15.b 20/05.
   Miscellaneous. 52 Bty reports houses marked on map at K.31.b 6/1 and K.31.b 7/1 to be wrongly marked. They appear to be at K.31.b 4/1 and K.31.b 6/1 respectively.
   At 3.30 a.m. an enemy party of 3 men attempted to raid our extreme right post on the canal. All three were killed by L.G. fire and their bodies brought in. They belonged to the 140 I.R., 4th Div. (Normal).
   LATER. Inf. report H.B. seen firing T.B. 76 degs. 50' from K.14.a 75/75, at VIEUX MOULIN.

14th May, 1918.   sd. R.F. MASON, I.O. 5 D.A.

5TH DIVISIONAL ARTILLERY INTELLIGENCE SUMMARY
6PM 14/5/18 TO 6PM 15/5/18.

Secret.

1. SITUATION. Unchanged. The 3-man raid reported on our extreme right post yesterday appears to have been made by a "Sturm - Truppe" collected from 2 battalions of 140 I.R. 4th Division, consisting of considerably more than 3 men. Immediately on being challenged, they threw a dozen bombs which all fell short of the post, and then retreated hurriedly under L.G. and rifle fire, leaving 3 dead behind them.

2. OUR ARTILLERY. Besides the usual harassing fire during the night, A/15 and D/15 fired in support of raid by Brigade on our right at 11.30 p.m., engaging enemy M.G's. Today mainly harassing fire and ammunition - testing. 80th Battery set fire to house at K.26.c 6/6.
   Trench Mortars. X/5 engaged M.G. at K.26.c 8/7 during the morning and silenced T.M. at K.32.a 8/7 (ELSIE) at 2.15 p.m.

3. ENEMY ARTILLERY. Much quieter on the Left Brigade front, but more persistent on the Right Brigade front. 4.2's harassed lightly HAVERSKERQUE, CROIX MARRAISSE and J.28.a and the HAVERSKERQUE - ST VENANT Road during the night. Intermittent shelling of edge of wood and open fields in K.25.a by 4.2" and 5.9"., some 4.2's on K.15.a, and 5.9's on J.27.b and J.28.a during the morning. 12 Noon eight 4.1" H.V. shells on bridge at J.26.c 5/1 - one direct hit but no substantial damage and 12 5.9's on road J.28.b 2/0 at 12.45 p.m. This afternoon some 4.2's and 77mm on Canal bank in K.31. and J.36. Some shrapnel on K.14.b and BEDFORD FARM, and 4.2's on J.33.d 8/3. Most of this light shelling had the appearance of registration - but may have been/harassing fire. only

4. INTELLIGENCE.
   Batteries. Infantry report A.A. Battery flashes seen at K.33.c 2/9. Also battery T.B. 76 degs. 5 mins from K.8.c 75/75.
   Aerial. E.A. busy bombing back areas during parts of the night. One E.A. flew low over J.29. at 8.0 p.m. - was driven off by M.G. fire. E.A. over CORBY three times today. One flying high W. to E. probably photographing the Forest at 5.0 p.m. One E.A. is reported brought down near Left Battn Right Brigade H.Q. between 6 p.m. and 7 p.m. yesterday (confirmation needed).
   Balloons. 5 p.m. T.B's 76 and 101½ degs. from J.33.b 7/4 and all the morning T.B's 65 (2), 71, 62 (2), from J.36.b 7/9 and 102 (2) from J.28.a 3/0. These last eight were pulled down at 4.0 p.m.
   M.G's. (From Div. Summary). Very active during the night from K.26.b 7/7, K.21.a 5/3, K.26.c 6/6 and 40/15, K.26.b 70/25, K.15.b 60/25 and K.21.a 7/5 (the last three new emplacements).
   Movement. etc. House at K.6.d 75/95 occupied.
   Defences. Thick wire is visible along ditch in K.26.a and d. Fresh earth in K.21.a 5/3.
   Light Signals. Enemy put up RED very lights from forward positions and GOLDEN RAIN and DOUBLE GREEN from places in rear, when our barrage opened at 11.30 p.m. Strings of white lights continually seen E. of MERVILLE when enemy bombing planes were about. GREEN very lights were sent up by the enemy to denote short shooting.

(continued).

5.   MISCELLANEOUS.
     One German Div. has arrived from Eastern Theatre making 207 on Western front.   124 are in line and 83 in reserve, of which latter, 12 are fresh, one is a Landwehr Division and 70 are tired withdrawn from the battle. Of these 70, 53 have been refitting for 10 days or more. There are 25 fresh Divisions in the line which have not yet been drawn into the fighting.

Headquarters.   sd. R.F. MASON.   Lieut. R.A.
R.A. 5th Divn.   Intelligence Officer,
15th May, 1918.   5th Divisional Artillery.

SECRET.
5TH DIVISIONAL ARTILLERY INTELLIGENCE SUMMARY.
6.0 P.M. 15/5/18 to 6 P.M. 16/5/18.

1. SITUATION. Unchanged.
2. OUR ARTILLERY. Harassing fire during night, on selected targets. Today lines and ammunition were checked and tested, some registration done, 120th Battery engaged H.B. at K.28.a 2/8 (reported by infantry), at 9.30a.m., and 80th Battery set fire to and burnt down house at K.26.c 68/41. All batteries fired 5-minutes concentration at 4.30 p.m. on trench from K.21.b 4/4 to K.21.c 7/9.
   Trench Mortars. X/5 fired 16 rounds at GABY at 1.0 p.m. - good shooting.
3. ENEMY ARTILLERY. Between 8.0 p.m. and 10 p.m. about 200 4.2" -&5.9" - gas shells (sneezing and mustard) on road at J.12.a 1/8, and five salvoes 4.2" and 77mm gas in vicinity of lock at LA MOTTE. Intermittent gas shelling D.28.d. during night. A 5.9" battery twice shelled edge of wood in K.25.a today while our batteries were shooting - probably suspects O.P's here. The canal bank in K.31.a and J.26.d was again shelled between 7.0 a.m. and 9.0 a.m. During the day, some 5.9's on J.30.a 1/2 - near party working on support line - cross roads in LA MOTTE BAUDET, ST FLORIS and GRAND TREILLE (J.34.c) 4.2's W. of CORBIE, LES LAURIERS, and K.15.a., and 77mm on CORBIE. A 4.2" Battery put one round on bridge in J.27.c at 12.22 p.m., possibly checking its line, and a 5.9" was apparently registering on cross roads in LA MOTTE BAUDET at 3.0 p.m.
4. INTELLIGENCE. Batteries. K.28.a 2/9 reported by Infantry. Photos show many tracks and several short lengths of trench behind the hedge here.
   Aerial. E.A. busy bombing till past mid-night last night. E.A. flew high over our lines as far as CORBIE, and were driven back by A.A. fire at 6.30 a.m., 7.45 a.m., 9.15 a.m., and 9.45 a.m. Another over ST. VENANT at 10.10 a.m. and some high over ST. FLORIS during the afternoon. (The aeroplane reported yesterday as crashed near Left battalion H.Q. was one of ours.)
   M.G's. (From Div. Summary). Active at night from K.26.c 25/25, 30/25 and 7/7, K.26.b 70/25, K.21.a 5/3 and K.21.b 3/6. Another located at COURTFROIE Farm.
   T.M's. From K.21.b 2/2 and K.32.a 1/2.
   Defences. What appears to be a sniper's post is visible in a shell-hole at K.26.c 7/7. New work on trenches in K.26.d. Three knife-rests have been fixed on road at K.26.c 25/30.
   Fires. 3.20 p.m.- 3.30 p.m. column of black smoke rising T.B. 82½ from J.34.a 4/4. The Infantry report the barn at K.26.c 6/7 has been completely burned out.

                                               sd. R.F. MASON. Lieut. R.A.
                                                    Intelligence Officer,
16th May, '18.   5th Divisional Artillery.

**5TH DIVISIONAL ARTILLERY INTELLIGENCE SUMMARY 6 P.M. 16-5-18
to 6 P.M. 17-5-18.**

1. SITUATION.   Unchanged.

2. OUR ARTILLERY.   Special harassing fire during the night in anticipation of enemy relief opposite Right Brigade front. Left Group 4.5" Hows. engaged a enemy M.G. at K.21.b 4/6 at 7.15 p.m.   5-minute concentrations were fired at 3.15 a.m. on trenches K.26.d 2/5 - c. 6/3 and K.32.a 3/7 to 31.b 95/20 and at 4.45 p.m. on trench and shell-holes from K.16.c 3/3 to K.21.b 50/65.   In addition to harassing fire today, ammunition was tested and lines checked.
   Trench Mortars.   Inactive.

3. ENEMY ARTILLERY.   Quieter. A few gas shell on ST FLORIS and near LE VERTBOIS in the early morning and some 77mm on LES LAURIERS and sneezing gas-shell on D.28.a during the night.   Today some 5.9's on K.11.b., 4.2's and 4.1"" H.V.s on corner of wood K.25.a and CAUDESCURE and a small area shoot with 4.2's and 4.1's on Canal bank in K.31.b from 4.0 p.m. to 4.3 p.m.   No retaliation to either of our bursts of fire.

4. INTELLIGENCE.   Batteries. No information available.
   Aerial. E.A. busy bombing AIRE, and the FOREST, and near ARREWAGE during the night.   This morning several E.A. were over ST FLORIS, - this afternoon none were seen.
   Balloons. 12 Noon to 3.0 p.m. up at T.B's 54½, 57, 58, 60½, 61 62½, 66 and 69½ degs. from J.35.d 4/0. At 1.45 p.m. one of our planes flew over and frightened three enemy balloons which were pulled down - T.B's 74, 75 and 83 from J.34.a 4/4 .
   M.G's.   (From Div. Summary) Firing during the night from K.26.c 2/1 and K.26.c 6/6, - 2 are reported also in hedge between K.10.d 05/50 and K.10.d 0/2.
   T.M's   Inactive.
   Movement etc. Houses at K.15.d 8/3 and K.10.c 8/9 occupied.   Occupied posts at K.26.c 7/7, K.26.c 60/65 and K.26.c 65/50.
   Defences, etc.   Small working party at K.21.a 9/1 dispersed by infantry fire.
   Lights.   Again strings of white lights sent up from E. of MERVILLE while enemy bombing planes were over at night.   They may be used to show up our bombing planes.
   3.38 p.m. large cloud of smoke rose behind enemy's line, T.B. 101 from J.34.a 4/4.

5. MISCELLANEOUS.   2 photos, of squares L.26 and L.22 and 28 reveal a back - line of trenches being dug by the enemy, (approx. line L.23.c 0/0 to house L.32.b 6/8). Strong Points in the shape of circles of traversed trench about every 1000 yards, already dug, the joining trenches - traversed - not being yet completed.
   sd. R.F. MASON. Lt. R.A.
17th May, '18.   Intelligence Officer 5th Divnl Artillery.

5TH DIVISIONAL ARTILLERY INTELLIGENCE SUMMARY 6 P.M. 17-5-1918 to 6P.M. 18- 5-18.

1. **SITUATION.** Unchanged. A new trench has been dug and wired, and is occupied by Left Battn, Left Brigade, - from K.9.d 95/35 to K.10.a 35/15.

2. **OUR ARTILLERY.** Harassing fire as usual during the night. None during the day. 5-minute concentrations fired at 3.15 a.m. on trench and wire K.16.a 0/9 - K.15.b 55/75 - K.15.b 7/5 - K.15.b 5/1 and at 5.30 p.m. on trenches K.26.d 2/5 - 26.c 6/3 and K.32.a 3/7 to K.31.b 95/20. 120th Battery engaged T.M. "GERTIE" at 4.55 a.m. Today, lines were checked and ammunition tested. Also a little registration.
   Trench Mortars. Inactive.

3. **ENEMY ARTILLERY.** Active between 9.30 p.m. and 10.30 a.m. - quiet for the rest of the day. LA MALADERIE, Road in J.5.c., LE PARC., LA MOTTE BAUDET and CROIX MARRAISSE - L'EPINETTE area received doses of 5.9" and 4.2" fire - between 20 and 100 rounds on each. The HAVERSKERQUE - LE CORBIE ROAD was gas - shelled at midnight, and at the same time a 4.1" battery put 100 rounds on J.21.a (L'EPINETTE)
   6.45 a.m., - 8.30 a.m., and 9.30 a.m. - 10.30 a.m., 75 rounds 8" (or 11") on J.28.central - probably an observed shoot on battery position at J.28.c 90/82 as an E.A. was patrolling behind German front line during both periods. Damage - 50 rounds shrapnel in the position destroyed. About 40 rds. 4.2" on K.9.a. during the afternoon.

4. **INTELLIGENCE.** Batteries. 8" shelling J.28.central T.S.B.83 degs. from J.34.a.4/4. A T.B. of 100 degrees was taken from nose of one of these shell to opposite point of crater at J.28.c 55/98. These bearings however cross - bear on a point too near our lines to be the position of the Howitzer.
   11.45 p.m. gas shell (77mm?) shelling HAVERSKERQUE - LE CORBIE Road TSB 88 degs. from J.34.a 4/4.
   11.0 p.m. 4.2's shelling LA MALADERIE TSB 90 degs. from J.34.a 4/4.
   11.0 a.m. NF K.24.d 4/6.
   Aerial. E.A. busy bombing back areas, including PECQUEUR and near HOULERON, between 10 p.m. and midnight. One E.A. is reported flying very low over J.27.c at 10 p.m. Inactive during day. One "scrap" was heard somewhere high over MORBECQUI at 11 a.m.
   Balloons. Up at 5.10 a.m. T.B's 58, 58½, 63 and 60 degs. from J.35.d 4/0.
   M.G's. (From Div. Summary(. Active from K.26.c 6/6, K.21.a 55/35 and K.26.c 3/7.
   T.M's. Located at K.26.c 7/3 and K.32.a 2/1.
   Movement. etc.. Individual movement in brickfields.
   Defences. Wiring party found by patrols from K.26.b 60/55 - K.26.b 6/7. Patrols also located M.G. Posts at K.26.b 7/8 and K.31.b 7/7.
   Miscellaneous. A screen has been erected along road from K.5.d 4/4 northwards. Two bushes have been put up at approximately K.10.b 2/3.
   2.50 a.m. enemy put up one golden rain rocket and two green lights when a round from one of his guns fell short.

sd. R.F. MASON. Lieut. R.A.
Intelligence Officer,
5th Divisional Artillery.

18th May, 1918.

SECRET

5TH DIVISIONAL ARTILLERY INTELLIGENCE SUMMARY, 6PM 18/5/18 TO 6PM 19/5/18.

1. **SITUATION.** Unchanged.

2. **OUR ARTILLERY.** Night harassing fire. Two concentrations fired - 5 minutes each - on trench and wire K.16.a 0/9 - 15.b 55/75 - 15.b 7/5 - 15.b 5/1 at 3.4 a.m., and area K.33.a 30/85 - 33.a 9/9 - 33.b 0/6 - 33.a 4/4 at 2.0 p.m. During the day A/15 fired on house at K.33.b.0/5 with balloon observation, D/152 engaged H.B. at K.29.a.95/95 and A/152 H.B.No. K.D.21. 18-pdr battery of LEFT GROUP fired on houses in K.10.c., with good effect. One house was set on fire, and burnt to the ground. D/152 got 5 direct hits on Barn at K.15.b.98/28, 2 on house K.16.a.03/22 and 5 on farm K.15.b.50/05. COURTFROIE Farm and cottage K.15.b.8/2 shelled with 4.5's. A roving 18-pdr of Left Group, went out at 10.30 p.m., shelled enfiladed roads and tracks in Brigade Zone and returned at 2 a.m.. 120 Bty. answered NF K.23.d.5/0 at 12.29 pm. In addition ammunition testing was continued.

   Trench Mortars. X/5 fired 17 rounds at "ELSIE" (3 rds) on enemy front line K.15.b.8/8 to K.10.c.10/05 (8 rds several hits on trench and wire) and trench from K.15.b.75/55 to 5/2 and Orchard in K.16.a. (6 rds) Y/5 T.M.B. fired 21 rds. registering wire at K.15.b.6/5, trench K.15.b.6/3, and orchards in K.16.a. and K.21.d. 2/1.

   All this T.M.fire between 3 p.m. and 4.30 p.m.

3. **ENEMY ARTILLERY.** More active - probably stirred out of its legarthy by our concentrations and H.A. shooting. Some gas on Rue des MORTS area, and a considerable amount of harassing fire around HAVERSKERQUE. Details attached.

4. **INTELLIGENCE. Batteries.** KD.21 and 80, and batteries at K.29.a.95/95 and K.23.d.5/0 reported by aeroplanes as active. True bearing of 101 degs. taken from the groove of a blind 77 mm at J.28.a.2/5.

   Aerial. A large E.A. flew over our lines at 8.55 p.m. at about 900 ft. Driven off by L.G. fire. E.A. busy bombing during the night till 1 a.m. 1 E.A. over CORBIE at 7.30 a.m. Some over our lines in early morning, flying low.

   Balloons. 1.30 pm to 4 pm T.B's 75 and 76 degs. from J.35.a.4/0.

   M.G's. Active at K.26.b.7/4 and 6/4. Flashes of a troublesome M.G. located at K.26.c.55/40. A particularly active sniper is reported in the orchard at K.32.a.5/8. The brickfields M.G. (probably at K.32.a.12/20) was busy during the night.

   T.M's. Active from K.32.a.15/20 and K.15.b.50/25 (approx).

   Defences. O.C., X/5 T.M.B. reports wire along enemy F.L. in K.10.d. and K.16.a. appears to be very thin except for a stretch of 20 yards at K.10.d.20/01. O.C., Y/5 T.M.B. reports wire at and near K.15.b.6/5 should not be a serious obstacle to Infantry. Inf'y report 3 knife rests at K.10.c.5/8. No wire was found by patrols in front of house at K.26.b.65/75. Posts at K.31.b.9/9 occupied by day.

   Fires. 2.15 pm two fires broke out in enemy's lines T.B.86 and 91 degrees from J.34.a.4/4 and another at 2.50 p.m. T.B. 92 degs. from same place.

   O.P's. There is a hole facing West in the chimney in K.35.a, which is possibly used as an O.P.

   Miscellaneous. 1st Brigade R.A.F. report that during the 1st fortnight of May they accounted for 81 E.A. - 37 destroyed and 44 driven down out of control. Losses of 1st Brigade in that period 8 machines missing, 1 airman killed, and 8 airmen wounded in combat or by A.A.Fire.

   sd/- R.F.MASON. Lieut.R.A.
   19-5-18. Intelligence Officer, 5th Divisional Artillery.

HOSTILE SHELLING.

Time.	Calibre.	Area shelled.	No. of rds.	Remarks.
Midnight to 1.0a.m.	4.2"	HAVERSKERQUE - CROIX MARRAISSE Road.	100.	-
8.0 a.m.	77mm	J.28.c and d.	200	-
10 a.m.	4.1 HV	J.25.d & 26.c.	50 ?	Harassing.
9.30am - 10 a.m.	4.2" 77mm	P.3.b and 4.a.	30.	
During night	4.2" & 77mm gas.	BOIS CLOBERT. BOIS des VACHES and PAPOTE areas.	100 to 200.	sneezing gas.
11.30am	4.2" gas.	J.11.a and b.	30 to 50.	-
12 Noon	4.2"	J.11.a and b.	75.	Probably H.D.50.

5TH DIVISIONAL ARTILLERY INTELLIGENCE SUMMARY

6 P.M. 19/5/18 to 6.0 P.M. 20/5/18.

1. SITUATION. 1st E. SURREY REGT attacked and captured enemy front line from K.15.b 97/91 to K.15.d 55/90 at 4.30 p.m. Copy of wire timed 7.50 p.m. from O.C. 1st E. SURREY'S "All objectives taken - slight enemy opposition except in houses K.15.b 5/0 where first wave was held up temporarily by M.G. fire but only for a few minutes aaa On most of the front enemy fled aaa Many were shot down by M.G. and rifle fire aaa Prisoners not yet counted estimated about 30 aaa 6 M.G's reported captured aaa Casualties about 50 most of which suffered on the right aaa .... behaviour of troops magnificent."

2. OUR ARTILLERY. Night harassing fire on tracks, bridges, etc. 5-minutes concentration fired at 2.0 a.m. on trench and wire K.16.a 0/9 - K.15.b 55/75 - K.15.b 7/5 - K.15.b 5/1. From 6.0 a.m. 18-Pdrs (300 rounds) and 4.5" (115 rounds) of Left Group shot at enemy wire in K.15.b 70/60 to K.15.b 95/95, also fired 50 rounds Thermite at 4.15 p.m. on house at K.15.b 8/2 which was successfully burnt. Today batteries registered and checked ammunition, fired one instructional shoot and answered NF KD.50 (121 Bty - 40 rds). At 4.27 p.m. batteries started firing in support of operations, barraging till 4.55 p.m. Start of barrage reported very slightly ragged, shrapnel bursts good, with very few high bursts - in general, a good barrage.

   Trench Mortars. Y/5 fired 30 rounds into wire in K.15.b and X/5 60 rounds into wire from K.10.c 10/07 to K.15.b 80/05 - at 2.0 a.m. During operations at 4.30 p.m. X/5 and Y/5 T.M. Batteries barraged the enemy front line, lifting at Zero to the Orchard in K.16.a., firing 294 rounds from 6 guns in 23 minutes. The shooting is reported to have been excellent - accurate and bursting well, probably contributing largely to the demoralization the enemy apparently displayed. No information about the barrage or the state of the enemy's wire, has been received yet from the attacking battalion.

3. ENEMY ARTILLERY. Details shown on attached list.
   2 points for comment - one, a deliberated counter battery shoot on 121st Battery this morning, with aeroplane observation, the other, the extraordinary absence of heavy fire during our attack - a few 4.2's on our front line, and 1 5.9" every two or three minutes on K.9.c., for about half-an-hour after Zero. No attempt at an S.O.S. Barrage. It is noticeable that during the raid at 2.0 a.m., May 11th., there was also no Artillery retaliation of any sort.

4. INTELLIGENCE. Batteries. 7.4 p.m. NF K.D.50.
   2.27 p.m. NF K.36.a 60/99.
   Two bearings given in attached list.
   Aerial. E.A. bombed back areas up till 12.30 a.m. Several E.A. crossed our lines during the early morning, but were driven back by A.A. and M.G. fire. One E.A. was crashed by 3 Camels at 7.30 a.m. - in enemy's lines opposite Right Brigade. An E.A. was up East of MERVILLE observing C.B. shoot on Battery Position in J.29.c during morning. No E.A. seen during operations this afternoon.
   Balloons. Up all day T.B. 57½, 60, 63 and 66½ from J.35.d 4/0. 5.50 p.m. an enemy balloon was brought down by our planes - occupant jumped out, and, as far as could be seen, his parachute failed to open.
   M.G's. One reported at K.26.b 55/60.

Page 2.

T.M's. Fired from K.32.a 7/7 and K.32.a 15/20.
Movement. etc. Div. Summary states " About midnight parties of the enemy in single file could be seen silhoutted against the fires in MERVILLE moving in both directions across our front in K.21.b. Small parties - some carrying M.G's. - moved along hedge K.26.b 7/6 - 8/7". A relief ?
Defences. etc. Enemy was working on his line, which runs S.W. from K.21.c 50/85 during the night. Fresh earth visible at K.26.b 70/45.
Fires. 7.0 p.m. - 7.30 p.m. large fire in MERVILLE at K.29.a 9/2 approx.
Miscellaneous. The top of MERVILLE Church was knocked off by H.A. today. A prisoner taken and interviewed tonight belonged to 223 R.I.R. 48th R. Divn.

        sd. R.F. MASON. Lieut. R.A.
        Intelligence Officer,
20th May, 1918.   5th Divisional Artillery.

HOSTILE FIRE.

Time.	Calibre.	Area shelled.	No. of rds.	Direction and remarks.
9.15pm - 9.45pm	4.2"	B/152 Bty Position.	50	3 dumps put up - no casualties.
1.30am	T.M.	Right Bde F.L,	-	ELSIE & GIRTIE. - we retaliated.
4.20am	4.2" 77mm	HAVERSKERQUE & J.28. T.B. 99 from J.28.c 75/65. (from groove.)	250	
4.30am	4.2"	K.13.a central.	50.	
During night.	4.2"	K.19.d.	150.	Bursts of fire.
--"--	4.2" 77mm	J.5.c., J.11.b., D.29.d., D.22.c & d.	-	Harassing.
8.15am - 11.0am	5.9" 4.2"	J.29.c. Bty Position.	250.	Just S. of MERVILLE from J.29.c. C.B. shoot.
9.0am - 11.30am	5.9" 4.2"	J.34.	20.	Harassing.
10 - 11am	77mm	Canal J.26.b & d.	25.	Harassing.
10.40am	4.2"	J.27.b.	20.	TSB.95 from J.28.a 15/30.
12 Noon,	77mm	D.22.c & d.	30 ?	
1 - 2pm	4.2"	HAVERSKERQUE.	30 - 40	Intermittent.
3.0pm	4.2"	J.24.d 9/2.	1.	Dud.
4.35pm	4.2"	K.15.d and 16.c.	12.	
--"----	5.9"	K.9.c	20 - 30.	1 per 2 or 3 minutes.

WAR DIARY
or
INTELLIGENCE SUMMARY

Army Form C. 2118.

MAY 1918.

Map 1/40,000. 36.A.

Place	Date	Hour	Summary of Events and Information	Remarks and references to Appendices
CROIX MARMUSE	20/31	6am	Fine day. 121st Battery position heavily shelled by aeroplane observation. Position badly damaged but only one gun out of action, + no casualties to personnel.	
		22nd	Position moved to J.39.c.8/5.	
			4.30pm Batteries of Brigade cooperated in a very successful operation by East Surrey Regt. Enemy line in K.15.b being taken + 38 officers + 300 O.R. captured. Nothing to report.	
	21/22		Fine day	
	22/23	"	"	
	23/24	"	"	
	24/25	"	"	
	25/26	"	37th Bde moved a forward section to wood at J.30.a.5/5.	
	26/27	"		
	27/28	"	Battery cooperated in raid by 14th Warwick Regt + 1st Worcesters. Nothing to report.	
	28/29	"		
	29/30	"		
	30/31	"		

BL 27 Div & Secret
80 Bty.

Batteries taking part in
the Creeping Barrage this
afternoon must arrange
their first lift at a certain
few seconds before Zero+x to
allow for time of flight.

20/5/18   JW Carter
               Capt & Adjt
               Right Sec

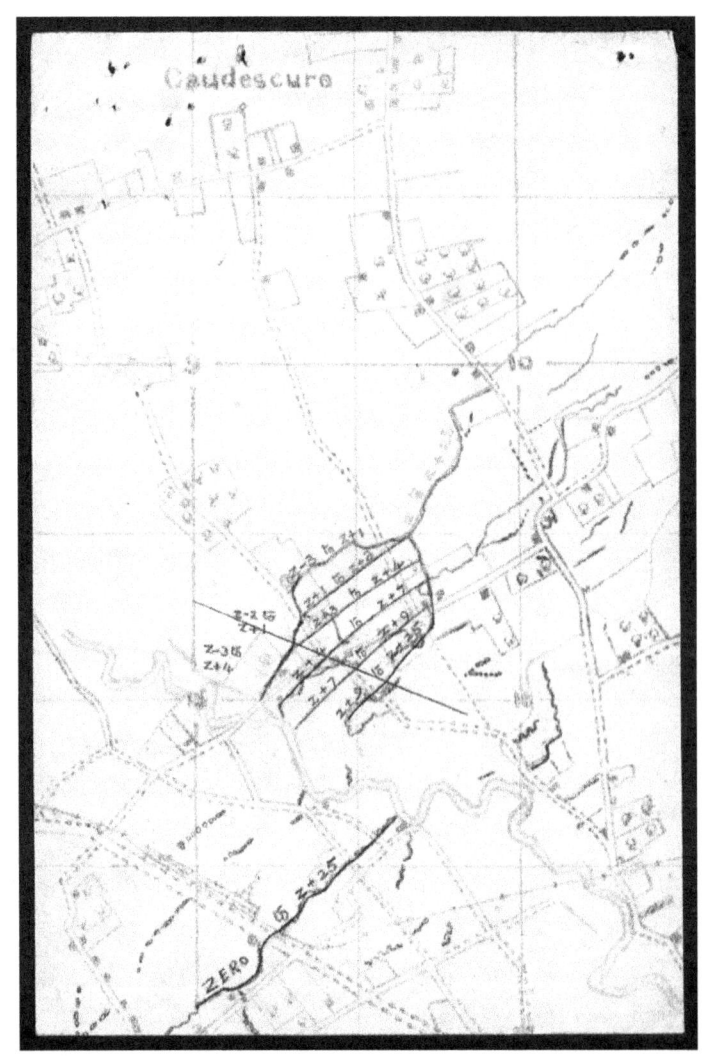

5th Divisional Artillery No. B.M. C.1

O.C. 27 Bde R.F.A.

S E C R E T.

Reference this Office No. AA 5/7.4

ZERO HOUR will be 4.30 pm May 20"

This paper must not pass through the hands of a clerk.

ACKNOWLEDGE.

Headquarters.
R.A. 5th Divn.
Date 20-5-18

M Parker
Capt
Major R.A.
Brigade Major R.A. 5th Division.

Adjt Night Sup

S E C R E T.

Officer Commanding

..........Battery RFA.   27th Bde. No. BM/195.

Reference attached 5th D.A. Operation Order No. 175.

1. With reference to para. 4.
(a)   The two 18-pdr. batteries barraging from K.21. central to K.15.c 25/30 will be 52nd and 120th batteries RFA.
      The 52nd Battery will take from K.21.c 0/1 to K.21.b 63/75
      The 120th Battery will take from K.21.b 63/75 to K.15.c 25/30.
      The 37th Battery will detail two howitzers (back position) and D/15 will detail two howitzers to participate in this barrage, 37th Battery taking the Left half as above and D/15 the Right half.

(b)   The Creeping barrage on Right Group Zone will be formed by 80th Battery and 121st Battery.
      80th Bty. - K.15.c 4/0 - K.15.b 50/15.
      121st Bty. - K.15.b 50/15 - K.15.b 65/35.

      Batteries will arrange for an overlap of 20 yards between batteries.

      The remaining 4 howitzers of 37th Battery and 4 howitzers of D/15 Battery will co-operate with the creeping barrage in accordance with para. 7 (b) and remainder of para. 7. 37th Bty taking left half as above and D/15 right half.

2. The times on the barrage lines are as under :-

   1st Line - Zero - 3 to zero plus 4
   2nd Line - Zero plus 4 to Zero plus 7.
   3rd Line - Zero plus 7 to Zero plus 9
   4th Line - Zero plus 9 to zero plus 25.

3. ACKNOWLEDGE.

                                            Captain R.F.A.

16-5-18.   Adjutant 27th. Bde. R.F.A.

S E C R E T.

15th Brigade R.F.A. No. A.A. 5/74.

O.C. २7th Brigade R.F.A.
~~52nd Battery.~~
~~8 0th Battery,~~
~~D/15 Battery.~~

Reference attached Order :-

1. ~~(a.)~~ With reference to Para. 4,
   (a.) The two 18-Pdr. Batteries barraging
        from K.21. Central, to K.16.c.25.30,
        will be ,
             52nd,
             /20 1, Battery, 27th Bde. R.F.A.
        52nd Battery will take from,
             K.21.b.0.1 to K.21.b.63.75.
        /20 Battery of 27th Bde. R.F.A. will take
        from, K.21.b.63.75 to K.16.c.25.30.
        27th Bde.R.F.A. will detail two
        Howitzers, and D/15 Battery will use two
        Howitzers, to participate in this barrage,
        the Battery of 27th Bde.R.F.A. taking
        the left half as above, and D/15 Battery
        the Right half.
   (b.) The Creeping Barrage on Right Group
        Zone will be formed by
             80th Battery,
             /21 a Battery of 27th Bde. R.F.A.

2. BATTERY ZONE-S FOR CREEPING BARRAGE,

   80th Bty, K.15.b.4.0 - K.15.b.50.15.
   Bty.27th Bd e R.F.A, K.15.b.50.15 -
                                K.15.b.60.33.
   Batteries will arrange for an overlap
   between Batteries of 20 Yards.
   The remaining 2 Howitzers of 27th Bde R.F.A.
   and 6 Guns, D/15 Battery, will co-operate
   with Creeping Barrage in accordance with
   para. 7, (b.) and remainder of para. 7.

   the 27th Bde RFA taking left half as above & D/15 right half

3. At Zero plus 25, 80th Battery, will act
   in accordance with para. 6 of attached
   order.

4. The times on the barrage lines are as
   under:-
   1st Line, Zero minus 3 to Zero plus 4,
   2nd Line, Zero plus 4, to Zero plus 7.
   3rd Line, Zero plus 7 to Zero plus 9.
   4th Line, Zero plus 9, to Zero plus 25.

                              M Parker
                              Capt. R.F.A,
                                Adjutant,
                                RIGHT Group.

18-5-18.

SECRET.

5TH DIVISIONAL ARTILLERY ORDER NO. 175
by
Brig-Gen. A.H. HUSSEY, C.B., C.M.G.
Commanding 5th Divisional Artillery.

18th MAY, 1918.

1. The 95th Infantry Brigade will capture the enemy front line from K.15.b.6/0 to K.15.b.95/95 on a day to be notified later.
The attack will be carried out by 1st Battalion, THE EAST SURREY Regiment.

2. Zero hour will be the time at which the assaulting infantry leave our trenches and will be notified later.

3. The attack will be covered by a barrage in accordance with the attached Barrage Map.

4. The barrage on the enemy trench North of the trench junction at K.10.c.4/0 will be formed by two 18-pounder batteries LEFT GROUP.
The barrage from K.21.central to K.16.c.25/30 will be formed by two 18-pounder batteries and four 4.5" Howitzers RIGHT GROUP.
The remaining 18-pounders of Left Group and two 18-pounder batteries of Right Group will form the creeping barrage.

5. The dividing line between Group Zones in the creeping barrage will be as shown on the attached Barrage Map.
Groups will arrange an overlap of 20 yards each.

6. After reaching the final protective barrage line one 18-pounder battery of Right Group will search the ground North of the River in K.15.d. and the Western half of K.16.c. N. of river.

7. 4.5" Howitzers.
   (a) Left Group, on 18-pounder opening barrage line as far North as K.10.c.4/0 from ZERO - 3 mins. to ZERO.
   (b) Right Group, (less 4 howitzers) on 18-pounder opening barrage line from ZERO - 3 mins. to ZERO plus 1 min.

4.5" Howitzers will lift (Left Group at ZERO. Right Group at ZERO plus 1) to the line from K.15.d.95/85 - along 18-pounder final protective barrage to K.16.a.45/75 thence along trench to K.10.d.2/3 to K.10.d.3/7.
From Zero plus 9 to ZERO plus 25 4.5" Hows. South of K.16.a.45/75 will search East as far as the LES PURESBECQUES ARREWAGE road paying particular attention to orchards and houses.

8. Rates of fire, ammunition etc. -

ZERO - 3 to ZERO	INTENSE	all H.E. 106 fuse not to be used
ZERO to ZERO plus 2	INTENSE	(18-pdrs all shrapnel (howitzers 101 fuze
ZERO plus 2 to ZERO plus 25	NORMAL	(18-pdrs all shrapnel (howitzers 101 fuze.
ZERO plus 25	STOP.	

9. H.A. XI Corps have arranged for 6" Howitzers to engage targets as under :-
   (a) Houses round cross-roads K.15.b.9/3 from Zero minus 3 mins. to ZERO plus 1 min.
   (b) Houses at K.16.a.8/6, K.21.b.9/9, K.10.d.2/1, K.16.b.5/6 from ZERO to ZERO plus 5 mins.

10. Details of Trench Mortar Targets will be issued later.

11. H.Q., will be -
    95th Infantry Brigade forward H.Q.   Estaminet K.8.c.70/25.
    1st East Surreys   K.9.d.1/0.

Page 2.

12. Liaison Officers will be found by Left Group with 95th Infantry Brigade forward H.Q. and with 1st East Surreys, the L.O. with the latter not to be below the rank of Captain.

13.   A counter battery programme will be carried out from Zero. to Zero. plus 25.

14. Acknowledge.

                                                      Wallace
                                                     Major R.A.

18th May, 1918. Brigade Major Royal Artillery 5th Division.

COPIES TO :- O.C. Right Group. (10 copies).
              -"- Left Group. (10 -"-).
              13th Inf. Brigade.
              15th -----"-----
              95th -----"----- (7 copies).
              XI Corps R.A.
              -"----- H.A.
              -"----- C.B.S.O.
              5th Division 'G'.
              R.A. 61st Divn.
              -"- 29th -"-
              42nd Squadron R.A.F.
              79th Brigade RGA.

Officer Commanding 119
                    120
                    121
............Battery R.F.A.   37   27th Bde. No. BM/203.

1.   The 121st Bty. will move their guns at once to
J.29.c 80/55 and will register their new S.O.S. Line, (Kempenay)
        (K.27.a 05/80 to K.21.c 5/9.)

2.   The 121st Bty. will not take part in this aft noons
operation (BM/195)

3.   The 120th Bty. will carry out those orders laid down for
121st Bty. in BM/195.

4.   Reference BM/195/1.   S.O.S. Orders.
     After Zero plus 25 the 120th Bty. will cover from
K.21.b 3/6 to K.16.c 0/5 and the 121st Bty. from
K.27.a 05/80 to K.21.c 5/9.

5.   Batteries taking part in the creeping barrage this
afternoon must arrange the first lift at a certain few
seconds before Zero plus 4 to allow for time of flight.

                                    [signature]
                                    Captain R.F.A.

                                    Adjutant 27th. Bde. R.F.A.

Officer Commanding,
    Battery R.F.A.   27th Bde. No. BM/178/1

Subject S.O.S.

1. The N. Group Boundary an E. and W. Line through K.21.a 60/65.
   The S. Group Boundary is E. and W. Line through J.36. central.

2. S.O.S. Line on Group front now runs K.31.b 7/0 - K.27.a 0/7 - K.21.a 6/1 - K.21.a 85/40 - K.21.b 15/75.

3. This S.O.S. Line is allotted as under :-

   18-Pdrs.

   A/15 and 119th)
   Batteries   ) K.31.b 7/0 - K.26.c 95/50.

   119th Bty. will keep one gun enfilading N. bank of Canal.
   119th Bty. will keep one gun enfilading LE SART Road.

   52nd Bty. K.26.c 90/40 - K.26.b 6/3.

   120th Bty. K.26.b 50/20 - K.27.a 0/7 - K.21.c 1/0

   80th Bty. K.27.a 05/95 - K.21.c 55/95.

   121st Bty K.21.c 50/85 - K.21.a 6/1 - K.21.a 85/40 - K.21.b 15/75

4. 5" Hows.

   D/15 Bty. 2 guns, Brickfield, K.32.a 1/1.
             1 gun , Farm, K.26.d 4/6.
             3 guns , round Houses and Cross Roads K.26.c 80/05.

   37th Bty. 2 guns , K.27.a 1/3 (Farm)
             2 guns , Cross Roads   K.21.b 7/5.
             2 guns , K.21.d 1/5 and K.21.d 5/1 (Houses).

4. The above will come into force at 7.30 p.m. to-night.

                                                          Captain R.F.A.

22-5-1918.   Adjutant 27th Bde. R.F.A.

Cancelled
31/5/18

Office 119
120
127
37

Officer Commanding

............Battery R.F.A.   27th Bde. No. BM/243.

1. A Patrol of the West Kent Regiment will rush a hostile machine gun at K.21.c 30/55 tonight 27th/28th inst.

2. Four guns of 126th Battery will co-operate by firing a barrage from K.21.a 60/10 to K.21.c 80/75.

    Ammunition all "A"   (50% grazes).
    Rate of fire :-
        Zero to Zero plus 5   NORMAL.
        Zero plus 5 to Zero plus 15   SLOW.
        Zero plus 15   CEASE FIRE.

3. Zero hour will be notified later by phone in the following manner :-

    12.30 a.m. will be sent as " Your BM/12/30 received ".

    1.0 a.m. will be sent as " Your BM/1 received ".

                                           Captain R.F.A.

27-5-18.   Adjutant 27th. Bde. R.F.A.

SECRET.

To 2nd R.S.R.

14th Inf. Bde. S.G. 871.

Two small raids will take place tonight, night 28/29th :

1. On the enemy post at about K.21.c.7.7. to be carried out by 1/A.W.Kent R.

2. A raid on the two enemy posts at about K.21.b.95.70. and K.22.a.15.70. to be carried out by 1R/R.War.R.

There will be Artillery and M.G. co-operation for both raids.

Zero hour for raid to be carried out by 1/A.W.Kent R. will be 1 A.M.

Zero hour for raid to be carried out by 1R/R.War.R. will be 12 midnight.

B Luke
Captain.
Brigade Major, 14th Infantry Brigade.

28th May 1918.

Office 119
170
Officer Commanding 171
37
............Battery RFA.   27th Bde. No. BM/250.

1.   Reference 15th Infantry Brigade Operation Order No. 3 para. 8.

   Zero hour for this raid, the 15th R. Berwick Regt. will be at 12 midnight 28th/29th.

2.   Reference 15th Infantry Brigade Operation Order No. 3 para. 9 and this Office No. BM/243.
   Zero hour for the raid by the 1st R.W. Kent Regt. will be 1.0 a.m. 28th/29th.

                                        [signature]
                                        Captain R.F.A

28-5-18.   Adjutant 27th. Bde. R.F.A

COPY No. 8

S E C R E T.

15th Brigade R.F.A. No. A.A. 5/112.

O P E R A T I O N   O R D E R   No. 3,
By
Lieut-Col. C.StL.G.HAWKES, D.S.O., R.F.A,
Commanding RIGHT Group, 5th Divl. Artillery.

(1.) The Raid will take place tonight, 28th/29th May, by the 15th R.Warwick Regt. on the Posts at K.31.b.8.8 and K.31.b.9.9.

(2.) RIGHT Group, 5th Div. Artillery, will co-operate with destructive fire on the Posts, followed by a Box Barrage, as under:-

Zero to Zero plus 2,

	119th Bty,	K.31.b.55.55 to K.31.b.75.80.
52	120th Bty,	K.31.b.75.80 to K.31.b.9.9.
	A/15 Bty,	K.31.b.9.9. to K.32.a.10.99.
120	52nd Bty,	K.32.a.10.99 to K.26.c.4.1.
	80th Bty,	One Gun only, on K.31.b.5.5.

Zero plus 2 to Zero plus 30. ?

	119th Bty,	K.31.b.63.66 to K.31.b.95.60.
52	120th Bty,	K.31.b.95.60 to K.32.a.25.75.
	A/15 Bty,	K.32.a.35.75 to K.32.a.38.80 to K.32.a.38.88.
120	52nd Bty,	K.32.a.38.88, along Hedge to K.26.c.4.1. to K.26.c.25.15.
	80th Bty,	One Gun only on K.31.b.5.5.

(3.) AMMUNITION.

Zero to Zero plus 2,

    75% H.E.   25% Shrapnel.

Zero plus 2 to Zero plus 30,

    50% H.E.   50% Shrapnel.

106 Fuze may be used after Zero plus 2.

(4.) RATES OF FIRE, (including Howitzers.)

Zero to Zero plus 5,	INTENSE.
Zero plus 5 to Zero plus 20,	NORMAL.
Zero plus 20 to Zero plus 30,	SLOW.

(1.)

(5.) 4.5" Howitzers.

    D/15 Battery will harass area round cross Roads in
        K.26.c.
    One section of the 37th Battery will fire on
        Brickfields.

(6.) 16th Divisional Artillery has been asked to fire on
    Houses on Southern Edge of Canal Bank in K.31.d. and
    K.32.c.

(7.) Watches will be synchronised at this Office at 7-0 P.M.
    today, 28th instant.

(8.) Zero Hour will be notified later.

(9.) The small enterprise arranged with the West Kents
    will take place at Midnight, 28th/29th May.
    The 120th Battery will co-operate.

                                              A K Scott

                                        Lieut. R.F.A,
                                        a/Adjutant,
28th May 1918.   RIGHT Group.

Copies to :-   Brigade Major, 5th Div. Artly.   (No. 1)
             Brigade Major, 16th Div. Artly. (No. 2)
             Brigade Major, 13th Infy.Bde.   (No. 3)
             O.C. 27th Brigade R.F.A.   (Nos. 4 to 8).
                52nd Battery.   (No. 9)
                80th   "   (No. 10).
                A/15   "   (No. 11)
                D/15   "   (N°. 12)
                15th Battln. R.Warwick Regt.   (No. 13)
           File.   (No. 14).

SECRET

5TH DIVISIONAL ARTILLERY INTELLIGENCE SUMMARY 6 P.M. 20-5-18. TO 6 P.M. 21-5-18.

1. **SITUATION.** Extracts from Div.Summary "The attack barrage at 4.30 pm. 20th was excellent and enormously facilitated the Inf'y advance...... At 3 a.m. 21st a party of the enemy gained a footing under cover of a heavy mist in our recently captured trench at K.15.b. 9/9. They immediately commenced bombing down the trench towards the orchard and were held up by a block formed at K.15.b.8/8; our bombing sections attacked, killing 12 of the enemy and completely restoring the situation. The line gained was consolidated during the night and the Right Battalion of the Left Brigade advanced their line from K.15. d.6/8 to K.15.c.9/0 to keep touch with the battalion which had attacked".

2. **OUR ARTILLERY.** Harassing fire during the night. Left Group increased their fire and paid special attention to bridges over stream in K.11.b. d. & c. and K.16.b. & d. "SUNNY JIM" - Left Group's roving 18-pdr. - went out at 9 pm and returned at 3 am and engaged targets K.17.b.5/5, K.17.b.8/6 and K.29.a.95/95. At 3.5 a.m. Batteries concerned opened up on S.O.S., L.3. - barraging till 3.50 a.m. Right Group fired on S.O.S. lines from 3.5 am - 3.10 am when it was ascertained all was quiet on Right Brigade Front. During night Left Group fired on T.M's at K.16.a.0/4 and K.16.a.3/4 and M.G. at K.10.d.1/1. Today in addition to line-checking and ammunition-testing, a C.B. shoot on K.D.32 and K.D.50 was fired by 37th Battery, D/15 fired an instructional shoot, and A/15 retaliated on T.M's.
   Trench Mortars. X/5 fired 8 rounds on GABY, ELSIE and T.M. in house at K.26.d 35/60 - registration during afternoon. Good results.

3. **ENEMY ARTILLERY.** Busy night and quiet day. Heavy fire on Left Brigade front at mid-night - dealt with by Counter Batteries, and a barrage covering the counter-attack at 3.0 a.m. - lasting till 3.45 a.m. (approx.) T.M's were active on Right Brigade front in the early morning. Right Group silenced them. Details attached.

4. **INTELLIGENCE.** Batteries. Bearings are reported in list attached.
   Aerial. 1 E.A. over our lines low at 4.15 a.m. - driven back by L.G. fire. 2 E.A. high over our lines at 11.30 a.m., 4.30 p.m. and 6.45 p.m.
   Balloons. 7 p.m. - 9 p.m. T.B. 103 from J.34.a 4/4.
   One up all day T.B. 101½ from J.33.b 7/2.
   3.30 - 5.0 p.m. grid bearings 69 (2) and 73 (1) from J.35.d 4/0. 4 p.m. - 5.0 p.m. grid bearings 70 and 71 from same place.
   5.30 - 6.0 p.m. all the above up again.
   M.G's. (from Div. Summary) seen firing on our planes from T shaped trenches near hedge K.10.c 5/1 - 6/2.
   T.M's. ELSIE K.32.a 6/7 and GABY K.26.b 95/30 active during early morning.
   Defences. The strong point at K.16.c 15/90 was the scene of much movement during the attack yesterday. Small trench at K.31.b 7/1 now occupied by enemy. Strongly held enemy post at K.21.c 3/7. House at K.31.b 6/1 probably used as an O.P.
   Miscellaneous. Double-green and double-red rockets were used apparently as S.O.S. Signals during the attack.
   8.35 p.m. thick black cloud of smoke T.B. 106 degs. from J.34.a 4/4.

21st May, 1918.

sd. R.F. MASON. Lieut. R.A.
Intelligence Ofr 5th Div. Arty.

HOSTILE FIRE.

Time.	Calibre.	Area shelled.	Rds.	Direction.	Remarks.
6.30pm	4.2"	LA MOTTE.	30		
8.45pm	77	LE CORBIE.	20	TSB 73 from J.34.a 4/4.	
9.30pm	77	LA MOTTE BAUDET.	20		
11.15pm	4.2"	J.34.b.	30		
11.30pm - 12.1am	5.9"	J.10.d 65/65.	40.		
11.55pm	4.2"	MORBECQUE.	10.	125 grid from D.28.b 8/38.	
12.30am	4.2" gas.	D.22.central.	20.	125 grid from D.28.b 8/38.	
---"---	5.9"	D.24.a.			
2.30am		D.22.central. (4.2 Gas)	30	119 grid from D.28.b 48/38.	
3.35am- 7.0am	77mm 4.2"	J.26.	100	TSB 73 from J.34.a 4/4.	
4.11am- & 5.27am	77mm 77mm	K.31.a.	10 min. barrage.		
Night.	77mm	P.5.a and b. S. of Canal.			Intermittent.
8.35am	77mm	ST VENANT.	50.	TSB 78 from J.34.a 4/4.	
8.30am	4.2"	D.22.central.	8.		
9.10am	4.2"	Cross Rds K.8.d	50.		
9.30am	77mm & 4.2"	HAVERSKERQUE.	"	A few rds.	
9.45am	4.2"	Supports in J.36.	6.	TSB 90 from J.35.d 4/0.	
10.20am	4.2"	K.15.b 55/15.	10.		
11.30am	4.2"	HAVERSKERQUE.	1	MERVILLE.	
12.30pm - 5.30pm	4.2"	K.9.a & d and K.15.b.	50.	Intermittent.	
3.30pm	4.1HV	J.31.c.	2.	VIERHOUCK.	
4.30pm	4.2"	ST VENANT.	4.		
5.45 - 6.5pm	5.9"	LE CORBIE and VICTES.	30.		
6.10pm -6.50pm	5.9"	---do------	12.	TSB 80 degs. from J.35.d 4/0.	

SECRET.

5TH DIVISIONAL ARTILLERY INTELLIGENCE SUMMARY

6 P.M. 21/5/18 to 6 P.M. 22/5/18.

1. **SITUATION.** Our new line now runs as follows :-
K.9.d 94/36 - K.15.b 99/97 -
K.15.b 95/72 - K.15.b 71/42 - K.15.b 71/17 - K.15.d 52/81.
There are two German posts containing Heavy M.G's at
K.10.c 47/31 and K.10.c 37/21. The Infantry are anxious
to have them knocked out.
The enemy's front line is probably trench line running
through K.10.c 62/75 - K.10.c 21/20 - K.16.a 45/72 -
K.16.a 44/40 - K.16.c 02/92 - K.16.c 0/4. Thence posts at K.15.d.72/41,
K.15.d 35/05, K.21.b 0/8 - thence along original line of posts.

2. **OUR ARTILLERY.** Harassing fire continued by night -
special attention to footbridge opposite
ground recently captured. 18-Pdrs Left Group engaged
M.G's at K.16.a 5/4 and K.16.a 2/9 at 10.30 a.m. and fired
60 rounds on H.B. suspected at K.10.d 71/06.
11.42 p.m. - 12.5 a.m. Left Group fired on S.O.S. lines
in response to a suspected S.O.S. Signal from CHAPELLE BOOM.
37th, 121st, 80th and A/15 Batteries retaliated on
Trench Mortars during the night. 1 instructional shoot, and
ammunition testing and line-checking today. Left Group's
peripatetic 18-Pdr fired during the night on the VIERHOEK -
PONT ROUDIN Road, and in K.16.B and c.
Trench Mortars. X/5 registered on chimney K.32.c
10/18 and retaliated at 4 a.m. on Trench Mortar at K.26.d 35/60.
Y/5 inactive.

3. **ENEMY FIRE.** Rather heavy 5.9" fire on K.15.d. front
line from 3.0 p.m. onwards, and 77mm on
K.15.b front line from 3.0 p.m. to 4.30 p.m. - thought to
be registration. (Suggested that too many rounds were fired
for that). Otherwise only light shelling.

4. **INTELLIGENCE.** <u>Batteries.</u> 7.55 p.m. N.F. K.36.a 4/7.
Flash spotters placed a
77mm battery at K.10.d 6/1 this morning. This was confirmed
by Left Group Observers, and photo No. 42.A 699 shows two
possible gun-pits in trench at K.10.d 55/08.
Bearings of dud 77mm - 112 degs. True from K.13.b 8/6.
Flashes seen during night from K.35.d 4/0 :-
9.48 p.m.   4 at T.B. 73 degs.
10.10pm-11.31pm.   9 ---"--- 62 -"--
10.17 p.m.   2 ---"--- 106 -"-
10.22pm-10.56pm.   1 ---"--- 60 -"-
10.45pm-11.27pm.   2 ---"--- 57 -"-
<u>Aerial.</u> 2 E.A. were high over our lines 6 times during the
day. E.A. did a certain amount of bombing during the night,
dropping, amongst others, 10 bombs 4 in J.36, 2 near HAVERSKERQUE
and 4 in J.28.d.
<u>Balloons.</u> 5 rose opposite our front between 5.0 a.m. &
6.0 a.m. and remained up during day.
9.55am - 2 p.m. 107 degs. and 95 degs. Grid from J.33.b 7/5.
10.0a.m. - 11.40 a.m. 94 degs grid from J.33.b 7/5.
<u>M.G's.</u> (From Div. Summary) fired from K.16.a 05/55 - K.26.c
65/70, and 3 from hedge running N.E. from K.16.a 05/55 to road
at K.16.a 3/7.

INTELLIGENCE. (Continued).

Trench Mortars. Located at K.16.a 75/65 (H.T.M.)
Trench mortars fired from K.21.d 5/9, K.32.a 2/1 and K.32.a 8/7 between 2.0 a.m. and 3.0 a.m.

Movement. etc. Considerable movement in circular trench at K.15.c 05/90 and in wood in K.16.a. screen at K.6.b 8/0 has been repaired. O.P. is suspected at K.26.c 4/1.

Defences. Patrols found enemy wiring party at K.21.a 9/2. Work is in progress on trench at K.21.c 2/8 and trench and wire entanglements are being constructed northwards from K.26.b 75/70.

General. 10.30 p.m. A yellow light up, remaining stationary in the air for 3 minutes, grid bearing 99 degs. from J.34.a 4/4.

5. **MISCELLANEOUS.** Two badly wounded prisoners of 223 R.I.R. 2nd Btn (which met our attack on the 20th) were picked up in shell-holes yesterday. They state they expected their Battalion to be relieved on night 20th/21st but do not know if it happened.

sd. F.F. MASON. Lieut. RA
22nd May, 1918.   Intelligence Officer 5th Divnl Arty.

HOSTILE FIRE.

Time	Calibre	Area shelled	Rds.	Direction	Remarks
6.15pm	5.9"	LA MOTTE BAUDET.	15		Air bursts.
1.0am	HAVERSKERQUE. (4.2")		20		
1.10am	77mm	CORBIE.	15	N. of MERVILLE.	
2.0am	77mm	HAVERSKERQUE.	20.		
2.50am	4.2"	J.27.c and d. (4.2")	30.	TSB 111 degs. from J.27.c 4/9. 2 guns.	
3.30am	4.2"	Main Rd J.27.b.	7.	------do------	
3.38am	4.1"	J.27.c and d.	4.	TSB 111 degs. from J.27.c 4/9. 4 guns firing.	
4.0am	4.2"	LA MOTTE BAUDET.	20.		
4am-9am	4.2" 77mm	K.25. and 26.a. (southern).		Occasional.	
4 - 4.45am	77mm	K.29.central.	30.		
5 -7am	4.2" 5.9"	J.28.	) 30.		
Night.	Wood K.13.b. (77mm)			Occasional searching.	
5.15-5.45am	5.9"	J.22.d 0/0.		Occasional.	
During night.	5.9"	D.30.c.	100 ?	H.E. and gas.	
--"---	77mm) 5.9")	LA MOTTE - PAPOTE Road.	) 100 ?	Thought to be 18-Pdr.	
9.0am	Shrap.	LE PARC.	6.		
11am-Nn	77mm	ST FLORIS.	12.		
11.55am-12.10pm	4.2"	ST FLORIS.	6.		
12.15pm	5.9"	K.31.c & J.36.d.	20.	TSB 93 degs. from J.27.c 4/9 2 guns firing.	
12 Noon.	4.2"	J.5.d.	24		
12.15-12.45pm	4.2"	K.25.central.		Occasional bursts.	
12.17-12.50pm	4.2"	J.36.d 5/5.	15.	Registration.	
2.45pm	77mm	House K.25.b6/5	8.		
3pm onwards	5.9"	F.L. K.15.d 6/9 & house.	200.	Registration ?	
3-4.30pm	77mm	F.L. K.15.b 80/50.	150.	Gridbearing 106 from K.15.a 00/45. Regstn.	
4.0pm	77mm	K.25.d 40/83. House.	12.	Registration.	

SECRET.

5TH DIVISIONAL ARTILLERY INTELLIGENCE REPORT
6PM 22/5/18 to 6PM 23/5/18.

1. **SITUATION.** Unchanged. At mid-night, a raiding party went out, under cover of M.G. and L.G's and artillery fire, and finding the house at K.26.b 65/75 empty, moved on to within 10 yards of hedge K.26.b 8/7 - K.26.b 7/6, but found no working party.

2. **OUR ARTILLERY.** Night harassing fire. "Sunny Jim" went out between 10 p.m. and 3 a.m. and fired 150 rounds on the LA MOTTE - MERVILLE Road and on K.29.a. 120, 80, and D/15 batteries fired at ELSIE and GERTIE during the early morning - 120th covered the raid mentioned above. Today Left Group fired at a suspected 77mm battery at K.16.d 8/0, - and all batteries continued registrating and ammunition-testing.

   Trench Mortars. X/5 fired 20 rounds into MOATED GRANGE and K.26.d 35/60 in retaliation for enemy T.M. fire at 12.10 a.m. and 1.20 a.m. Y/5 registered on K.16.a 5/6.

3. **ENEMY ARTILLERY.** A 4.1" gun seems to be regularly employed at night harassing the HAVERSKERQUE Area, together with another 4.1" gun further that fires north. Last night a good deal of shrapnel was used. Other details of fire in attached List.

4. **INTELLIGENCE.**
   Batteries. T.B. from grooves in two shell-holes caused by above 4.1" gun at J.27.c 4/9 111 degs. (approx.).
   Flashes seen from J.35.d 4/0. :-
       9.30 p.m. TB 58 degs. 11 p.m. TB 64 degs.
   12 Mn T.P. 55 degs.
   Aerial. 6 E.A. crossed our lines at about 2,500 ft. between 7 p.m. and 8 p.m. yesterday. A few E.A. over back areas about 1.0 a.m. None seen today.
   E.K.B. 8 p.m. - 9 p.m. grid bearings 74, 80, 94½ and 98 degs. from J.34.a 4/4.
       4.30 a.m. - 11.30 a.m. grid bearings 66 and 66½ and 7 a.m. - 11.30 a.m. grid bearings 65, 68, 71, 74, 77½, 90, and 93, all from J.36.b 55/87.
       After 11.30 a.m., none up.
   M.G's. (From Div. Summary) Fired from K.16.a 9/4 and K.16.a 10/55, K.26.c 6/7, and K.32.a 4/2.
   T.M's. Reported by Infantry at K.21.b 6/4, K.21.b 2/2 K.32.a 2/1 K.32.a 8/7 K.27.a 05/50 and K.32.c 80/95.
   Movement. etc. Houses at K.26.c 6/6 and K.22.b 70/65 apparently occupied. 4 men seen fixing a screen at house K.6.d 9/9.
   Defences. etc. House at K.10.c 8/9 is reported to be either an O.P. or a sniping post.
   General. 8 - 8.10 p.m. considerable amount of white smoke at 83 G.B. from J.34.a 4/4.
   11.10 p.m. one golden-rain rocket over L.1.

                                sd. R.F. MASON. Lieut. R.A.
   23rd May, 1918.   Intelligence Officer 5th Divnl Artillery.

Time.	Cal.	Area shelled.	Rds.	Direction.	Remarks.
3-5 am	77mm	J.28.b.	100		Gas.
12 m.n.	77mm	L'EPINETTE and C. MARAISSE area.	30.	TSB 102 from J.15.b 2/0.	
12 m.n. & 3.15am	4.1"	J.21.d & 22.c.	30	TSB 90 from J.36.b 55/87.	
4.0am	MTM	K.31.b 6/0.	3.		
--"--	Gas	J.28.b.	60.		Gas shell barrage.
6.30am		K.31.b 6/0. (M.T.M.)	9.		E.A. overhead at the time.
6.45am	5.9"	K.35.d.	11.		1 gun firing.
8 - 9am	4.2"	ST FLORIS.	15.		
9.15am	4.2"F.L.	in K.26.a and K.20.d.	7.		Probably registration.
10-12Noon	77mm	ST FLORIS.	30.		
11.0am	LTM	K.31.b 1/3.	13.		
11am to Noon.	4.2" 77mm	) K.26.a and) K.20.d.	30.		
1.0pm	5.9"	J.10.a Canal.	15.		
2.0pm	4.2"	----"----	8.		
2.0pm	LTM	K.31.d 2/9.	7.		

SECRET.

5TH DIVISIONAL ARTILLERY INTELLIGENCE SUMMARY. 6.0 P.M. 23/5/18
TO 6 P.M. 24/5/18.

1. **SITUATION.** Unchanged.

2. **OUR ARTILLERY.** Harassing fire during the night on selected
targets.   Left Group retaliated at 11.0 p.m.
at Infantry request, and fired 2-minute bursts of fire on
K.18.c 9/8, K.18.c 23/42, K.17.d 75/45 and K.17.d 25/20 at
4.30, 4.50, 5.5, and 5.23 p.m.   Today a little registration
and ammunition-checking - no special shooting owing to bad
visibility.
    Trench Mortars. Y/5 registered on K.16.b 5/7 at 7 p.m.
- otherwise inactive.

3. **ENEMY ARTILLERY.** Considerable amount of gas-shelling last night
in K.13.d and 19.b, and 5.9's and 4.2's on Left Brigade trenches
most of the night.   Today comparatively quiet.   Details
attached.

4. **INTELLIGENCE. Batteries.** 4.30 a.m. flash of 4.2" shelling
    J.34.b 3/3 T.B. 86 degs. from J.34.a
4/4. Several sound bearings are given in attached list.   Flashes
9.45 p.m. 73½ T.B. from J.35.d 4/0.   10.30 p.m. 62 degs. T.B.
from J.35.d 4/0.
    Some bombing planes crossed our lines at night.
    E.K.B. 2 up in early morning - down by 6.0 a.m.
    M.G's. (From Div. Summary) fired during the 24 hours from
K.26.c 6/7, K.26.b 7/8, K.16.c 1/9, K.16.a 8/7, K.10.c 65/80
and K.10.c 80/85. Another reported on Canal Bank at
K.32.a 4/0.
    T.M'S. Reported at K.32.c 8/8 and others firing from
K.21.b 2/2, K.32.b 3/9 and K.26.b 8/2 (approx.).(This last
apparently registering on front and support lines of L.2.
sector.) Max
    Movement. etc. Infantry report 40 Germans in full marching
order moving along hedge at K.16.c 2/1, carrying rifles
slung.   Movement seen in trench at K.11.a 5/6, at K.10.b 7/6,
on roads at K.18.c 9/4 and K.23.b 5/9 and at road junction in
K.17.b.
    Defences. A trench is apparently being dug connecting
COURTFROI Farm with house at K.26.b 80/87.   Infantry report
enemy posts in K.10.b are being linked up.   New wire visible
in front of house at K.16.a 4/5 (approx).   Patrols found
some English wire and Screw Pickets at K.31.b 3/5.   It is
believed that there is a trench running behind hedge at
K.31.b 3/5 which is held.   House at K.26.b 78/58 (not
marked on map) is said to be an O.P.   Lieut. WOOD, A/15
Battery reports that conveniently - placed shell holes in
the factory at K.35.a 6/6, the house at K.29.c 6/0 and the
chimney at K.34.b 3/4 are very probably used for observation
purposes - and that MERVILLE Church and the Brickfields
Chimney are too much knocked about to be used as O.P's.
    General. Fires were burning all night in the enemy's
lines T.B. 79 degs. and 67½ degs. from J.34.a 4/4 and another
T.B. 71 degs. from J.35.d 4/0 - probably house at K.29.a 6/8.

24th May, 1918.
sd. R.F. MASON. Lieut. R.A.
Intelligence Ofr 5th Div. Arty.

HOSTILE FIRE.

Time.	Cal.	Area shelled.	Rds.	Direction. Remarks.
7.30 pm	4.1"	J.34.a.2/3.	9.	
7.45 p.m.	77mm	J.34.a.	14.	
9 p.m.	4.2"	---"---	12.	
9.30 pm - 3 a.m.	77mm 4.2"	Roads in J.30 & 36.	100.) 30.)	Gas and shrapnel mixed.
9.45 - 10.15 pm.	4.2"	K.34.d.	40.	
10.45pm.- 2.5 a.m.	77mm	J.18,24. K.19.		7 per minute Mustard Gas and sneezing T.S.B.110° from Left Battalion.
11pm to midnight.	5.9") 4.2")	Left Bde.F.L.	?	Fairly heavy.
Overnight.	4.1"	J.28.d. (N.E.)	30	
4 am-6am.	77mm 4.2 gas	J.5.c.	150.	
4.30 a.m.	4.2"	J.34.b.3/3	12.	Flash TB 86° from J.34.a.4/4.
8.10 a.m.	77mm	LA MOTTE	150-200.	Probably K.23.d.
9 a.m.	4.2"	K.19.d.	20.	
10.30 am	4.1"	J.28.d.	30.	TSB 86° from J.28.c.
10.30 am	4.2"	K.2.d.	40.	75/15.
11 am.	77mm	J.28.a.	40.	
11.15 am	4.2"	J.29.c.	12.	TSB 90° from J.34.a.
1.15 pm	4.2"	K.8.c.8/1	20.	4/4
2.30 pm	4.2"	K.15.b.& c.	20.	
2.30 pm	77mm.	J.34.a.8/5.	6.	Shrapnel.

5TH DIVISIONAL ARTILLERY INTELLIGENCE SUMMARY 6 P.M. 24-5-18 TO 6 P.M. 25-5-18.

1. SITUATION.   Unchanged.

2. OUR ARTILLERY.   Harassing fire at night with special attention to Factories and College N. of MERVILLE and tracks and roads leading up to the enemy's line.   D/160 fired 350 rds. in bursts during the night on HB at K.18.c.1/8 and at 7.50 a.m. D/152 answered NF call KD.10.   Left Group 18-pdrs. put 200 rds. into Orchards, and road in K.16.b and d. during the morning, in retaliation for shelling of K.15., and fired an observed shoot on K.21.b 95/95 with good results - house there set on fire. Right Group registered and tested ammunition during the day. "Sunny Jim" was out between 10 p.m. and 3.0 a.m. and fired 150 rounds on K.R.21, K.D.32, K.29.a 8/6 and cross roads L.13.a 2/9.

    Trench Mortars. X/5 registered on ELSIE yesterday afternoon. No firing today.

3. ENEMY FIRE.   Some gas shelling on the LE PARC - LA MOTTE Areas, sharp bursts of fire on front and support lines in K.15.b and c., and harassing fire S. and E. of HAVERSKERQUE during the night. A captured 9.2" or an 11" put 20 - 25 rounds on to J.34.a and 33.b. in the early morning, probably searching for a heavy battery there.   A little gas shelling on J.29.c during night. Details attached.

4. INTELLIGENCE, BATTERIES. (Bearings of 77mm and 11" shelling J.33.b sent on to G.B's).
    FLASHES. T.B's from J.35.d 4/0.
    9.20 p.m. 65 degs., 9.30 p.m. 70 degs., 9.45 p.m. 75 degs., 12.34 a.m. 75 degs.,
    AERIAL. 9 E.A. crossed our lines, high, during day, but did not penetrate far.   No bombing on back areas during night.
    BALLOONS. None reported.
    M.G'S. (From Div.Summary) Fired during night from K.26.c 7/4 and 60/65, K.16.c 1/9, K.15.d 80/35, K.10.c 65/80, and 5/3 and K.4.b 4/0.   L.O. Right Brigade reports M.G. very active during night from hedge at K.26.c 24/20.
    T.M's. At 2.30 a.m. one fired 20 rounds from K.32.b 3/9.
    MOVEMENT. Seen at L'EPINETTE and at K.16.a 1/2 "Where some commotion was caused by our Artillery fire".   Movement seen on roads leading to CORNET PERDU and VIERHOEK and at houses at K.16.b 5/1 and K.11.d 7/3.
    DEFENCES. Post occupied at K.31.b 8/8, and a line of posts behind hedge K.31.b 3/5 to K.31.b 3/4 held at night.   House at K.10.d 6/5 is being loopholed and is apparently used at night.   Another loophole in post at K.10.b 7/6.

    Infantry report cook-house at K.16.b 5/1. Camouflage on road in K.17.b has been blown down. (18-Pdrs are sprinkling this road with shrapnel tonight).   Patrols report belt of wire along hedge K.31.b 40/45.   Houses at K.21.a 40/35 and 6/2 and trench K.21.c 3/7 found unoccupied.

    Little new work is visible in enemy's lines except wiring.
    GENERAL. Infantry report GOLDEN RAIN Rockets were fired when enemy artillery put a few rounds short at about K.26.central. Right Group report 12 GOLDEN RAIN rockets on line S. of CANAL in K.33.c at 1.40 a.m. followed immediately by several rounds of 77mm shrapnel.

                                            sd. R.F. MASON. Lieut. RA
25th May, 1918.   Intelligence Ofr 5th Div. Arty.

HOSTILE FIRE.

Time.	Area shelled.	Rds.	Cal.	Direction & Remarks.
8pm	J.28, J.22.d.	200	4.2"	
8.20pm	J.34.a.	4	11"	E. of MERVILLE.
		8	4.2"	
		50	77mm	TSB 90 from J.34.a 4/4.
8.30pm - 10pm	J.29.c.	90	77mm	Just N. of MERVILLE. Phosgene - in intermittent bursts.
9.8pm	HAVERSKERQUE - ST VENANT Rd.	10	77mm	
9.20pm	----do----	20	77mm	TSB 95 from J.34.a 4/4.
9.30pm	LA MOTTE BAUDET.	20	gas.	
9.40 - 10.20pm	K.8.c and 14.c.	80	4.2"	2 rds per minute.
9.50pm	J.34.a.	5	11"	Behind MERVILLE.
10pm - 2.0am	LA MOTTE - LE PARC area.	100	4.2" gas.	Harassing.
10.10pm	LA MOTTE BAUDET.	20	Gas.	
12.40am	K.15.d School.	10	5.9"	
1.10am	K.9.b	5	5.9"	
1 - 1.30am	F.L. and S.L. in K.15.b and c.	-	4.2" 77mm	Shrap bursts.
3.0am	J.34.a and b.	50	77mm	
3.31-4.1pm	School K.16.d.	44	5.9"	GSB 92 degs. from J.10.a 7/6.
4.25am	LA MOTTE BAUDET.	40	77mm	
4.40am	J.34.a.	20	11"	E. of MERVILLE.
5 - 5.30am	J.17.a 3/8.	4	8" How.	TSB 95 from J.17.a 8/8
7am	J.28.a	30	77mm	Gas.
10am	J.28.a	20	77mm	H.E.
10am	K.15.b 6/2.	30 ?	5.9"	N.E. Intermittent.
10.30am	K.25.a 6/5.	20	4.2"	2 guns firing in salvoes.
10.30am	K.36.a	40	77mm	
11.30am - 4.0pm	ST FLORIS. P.6.a.	50	5.9" 4.1"	
Noon - 4.0pm	ST VENANT.	50	4.2" 5.9"	
4.35pm	K.8.c.	20	4.2"	
5.45pm	K.9.a.	10	77mm	

SECRET

5TH DIVISIONAL ARTILLERY INTELLIGENCE SUMMARY 6 A.M. 25-5-18 TO 6 A.M. 26-5-18.

1. SITUATION. Unchanged. Div. on our left fired 500 gas projectors on to VERTE RUE and VIEUX BERQUIN at 2 am yesterday. No retaliation.

2. OUR ARTILLERY. Harassing fire during night on selected targets. Left Group 4.5" Hows. engaged M.G. K.10.d.0/6 at 9 pm, - infantry report gun knocked out and 18-pdrs shot at K.10.c.9/0 (suspected T.M.).
At 9.30 p.m. Left Group fired 800 rds on S.O.S. lines sweeping 300 yards E., and another 400 rounds at 10.15 pm in retaliation for heavy shelling of our support lines in K.9 and 15. "SUNNY JIM" fired on K.6.c., K.12.a. and K.23.d., E.30.a. and L.13.a. and 14.c during night. 27th Brigade engaged GERTIE at 12.30am and 37th Battery fired 210 gas shells at H.Q., K.22.d.7/9 and road in K.28.c. During day some registration and ammunition-testing. Left Group again searched E from their S.O.S. lines at 3.45 pm and 6.15 pm in reply to enemy activity on Left Brigade front, while Right Group 4.5" walked up and down the new C.T. in K.21.b.& d. and K.22.c. at 5.45 pm.
Trench Mortars. During the very early morning JIM (X.5.) put 5 rounds into GERTIE, which settled her for the night.

3. ENEMY FIRE. Heavier, specially on Left Brigade support lines - 6 bursts of heavy fire 5.9" and 4.2's were put down in K.9. and K.15 last night and this afternoon. Apparently the enemy either expects another small attack by our Left Brigade or contemplates one himself.
The areas S. and E. of HAVERSKERQUE were rather heavily harassed during the early morning and evening. T.M's were busy on right brigade front at 1.0 a.m.

4. INTELLIGENCE. Batteries. The batteries firing so often on K.9 and 15 seem to be in the NEUF BERQUIN area. K.D. 50 was active this afternoon and is thought to fire on J.33.b at night, as well as Q.B. 12 or 21.
Flashes. T.B's from J.35.d 4/0 9.5 p.m. 71 degs., 9.10 p.m. 59 degs., 11.0 p.m. 80 degs., 11.0 p.m. 74 degs. Reported by Infantry 8.45pm 4.2" shelling K.4.c TB 122 degs. 9.0 p.m. 5.9" -- --- K.10.a 0/5 TB 153 degs. Both from K.10.a 5/2.
Many sound bearings are given in attached list.
Aerial. At 1.0 p.m. and 3.35 p.m. one E.A. patrolled our lines flying low. 2 flew high over our trenches at 6.20 p.m.
E.K.B's. 3.20 - 3.50 p.m. 72 degs. 10 mins. and 4.25 p.m. - 6.10 p.m. 78 degs. 20 mins. T.B's from H.35.d 4/0.
M.G's. Fired from K.10.d 0/8 at night and was silenced by our 4.5's. Guns at K.26.b 8/7 (JOSEPH) and K.21.c 80/65 also fired during night. Infantry report active M.G's at K.26.c 7/4, K.26.c 3/2 and 60/65, K.15.d 7/2, K.10.c 3/0.
T.M's. GIRTIE fired a few rounds at 1.0 a.m. GABY was lined by two 18-Pounders all night at Infantry request, but did not speak. An H.T.M. fired from behind house at K.16.a 85/60. Several T.M's are reported in this Orchard. Infantry report T.M's at K.32.b 3/9 and K.32.a 2/1 active during night.
Movement. etc. A working party of 30 seen at K.26.b 90/45.
General. Patrols brought in an identification of 4th German Division opposite our Right Brigade front (normal).
During enemy barrage on Left Brigade lines at 10 p.m., a GOLDEN RAIN and 4 SINGLE RED Rockets were sent up from K.15.d and 21.a.
/Fires seen in enemy's lines

Page 2.

INTELLIGENCE.

Fires seen in enemy's lines (T.B's from J.35.d 4/0).

9.30pm 58 degs., 11.5 p.m. 77½ degs., 10.30 pm - 12.30 a.m. 48 degs. (apparently a dump).

Smoke as of a burning dump seen T.B. 85 from J.35.d 4/0 during afternoon.

sd. R.F. MASON. Lieut. R.A.
Intelligence Officer 5th Divnl Arty.

26th May, 1918.

HOSTILE FIRE.

Time.	Area shelled.	Rds.	Cal.	Direction & Remarks.
5.45pm	K.14.a 5/8	10	5.9"	TSB 100 degs. from K.13.d 90/40.
6.22pm	K.15.a	20	10.5" How.	
6.30pm	J.38.a.	10	5.9"	TSB 82 degs. from J.5.d 4/0.
6.30 - 7.0pm	D.28.d 5/5	6	15cm How.	∅ 104 degs.
7.10pm	J.30.a 7/4.	20	59"	TSB 94 degs. from J.28.a 3/0. TSB 101 degs. from J.34.a 4/4
7.15pm	J.30.b 4/9.	7	5.9"	TSB 130 from J.34.a 4/4.
7.15pm	J.34.d	20	4.2"	81 degs. from J.35.d 4/0. 85 degs. from J.33.c 9/8.
7.20pm	J.34.a 2/4.	24	4.2"	TSB 122 degs. from J.34.a 4/4.
8.25pm	GAUDESCURE.	40	10.5" How.	X 118 degs.
8.35 - 8.55pm	K.15.a and b.	100	77mm & 10.5"	10 flashes observed from K.15.a 0/4 at 97 degs. from X
8.30 - 8.40pm	LE PARC, RUE DES MORTES, J.11.a & J.17.a.	100	21cm 77mm 10.5"	
8.30 - 8.45pm	D.28.d 5/5.	15	15cm How.	∅ 124 degs.
8.40 - 8.50pm	D.24.b and c. and D.23.b and d.	6	15cm How.	∅ 98 degs.
9.0pm.	ST VENANT.	3	5.9"	
9.0pm	K.21.a 5/8 - K.15.b	-	-	10 mins. 5.9" & 4.2" barrage.
9.10 - 9.40pm	J.5.a and b.	20	10.5" How.	∅ 110 degs.
9.10pm	Back areas.	3	8"	86 degs. TSB from J.35.d 4/0.
9.20pm	K.21.a 5/8 - K.15.b	-	-	10 mins. 5.9" & 4.2" barrage.
10 - 10.10pm	K.15.a.	-	77mm 10.5 & 15 cm.	Heavy barrage.
10 - 10.45pm	J.4.a.	15.	77mm	
11.35 pm	J.30.a.7/4 and J.34.a.3/5	30.	77mm	

Cont'd.

Page 3.

Time.	Area shelled.	Rds.	Cal.	Direction & remarks.
10.45pm	RUE DES MORTES.	20	5.9"	73 degs. TSB from J.35.d 4/0.
11.40pm	J.34.a 3/5.	10	4.2" H.E.	
11.40pm	D.22.b	10	15cm	∅ 98 degs.
12.15am	J.34.a	30	4.2"	H.E. and Gas.
1.0am	D.22.b	4	15cm	∅ 98 degs.
1.25- 1.40am	J.5.a & D.29.d.	20	10.5 cm gas.	∅ 98 degs.
2 - 2.10am	-----do-------	10	15cm	∅ 104 degs.
2.20- 2.30am	------do--------	20	10.5 & 15cm	∅ 98 degs.
4.10am	K.15.b.	30	77mm	X 105 degs.
4.15- 4.45am	J.2.d	40	10.5 & 15cm Gas.	∅ 110 degs.
4.30-5am	LE PARC., RUE des MORTS and J.10.d 7/6.	60	105mm & 15cm	
4.35am	J.33.d and J.36.c.	35	77mm	Gas.
4.40am	J.34.d	30	77mm	82 degs. TSB from J.35.d 4/0.
5.0am	J.34.a	20	4.2"	H.E. and Gas.
5.0am	J.22.c and J.29.a.	10	5.9"	
5.15am	K.15.b	30	10.5"How.	X 112 degs.
5.15am	J.5.a & D.29.d.	20	15cm	∅ 104 degs.
7.50- 8.5am	J.5.a	20	10.5cm	∅ 117 degs.
--"---	J.4.a.	15	15cm	∅ 104 degs.
7.50- 8.5am	STEENBESQUE.	15	?	∅ 117 degs 30 mins.
8.20- 8.25am	D.22.b & D.23.a.	12	10.5cm	∅ 117 degs.
8.35am	K.26.c.	10	4.2"	
9.0am	K.31.a.	5	4.2"	
9-9.10am	J.34.d.	20	4.2"gas	62 degs. TSB from J.35.d 4/0.
9-9.45am	D.20.a 8/3.	5	10.5cm	∅ 107 degs.
9.45- 10.0am	K.31.a.	10	4.2"	Rapid bursts.
10-10.15 am & 11.20- 11.23am	D.8.d 8/4.	10.	10.5cm	∅ 107 degs.
11.10- 11.15am	D.21.d 8/8.	6	77mm	∅ 115 degs.
11.35- 11.40am	D.22.d 9/9.	2	15cm	∅ 104 degs.
11.45am -12.5pm	LE PARC, RUE DES MORTS & J.11.a.	50	10.5cm	
12 - 12.22pm	D.22.d 9/9.	2	15cm	∅ 104 degs.
12.55pm	-----do-----	4	15cm	∅ 107 degs.
1.20pm	-----do-----	1	21cm	∅ 104 degs.
2.28- 2.37pm	K.8.d, K.9.a &c. & K.15.b.	-	10.5" 15cm	NEUF BERQUIN. Heavy barrage.
2.45pm	J.29.c.	6	4.2"	shrap.
3.15pm - 3.30pm	K.8.d, K.9.a &c. and K.15.b.	-	10.5& 15cm	Heavy barrage. NEUF BERQUIN.

Page 4.

Time.	Area shelled.	Rds.	Cal.	Direction & Remarks.
3.30pm	ST FLORIS.	50	4.7" 5.9"	
3.45pm	K.31.a.	5	4.2"	
3.50pm	CORBIE. K.36.c 80/80	25	4.2"	Huricane fire. TSB 53 dogs. from J.35.d.
4.10pm	ST VENANT.	6	77mm	
4.45am	J.10.c 80/35	12	8"	
4.50pm- 4.55pm	K.8.d, K.9.a and c. and K.15.b.		10.5" 15cm	Heavy barrage NEUF BERQUIN. - from K.15.a 0/4.
5.28- 5.33pm	-----do-----	-	-"---------"------	
6.34pm - 6.42pm	-----do-----	-	15cm	----do-----
Afternoon	J.29.d 1/3. Cross roads.		4.1"	Occasional shrapnel.

ø Grid bearings from D.28.d 5/5 .

X ------"------ from K.15.a 0/4.

SECRET.

5TH DIVISIONAL ARTILLERY INTELLIGENCE SUMMARY

6 PM 26/5/18 to 6PM 27/5/18.

1. SITUATION. Unchanged.
2. OUR ARTILLERY. Harassing fire at an increased rate during the night. All batteries "Stood to" at dawn this morning. Left Group batteries retaliated to heavy enemy fire on Left Brigade support lines, at 7.5 and 10.50 p.m. firing on S.O.S. lines and sweeping 500 yards East. Also engaged H.T.M. at K.16.d 85/15 at 11.30 a.m. and fired an unsatisfactory observed shoot on K.17.a 7/40 at 12.30 p.m. - 13 rounds fired. Some registration and ammunition testing was done during the day.

    Trench Mortars. Inactive.

3. ENEMY FIRE. Some fairly heavy 4.2" and 5.9" fire on Right Brigade forward areas during early morning. Between 12.25 p.m. 26th. and 4.30 a.m. 27th seven heavy bursts of 4.2" and 5.9" fire lasting 5 - 10 minutes, were put down on support lines in K.9 and 15. A counter battery shoot by an 8" How. on an 8" How. S. of HAVERSKERQUE this afternoon, after registration during the morning. Otherwise nothing unusual.

    INTELLIGENCE. Batteries.

    4.10 a.m. 4.2" shelled HAVERSKERQUE flash 95 degs. grid from J.34.a 4/4

    10.10 p.m. 4.2" shelling S. of ST. VENANT flash 99 degs grid from J.34.a 4/4.

    Infantry report following flashes :- 1/7.
    During afternoon 5.9" shelling K.9.c and 15.a TB 124 from K.15.b
    ---"---------------- 77mm ----------"-------------/95degs.from
    125 &   K.9.d 8/2.
    ---"---------------- 77mm ----------"----------TB 125 from K.15.b1/5.
    10.15pm 4.2." shelling K.4.c TB 78 degs. from K.10.a 7/3.
    --"---- ?   -----"-- K.10.a 2/0 TB 153 degs. from K.10.a 7/3.

    Aerial. E.A. were over enemy trenches in evening, and another over ours at 6 a.m., flying low. 35 enemy machines were counted over our lines today at different times including one flight of 6 (at 10.30 a.m.) and 3 of 5. One dropped two small bombs in K.9.d at 11.30 a.m. E.A. observers very active during the morning using the following calls :- NTD, WNA, SCP, WHA, NCP and AD.

    E.K.B's. Up at 10.15 a.m. T.B. 80, 77 and 73 degs., 11.30 a.m. 75 degs., 12.30 p.m. 70 degs. (2) and 4.30pm 71 degs. from K.35.d 4/0. remaining up throughout the day.

    M.G's. (From Div. Summary) Active at K.26.c 7/4 and 60/65, K.26.a 6/7, in the orchard at COURTFROI Farm, at K.10.c 3/6 (?) and 80/93.

    T.M's. Fired from K.32.b 3/9, K.32.a 2/1, K.26.b 9/4, K.16.a 5/5 (HTM) and K.16.a 3/3 (MTM). The Infantry report that ELSIE seems to have been driven out and to have moved to garden at K.32.b 22/82.

    Movement. etc. Trenches at K.10.c 6/5 and K.10.b 6/4, wood at K.16.b 7/3, ruins at K.26.c 7/4 occupied.

    10 dugouts found by patrols at K.21.c 05/85, but immediately a wire was touched here a M.G. opened fire on the patrol.

    Trench K.21.c 5/3 to K.21.c 8/8 thought to be occupied by the enemy.

    Defences. Enemy line from K.31.b 6/6 to K.26.c 4/1 is reported wired with English wire - thickest in front of enemy posts.

    Camouflage about 15 ft. high has been put up along road from K.11.b 5/6 to K.11.d 8/9. Enemy sniper busy last night at K.26.b 7/7. A dead tree at J.26.c 3/2 looks like a camouflaged O.P. and has a loophole near the top. two bits of paper fluttered out of slit in small cabin built in wall of house at K.25.a 6/6 previously reported (on the 23rd May) as an O.P.

    General. GOLDEN RAIN Rockets sent up yesterday afternoon where enemy artillery shot short.

    3.30 - 4.30 p.m. heavy smoke and fire T.B. 65 degs. 40 mins. from K.36.b 7/8.

    sd. R.F. MASON. Lieut. R.A.
27th May, 1918.   Intelligence Officer 5th Divnl Artillery.

SECRET.
5TH DIVISIONAL ARTILLERY INTELLIGENCE SUMMARY, 6.0 P.M. 27/5/18 to 6.0 P.M. 28/5/18.

1. SITUATION.   Unchanged.
2. OUR ARTILLERY. Harassing fire 40 rounds per gun during the night. B/152 fired 33 rounds on H.R. aeroplane K.17.a 67/40 at 6.0 p.m. and 52 rounds at 7.0 p.m., with observation. The first shoot was unsatisfactory owing to poor visibility from the air.   During the second 6 Y's., one Z., and 13 A's were registered.   Batteries left group fired on and east of S.O.S. Lines at 10.20 p.m., 2.50 a.m., 2.40 p.m., and 3.45 p.m., in retaliation to enemy fire and at Infantry request. "SUNNY JIM" fired 150 rounds on K.29.b., 3 battery positions in K.17.b and roads and tracks at K.23.b 5/9.   B/152 fired 20 rounds and D/152 30 rounds on H.T.M. K.16.a 8/3 during the night.   At 8.3 p.m. 37th How. Battery answered NF   K.D.21 firing 50 EX and at 4.30 p.m. burnt, with incendiary shell, houses at K.27.c 7/6, K.27.d 2/1.   In addition today batteries checked lines and tested ammunition.

   Trench Mortars. X/5 fired 10 rounds at GERTIE at 2.15 a.m. Y/5 did no firing.

3. ENEMY ARTILLERY.   Left Brigade support lines were again fairly heavily shelled at intervals, about 200 rounds 4.2" and 77mm dropped in J.5.c during the evening, and the LA MOTTE - RUE DES MORTS area was shelled this afternoon.   The LA MALADERIE Line S.E. of HAVERSKERQUE was subjected to a heavy burst of 77mm and 4.2" fire at 8.25 a.m. A small area shoot on LA MOTTE BAUDET at noon and the apparent registration of a H.A. Battery position in J.28.a. by a 4.1" gun were the main features of enemy fire during the period.

4. INTELLIGENCE. Batteries. A bearing of 91 degs. true was taken from groove of a dud 4.2" which dropped at J.28.a 3/3 at 5.30 p.m.   Angle of descent 18 degs. 45 mins.

   - and of a dud 77mm at J.35.a 6/2 T.B. 86½ degs.

   Flashes seen during night T.B. 63 degs. from J.35.d 4/0 - possibly battery at K.18.c 3/4.   Flashes seen during night 26/27th sent on to C.B.S.O.

   Aerial. 50 E.A. were counted mostly flying high over our lines between dawn and noon today.   A few were over back areas last night bombing.   One is thought to have landed in our lines S. of the Forest, but there is no confirmation. 34 calls were picked up from an E.A. by our wireless between 8.50 and 10 a.m.   Details sent on to C.B.S.O.   Two E.A. were over J.34.a at 4.30 p.m. - high - and two over J.28.a at 5.25 p.m.

   E.K.B's.   11 were up between LESTREM and DOULIEU during the day. One went up at 3.0 p.m., the occupant parachuted out at 3.10 p.m. and the balloon descended at 3.15 p.m. - T.B. 97 degs. 15 mins from HAVERSKERQUE Church.

   M.G's. (From Div. Summary) Fired from K.31.b 6/6 and several from trench in K.10.a.

   Movement, etc. Sentry seen in trench at K.27.c 3/1 - a german at K.26.c 5/4 was hit by snipers.   During our shelling at 6.30 p.m. two Germans ran from house K.16.d 15/55 into the trench nearby.   Estaminet at K.18.b 4/3 had door open at 6.45 p.m.: this had hitherto always been shut.

   Defences. New wire has been put up in rear of enemy outpost line at K.26.b 8/4.   House at K.16.b 4/7 is said to be an O.P.   Loopholes visible at K.26.b 8/4.

   General.   Searchlights busy during night T.B. 78 degs. and 80 degs. from J.35.d 4/0.

   1.30 p.m. fire in enemy lines T.B. 56 from J.35.d 4/0.

5. MISCELLANEOUS.   A document taken off a prisoner of 121 German Division by the French on May 20th. show that the following Light Signals came into force on 21st May '18 :-

   Double Red Star ... ... BARRAGE.
   --"--- Yellow Star or Yellow Light
   Balls with parachute. ... ... COUNTER PREPARATION.
   Double Green Star ... ... LENGTH AND RANGE.
   White Star with Pearls. ... ... SHORTEN RANGE. (only to be used when outpost line has been evacuated).

   Sd. R.F. MASON. Lieut. R.A.
   28th May, 1918.   Intelligence Officer 5th Divnl Artillery.

SECRET.
5TH DIVISIONAL ARTILLERY INTELLIGENCE REPORT
6 P.M. 28/5/18 to 6.0 P.M. 29/5/18.

1. SITUATION.   Two raids were carried out during the night by the Right Brigade.   At mid-night a party of our troops rushed the M.G. post at K.31.b 9/9.   Several of the enemy were killed and 5 prisoners taken (2 wounded) At 1.0 a.m. another M.G. post at K.21.c 25/70 was rushed but no enemy were found there.   Our casualties reported to be 3 slightly wounded.

2. OUR ARTILLERY.   6.3 p.m. batteries answered XX Call K.23.c 4/8.   During night 25 rounds per gun harassing fire on selected targets.   Right Group supported Infantry in raids at 12 mid-night and 1.0 a.m.   129th Battery ran out a roving gun during night and harassed NEUF BERQUIN and eastern approaches to MERVILLE.   At 1.5 a.m. Left Group fired 800 rounds on enemy front line searching 500 E.   To-day some registration and ammunition testing.   37th Bty. fired incendiary shell at houses in K.27.c., K.26.d. and factory K.35.a.5/6.   First two burnt to ground, second contained bombs - 5 explosions.   Large fire caused in factory.

Trench Mortars.   X/5 Bty. cut wire in K.31.b. yesterday previous to the raid.   Also registered on GERTIE, GABY and NELLIE.   Between 12 mid-night and 12.30 a.m. fired 61 rounds on GERTIE and BRICKFIELDS in support of raid.   Y/5 Battery inactive.

3. ENEMY FIRE.   In general heavier but no exceptional crumping of any particular place.   LA MOTTE, LE PARC and LA MOTTE BAUDET each received about 100 rounds 77mm during the day and night.   Details attached.

4. INTELLIGENCE.   Batteries.   Flash seen 8.45 a.m. 77 m/m shelling J.36.central W.B. 107 degs. from J.36.b 7/9. No information as to approximate range can be obtained yet.

Flashes seen during night from J.35.d 4/0.
9.30 p.m. 62½ (5), 9.40 p.m. 56½ (3), 3.15am-3.30am 70 (20),
3.20 - 3.40am 53 (6), 3.45-4.5am 55 (10). - (All true bearings).

Aerial.   E.A. active this afternoon, one crossing our low lines 4 times.   1.0 p.m. and aeroplane dropped in flames in enemy's lines in line with BRICKFIELDS Chimney from J.34.a4/4. A German plane descended at 5.15 p.m. at T.B. 90 from J.34.a 4/4. 5.30 p.m. three E.A. attacked an R.E.8 over J.34., but our machine drove them away.   One E.A. dropped three bombs in BOIS MOYEN at 12.30 p.m.

LATER.   An E.A. brought our STEENBECQUE Balloon down in flames at 8.55 p.m. today, and got away safely.   Two more of our balloons were brought down in flames near HAZEBROUCK at 3.20 p.m.

E.K.B's.   T.B's from J.35.d 4/0.   70 degs., 10.30 a.m. 4.30 a.m. - 6.20 a.m.   10.50 a.m. onwards 71 degs., onwards 74 degs. 40 mins.   11.40am onwards 11a.m. - Noon & 12.15p.m. onwards 70½ degs.   71 degs., 12.35 p.m. onwards 69 degs., 12.55 p.m. onwards 75 and 76 degs.

M.G's.   Reported firing from K.26.c 60/65, K.21.a 95/90, and 85/15, K.10.c 5/4 and K.10.b 6/4.

T.M's.   Fired from K.16.a 7/4 and 1/2 and K.16.c 8/8. It is thought that a premature "happened" at one of these guns this morning.

Movement, etc.   Men seen walking through LE SART and in trench K.28.b 75/35 and on screened road K.11.c 1/9 - K.11.b 4/6.

Defences.   Post located at K.11.a 5/9.   House at K.10.d. 75/15 is a suspected O.P.

General.   Fires 4.30 a.m. T.B. 40 degs. from J.35.d 4/0. 12.5a.m. - 1.30 a.m. 121 grid from D.28.b 4/3,   Later 9.40pm large fire reported in MERVILLE.

During raid last night a number of RED and GOLDEN RAIN rockets were put up by the enemy.

5. MISCELLANEOUS.   Prisoners captured in K.31.b last night belong to 16 German Div. which relieved 4th Div. 9 days ago. Further details later

29th May, 1918.

ad, R.F. MASON. Lieut, R.A,
Intelligence Ofr 5th Divnl Artiller

SECRET.
5TH DIVISIONAL ARTILLERY INTELLIGENCE SUMMARY
6.0 P.M. 29/5/18 to 6.0 P.M. 30/5/18.

1. SITUATION. Reference the successful raid on
night 28th/29th. on enemy posts at K.31.b
8/8 and K.31.b 9/9 carried out by our Right Brigade, the
posts were well held by the enemy, 6 of whom were killed
in hand to hand fighting. One wounded man alone survived
of the post at K.31.b 9/9 and he was made a prisoner. A
M.G., too firmly clamped down for removal, was found in this
post. Of the post at K.31.b 8/8, one wounded and 1
unwounded man were taken prisoners, the remainder of the
garrison were killed. At Zero minus 4 a party of about
25 Germans were observed about to work near these posts.
They were caught by our barrage and those who fled towards
the Brickfields were heavily engaged by our Lewis Gunners
who claim several hits. The garrison of these posts
attempted to defend themselves with bayonets but caused no
casualty to our troops with them. An hour later a second
enterprise was carried out against the M.G. post at
K.21.c 25/75, but the enemy were not in occupation. Our
raiding party remained in the post in the hope that the
enemy would attempt to occupy it, but he failed to do so.

2. OUR ARTILLERY. Harassing fire during the night 25
rounds per gun on selected targets.
"SUNNY JIM" was out from 10 p.m. to 1 a.m., firing on roads
ELSIE and houses K.29.a and b., and K.22.a and d. D/15 fired on
T.B. at 11 p.m., and A/152 engaged H.B. K.B.81 at 12.30pm.
Todays ammunition testing and registration. D/160 fired a
very successful C.B. shoot on H.B. K.22.b 91/77 firing 300
rds between 4.25 p.m. and 5.30 p.m. No further details
available yet but said to be mostly O.K.
Trench Mortars. Y/5 fired 7 rounds at NELLIE at
2.45 p.m. at Infantry request - NELLIE silenced.

3. ENEMY FIRE. T.M's were active on Right Brigade front
between 10.30 p.m. and mid-night. Fairly heavy harassing fire
on BOIS CLOPERT area during night and a little sneezing gas
on J.22.c and d. at intervals in the early morning and
at 3.0 p.m. Otherwise normal. Details attached.

4. INTELLIGENCE. Batteries. Flashes seen during night
from J.35.d4/0 :-
9.35pm 63 degs. T.B.   10.2pm 80 degs. T.B.
9.48pm 61 -----"------   10.3pm 77 -----"----
10.13pm 57 -----"------   12.2am 67 -----"----
10.24pm 75 -----"------

1.4 p.m. NF K.D.91 received - out of range. Infantry
report flashes seen at 3.0 p.m. T.B. 133 degs. from K.4.c
6/5 and 71 degs. from K.14.a 7/9. Probable 4.2" dud
at J.36.b 5/8 gives T.B. 70 degs. angle of descent 44½ degs.
Aerial. 15 E.A. were seen high over our lines yesterday
evening, including one flight of 8. E.A. flew high over
HAVERSKERQUE at 11.25 a.m. but were driven off by A.A. fire.
Three E.A. crossed our lines at 4.45 p.m.
E.K.B's. All E.K.B's reported yesterday descended at
8.0 p.m. except the one at T.B. 75 degs. which descended
at 8.15 p.m., disappearing from view at T.B. 74 degs. 44 mins.
(bearings from J.35.d.4/0). Today E.K.B's rose 12.5 p.m.
T.B. 79, 12.15 p.m. T.B's 68, 66, 70 and 72 degs, and
12.45 p.m. T.B. 74 degs from J.35.d 4/0. Still up at
6.0 p.m.
4.55 p.m. E.K.B. brought down in flames by one of our
planes, near LESTREM.

M.G's. (From Div. Summary). M.G. at K.10.c 7/8 is
active and also one at K.10.c 8/9. There is a H/G.E. at K.21.
15/80 on the railway. 12.45 a.m. JOSEPH active on K.20.a.

T.M's. Fired from K.22.a 7/7 and K.32.a 15/20.

Movement. etc. Continual movement behind the hedges b. of
the road in K.16.a. Movement seen in trenches K.16.
K.10.c 85/15 and K.10.b 8/6 - and throughout the day at K.5.b 6/7,
K.17.d 3/4, at house K.11.d 7/4, and behind the hedges of orchard
at K.26.b 7/8.

Defences. Digging heard at K.32.a 2/7 at night. New work
visible at K.11.b 2/7 with new wire in front. The house at
K.5.b 77/72 is a suspected O.P. The house at K.26.d 80/05 is
occupied.

Fires. 5.30 - 8.0 p.m. fire in K.32.b reported - with
explosions, probably a dump on road. 6.1 p.m. large
explosion in a fire which started at 5.50 p.m. T.B. 88½ degs. from
K.25.a 2/7. Big columns of black smoke. 6.45 p.m. goods
station in MERVILLE reported set on fire. Today 1.35 p.m. small
fire T.B. 52 degs., and 1.47 p.m. and 2.20 p.m. another T.B. 75 degs.
All from J.35.d 4/0. 2.30 p.m. fire seen at about K.33.d 9/3
ceased. Another bearing to fire at 1.35 p.m. is 78 degs.
T.F. from K.14.a 7/8.

Miscellaneous. Golden Rain rockets sent up by the enemy 12.42
a.m. T.B. 67 degs. and 1.54am TB 60 degs. from J.35.d 4/0.
Searchlights 12.50 a.m. T.B's 73, 75 and 83 degs. from J.35.d 4/0.
It is suggested now that GOLDEN RAIN Rockets are now used
to make up shortage in Very Lights and that they have no special
significance.

GENERAL. There are now 14 fresh Division and 38 Divisions
which have been refitting for a fortnight   y or over,
in reserve, making a total of 52 Divisions in reserve in the
Western Theatre, available for immediate operations; of these,
however, at least 5 may have been already put on the AISNE front.

                                                sd. R.F. MASON. Lieut. RA
                                     Intelligence Officer 5th Div. Arty.

30th May, 1918.

5TH DIVISIONAL ARTILLERY INTELLIGENCE SUMMARY 6 P.M. 30-5-18 TO 6 P.M. 31-5-18.

1. SITUATION. Unchanged. The Div. on our left had no luck in their raid last night. The enemy raided one of the posts of the Div. on our right.

2. OUR ARTILLERY. Harassing fire by night - 25 rds. per gun. 52nd, A/15, 119th and 120th & D/15 batteries fired DRUM RIGHT scheme of retaliation at 3.30 a.m. 37th Battery fired at NELLIE during night and 120th Battery at AARON at 4.30 p.m. - scoring several hits. "SUNNY JIM" harassed cross-roads and houses in K.11.d. C/160 Bty. supported raid by Div. on our left at 12.30am. To-day mainly registration and ammunition-testing.
   Trench Mortars. X/5 Bty. checked lines during the afternoon.
   Y/5 Bty. inactive.

3. ENEMY FIRE. Considerable harassing fire during the night, especially on J.29.c & d., between 11.30 p.m. and 4.30 a.m. - mostly phosgene and BLUE CROSS gas. The area S. of PAPOTE, CHAPEL BOOM and BOIS des VACHES was also considerably worried with 4.2's and 77 mm and gas.. To-day has been comparitively quiet. Details attached.

4. INTELLIGENCE. Batteries. Flashes seen during night T.B's 64, 52, 56, and 73 degrees from J.35.d.4/0.
   Aerial. 20 E.A. were counted over our line at different times yesterday evening, including one flight of eight. This morning 6 were seen flying high over the lines. Some bombing-machines over during night - one dropped 2 bombs in STEENBECQUE at 11 p.m. killing 3 and wounding 36 civilians.
   E.K.B's. 7 rose at 7 a.m. T.B's 80, 81, 77, 75, 73, 70, and 68 degrees from J.35.d.4/0 - remained up during day. Div. state that two other E.K.B. are reported to have been shot down by Artillery fire at 5.5 p.m. yesterday.
   M.G's. (From Div.Summary) fired on our aeroplanes from K.10.b.9/1 during the day, and from K.10.c.65/80, K.10.b.55/45 and K.10.d.25/65 during the night.
   T.M's. One seen firing from FERME BEAULIEU. T.M. at K.32.a.7/7 reported active during the night.
   Movement etc. House at K.31.b.6/1 apparently occupied. Movement continues at the O.P. at K.5.b.77/72. The shutters in Chateau at K.22.d.5/3 occasionally open and close.
   Defences. O.P's. Some object can be seen in a tree about K.32.a.8/8 - possibly an observation 'nest'. A small hole has been made near the top of factory chimney K.23.c.4/8 - probably for observation purposes. A mound with a small square hole in front, has been constructed at K.32.a.8/8 probably a M.G.E.
   Rockets. Enemy sent up ORANGE lights bursting into GOLDEN RAIN during night when occasional rounds from his Artillery dropped short. DOUBLE RED Lights were put up during the raid on our left - apparently the enemy's S.O.S. signal.
   Miscellaneous. 10.45 a.m. our artillery started a fire in K.27.d. 12.30 a.m. - 3.15 a.m. fires seen 61 degs. T.B. from J.35.d.4/0. An explosion was heard at 5 a.m. T.S.B. 54 degs. from same place.
   Searchlights busy during night T.B's 73, 78, and 93 degs. from J.35.d.4/0.

sd/- R.F.MASON. Lieut.
Intelligence Officer, 5th Div'l Artillery.

31-5-18.

Army Form C. 2118.

WAR DIARY
or
INTELLIGENCE SUMMARY.
(Erase heading not required.)

May 1918.

Place	Date	Hour	Summary of Events and Information	Remarks and references to Appendices
			Casualties during the month :-	
			Killed Wounded Gassed	
			119 Battery 1 O.R. 1 O.R.	
			120 Bty 1 O.R. 3 Off. 25 other Ranks	
			121 Bty 1 Officer. 5 O.R. 19 " "	
			34 Bty 4 O.R. 4 " "	

Sheet sent for Colonel
Cundy 27 Bde R.F.A

Letters
27th Bde
R.F.A.

June 1918

Spare

Chapter XIII.

1915 - Vol II.

(1927 Revise.)

S/Lieut

27th Bde
RFA.

June 1918

Spare.

Chapter XIII.

1915 - Vol II.

(1927 Revise.)

Register No.
Part No.
Volume No.

WAR DIARY, (Original)

of

27th Brigade R.F.A.

for the month ending 30 June 1918.

1/7/1918.

Barkley Lieut Colonel
................Commanding
27th Brigade R.F.A.

WAR DIARY
or
INTELLIGENCE SUMMARY.

Army Form C. 2118.

JUNE 1918 Map 1/40,000 36ᴬ

Place	Date	Hour	Summary of Events and Information	Remarks and references to Appendices
CROIX MARAISE Bn. Hd. (J 26 b 4/3)	1/6	8am to 8am	The following mentions in despatches for work in Italy are announced. Lieut-Colonel J. BERKLEY. Major A.H. AREAH, 120ᵗʰ Bty. Major G.L. BUTLER, 121st " Lieut J.S. WILLIAMS, 37ᵗʰ " No. 41074 Fitter J.W. CUTFORTH 121st Bty. " 134969 Bdr H. PRIOR 120ᵗʰ " Very hot day. nothing to report	
	2/3	"	"	
	3/4	"	"	
	4/5	"	120ᵗʰ Bty. position was badly shelled during afternoon; no damage beyond some camouflage burnt.	
	5/6	"	Fine day, quiet.	
	6/7		"	
	7/8		"	
	8/9		"	
	9/10		Rain vaed	

Officer Commanding

.............Battery RFA. 119 / 120 / 131 / 37   27th Bde. No. BM/291.

1. Gas will be projected tonight 7th/8th inst. on the following targets :-

   (a) Cross Roads, K.26.c 80/15.
   (b) Area around Chimney, K.32.a 10/35.

2. Barrages will be fired as under:-

Zero minus 1 to Zero

   119th and 120th Btys. will fire bursts of H.E.
   119th Bty. will barrage K.32.b 3/7 to K.26.c 4/3
   120th Bty. will barrage K.26.c 4/3 to K.26.c 7/7 to K.26.d 1/4.

Zero plus 2 to Zero plus 5

   119th Bty. will barrage K.32.b 3/7 to K.26.c 4/3
   120th Bty. will barrage K.26.c 7/7 to K.26.d 1/4
   A/15 Bty. will barrage K.31.b 8/2 to K.31.b 8/8
   52nd Bty. will barrage K.31.b 8/8 to K.32.a 4/8

Ammunition :- 100% Shrapnel.

Zero plus 45 to Zero plus 47.

   120th Bty. will barrage Road, K.26.a 6/0 to K.27.c 5/0.
   A/15 Bty. will barrage Canal Bank, K.32.b 6/2 to K.32.a 5/2.

Ammunition :- 100% Shrapnel.

3. RATE OF FIRE :- INTENSE.
4. ZERO hour will be 1.30 a.m. 7th/8th June 1918.

Map - edition

                                 Captain R.F.A.

7th June 1918.   Adjutant 27th. Bde. R.F.A.

Army Form C. 2118.

WAR DIARY
or
INTELLIGENCE SUMMARY.

(Erase heading not required.)

JUNE 1918   Map 1:40,000 36.A

Instructions regarding War Diaries and Intelligence Summaries are contained in F. S. Regs., Part II. and the Staff Manual respectively. Title pages will be prepared in manuscript.

Place	Date	Hour	Summary of Events and Information	Remarks and references to Appendices
36 N 9/3	10/11	6am to 8am	Cold, some rain. Quiet day.	
"	11/12	"	" " Quiet day.	
"	12/13	"		
"	13/14	"		
"	14/15	"	13th Bty. heavily shelled overnight.	
"	15/16	"	Colonel BERKLEY to 16th R.F.A., to command Group during absence of Col. Hawkes acting CRA. Major G.H. BUTLER commands the Brigade.	
"	16/17	"		
"	17/18	"	19th & 87th Batteries to move to positions north of FORET de NIEPPE for special operations; two guns per battery move tonight. Seaborne move of battery completed.	
"	18/19	"	Capt J. WARRINGTON 119 Bty. wounded. 2/Lt. T.D. MARTIN " killed.	
"	19/20	"	no 55137 Sergt. J.W.T. AIREY. 120th Bty. awarded D.C.M. 119th & 87th Batteries return to former positions in Rges Group. Special operations cancelled.	

2353 Wt. W2514/1454 700,000 5/15 D.D.&L. A.D.S.S./Forms/C. 2118.

Army Form C. 2118.

WAR DIARY
or
INTELLIGENCE SUMMARY.

JUNE 1916

(Erase heading not required.)

Place	Date	Hour	Summary of Events and Information	Remarks and references to Appendices
J96 A2/3	20(b)	8am & 6pm	Fine day, cool. Epidemic of P.U.O. in 37th and 130th Batteries, 25 & 30 and 40 to 50 men respectively sick. Personnel of 130th Battery withdrawn to wagon line for rest. Guns remain in position. 7am for 10mins.	
"	21/22			
"	22/23			
"	23/24		Wet day	
"	24/25			
"	25/26		Major G.C. Biles (131 "B" Bty.) posted to England.	
"	26/27		37th and 119th Batteries move to pontoon fork of forts of NIEPPE for "BORDERLAND" operations. 131 "B" Battery personnel go into active again and move forward to new position for operation. Capt J.C.a'Arcy Jones 131 "B" Bty in command. Fine day. 6am 28th we attacked opposite CAUDESCURE. all objectives captured. Fine day.	
"	28/29		Battery outpoored (?)	

Army Form C. 2118.

WAR DIARY
or
INTELLIGENCE SUMMARY.

Maps 1.40.000. 36.A

(Erase heading not required.)

Place	Date	Hour	Summary of Events and Information	Remarks and references to Appendices
J26.b.7/8	29/30	8am	Fine day.	
"	30/April	8am	Fine day. 37th Bde return from BOREDERAND forming 119th Batty. orders to return rifles of the 1st July.	
			OPERATION ORDERS for BORDERLAND attack will be attached to July War Diary	

MESSAGES AND SIGNALS.

Army Form C. 2121.
(In pads of 100.)

Prefix......... Code.............m   Words.   Charge.   This message is on a/c of: Recd. at .... m.
Office of Origin and Service Instructions.
                                        Sent   Date...............
                                      At..........m.   Service.
                                      To............   From ....
                                      By............   (Signature of "Franking Officer.")   By................

TO { O/C "A" Coy Repeated and 3/4th   LIAISON OFFICER
     TEL1.   TEB1.   NOWR —

Sender's Number.   Day of Month.   In reply to Number.   AAA
*W.546.   2/6.

A fighting Patrol will be sent
out by you to-night consisting
of not more than one Officer and
ten O.R. AAA. To leave your trenches
between 9 and 10-30 p.m. AAA.
Exact time to be notified to these
HQ. and to flank Coys as early
as possible. AAA
OBJECT. AAA. To capture Post A
at K.21.c.2/4 as reported by
you in Patrol Report AAA. This
will be done by (a) Occupying
the post before the enemy arrive
there AAA or (b) cutting him off
when he is in occupation AAA.
You will arrange necessary L.C.

From
Place
Time
The above may be forwarded as now corrected.   (Z)
....
      Censor.   Signature of Addressor or person authorised to telegraph in his name.
* This line should be erased if not required.
(3198.) Wt. W12932/M1294. 375,000 Pads. 1/17. H.W.& V., Ld. (E. 815.)

MESSAGES AND SIGNALS.

Army Form C. 2121.
(In pads of 100.)

Prefix....Code....m	Words.	Charge.	This message is on a/c of:	Recd. at....m.
Office of Origin and Service Instructions.	Sent		....Service.	Date........
	At....m.			From........
	To....			
	By....	(Signature of "Franking Officer.")		By........

TO {

Sender's Number.	Day of Month.	In reply to Number.	**A A A**

covering fire for which the
L.Gs may be advanced if
necessary AAA. Harassing fire
by Howitzer on Orchard about
K.26.b 4/4 is being arranged
from Bde HQs AAA.
Notify B.H.Q. when Patrol
returns.

K.26.b 7.8 / 9.7 } M.G5

10.30 p.m. Slow fire
until J.O.

From JEL.1

Place

Time

The above may be forwarded as now corrected. (Z)

Censor.   Signature of Addressor or person authorised to telegraph in his name.

Capt

Officer Commanding,
    27th Brigade R.F.A.

Office 119
       120
       121
       37

1.   A small raid is being carried out tonight in K.21.c ; no firing is to take place in K.20.d or K.2 K.21.c between 10.30 p.m. and 3.0 a.m. unless especially asked for.

       No notice need be taken of Green Lights.

2.   A telephone line has been laid to H.Q. Left Company, Right Battalion ; this is a continuation of the Artillery line to Battalion H.Q.

       Any batteries wanting to observe from the neighbourhood of the front line can tee into this line.

                                        A.H. SCOTT Lt.
9-6-18.   A/Adjutant Right Group.
                                    - 2 -

Officer Commanding,
    Battery R.F.A.

       For information and necessary action.

                                        Captain R.F.A.
9-6-1918.   Adjutant 27th Bde. R.F.A.

Officer Commanding
....120th....Battery RFA

27th Bde. No. BM/269.

Copy

    A fighting patrol of the D.C.L.I. will raid Post "A" at K.21.c 2/7 tonight 2nd/3rd insts.

    The 120th Bty. will keep 2 guns on each of the Orchards at K.26.b 8/6 and K.26.b 8/3 from 10.30 p.m. onwards.

    Ammunition - on K.26.b 8/6 all "A".

                on K.26.b 8/3   50% A.; 50% A.X.

Rate of fire :-

Battery Fire 30 secs. on each target.

                                        Captain R.F.A.

2nd June 1918.   Adjutant 27th. Bde. R.F.A.

5th Division

27th Bde. R.F.A.

July to December
1918

MESSAGE FORM. Series No. of Message _____

| In CALL | v | Recd. At___ By___ Sent At___ By___ | Army Form C 2128 (pads of 100) |

PREAMBLE

M.M. Offices { Delivery _____ v
{ Origin _____

PREFIX | Words

TO | 5th Div A

FROM & Place | 5 D A

| Originator's Number | Day of Month | In reply to Number |
| KA 346 | 5th | |

Herewith War Diary of 27 Brigade R.F.A.

[signature]
CRFA
for BGRA

TIME OF ORIGIN | TIME OF HANDING IN (For Signal use only)

Originator's Signature (Not Telegraphed)

DAG
GHQ
2nd Echelon

Forwarded for information
of my AD/4050 of 7/4/19

[signature]
Major
Acting Emb't
Commanding 5th New Cadres

8/4/19

SECRET

Register No.: 603
Part No.: 7
Volume No.: 4

WAR DIARY, (Original)

of

27th Brigade R.F.A.

for the month ending JULY 1918.

J Berkley
Lieut. Colonel Commanding
27th. Brigade R.F.A.

31/7/1918.

Army Form C. 2118.

WAR DIARY
or
INTELLIGENCE SUMMARY.
(Erase heading not required.)

July 1918. Map Sheet 36ᴬ 1/40.000

Instructions regarding War Diaries and Intelligence Summaries are contained in F. S. Regs., Part II. and the Staff Manual respectively. Title pages will be prepared in manuscript.

Place	Date	Hour	Summary of Events and Information	Remarks and references to Appendices
CROIX MARAISSE J.26.b.2/3	1st/2nd	8am to 8am	Same day; quiet. Brigade disposition at beginning of month as follows:— 37th Bty in Farm house (J.15.d.6/4) B.de H.Q in farmhouse J.26.b.7/3 119 " on Lys Canal at S.R.c 9/8, position in wood. 121 " " " J.4.a.4/4. Position in hedge by towpath 120 " " " J.35.d.4/0. Guns shooting through Gatewash of trees & hotsen with 15th Bde R.F.A., Brigade forms Right Group, covering right Brigade 5th Div. Infantry	
"	2/3	"	Quiet: nothing to report.	
"	3/4	"	15th Bde R.F.A. Head quarters are withdrawn to rest billets, and H.Q.rs. 27 Bde take over command of Right Group. & Left Batteries. Lieut. E.P.M. Jones. M.C. 37th Battery, posted to R.H.A. 1st Cavalry Division	
"	4/5.	"	Very noisy night. Considerable hostile fire, harassing back areas.	
"	5/6	"	Capt. I.A. McGowan, from 4/15 Battery, posted second in command of 119 Battery.	
"	6/7.	"	Quiet: nothing to report	
"	7/8.	"		
"	8/9.	"	Very quiet period. Little activity on the front of the enemy. From previous statements it is known that 16th German Division, opposite our front, was relieved on or being relieved than the line owing to the numerous cases of P.U.O. Formations in batteries has so many sick even during June. The next enemy division the 93rd, a second-rate division, apparently would be brought up. Casualties from our harassing fire, and has adopted an extremely quiet attitude	
"	9/10	"		
"	10/11	"		
"	11/12	"		
"	12/13	"		

SECRET.   5th Divisional Artillery No. HBM/ 29/11.

15th Brigade, R.F.A. Headquarters will withdraw to their wagon lines on the 3rd instant, leaving a guard in their present Headquarters.

Lieut-Colonel J.BERKLEY, D.S.O., 27th Brigade, R.F.A., will command the Right Group from his present Headquarters in J.26.B.2/4.

The change will take place at 8 a.m. on the 3rd instant.

                                                                  A.H.Hussey B.G.
                                                                    CRA
2nd JULY, 1918.   5th Divisional Artillery.

Copies to:-   RIGHT GROUP.   XI Corps. H.A.
               LEFT GROUP.   C.B.S.O.,XI Corps.
               27th Bde. R.F.A.   O.C.42nd Squadron,R.A.F.
               5th Div."G".   66th Divisional Art'y.
               XI Corps R.A.   31st ----------"----------

SECRET   5th Divisional Artillery No. HBM/29/10.

1. 27th Brigade R.F.A. will be withdrawn from present positions under orders from O.C., 27th Brigade R.F.A.
2. Grouping will be as follows :-
   Right Group ... ... 15th Brigade R.F.A.
   Left Group   ... ... 295 and 296 Bdes R.F.A.
3. The principle will be to bring artillery barrage fire only on to the most important points on the front in accordance with XI Corps Memo. S.S.6/8 - the gaps being covered by M.G. fire.
4. At 8 p.m. July 15th dividing line between Groups Zones will become a line K.20.b. 9/1 - K.21.c. 65/90 - LOXTON HOUSE - Saw Mill (K.29.a. 1/6)
5. RIGHT GROUP :-
   (a) 2 18-pdr batteries will cover from CANAL to K.26.c.80/55 as at present.
   (b) 1 18-pdr battery will cover
       (a) K.26.c. 95/75 to K.26.b. 3/1.
       (b) K.26.b. 5/4 to K.26.b. 8/8.
   (c) 4.5" Hows. will be used to thicken 18-pdr barrage.
   (d) Gaps covered by M.G. Fire will be :-
       (i) K.32.a. 0/7 to K.26.c. 3/1.
       (ii) K.26.c. 80/55 to K.26.c. 95/75.
       (iii) K.26.b. 3/1 to K.26.b. 5/4.
       (iv) K.26.b. 8/8 to K.21.c. 75/90.
6. LEFT GROUP :-
   (a) 3 18-pdr batteries and 1 howitzer battery -
       K.21.c. 7/9 to K.16.c. 3/2 - special attention to be paid to area round MERVILLE - LA MOTTE road.
   (b) 2 18-pdr batteries - K.16.d. 15/60 to K.17.a. 10/85
   (c) 1 18-pdr battery - K.11.d. 6/8 to K.12.a. 1/4.
   (d) 1 4.5" How. battery will thicken (b) and (c).
   (e) Gaps covered by M.G. fire will be :-
       (i) K.16.c. 3/2 to K.16.d. 15/60.
       (ii) K.17.a. 10/85 to K.11.d. 6/8.
7. 27th Brigade Liaison officer at Left Battalion, Right Brigade will be relieved by Right Group at 8 p.m. 15th instant.
8. MOVES. Night 16/17th.
   (i) 80th Battery will relieve 120th Battery (J.35.d. 4/0) - not more than one section to be out of action at one time
   (ii) Advanced Section D/15 Battery will relieve section 37th Battery J.30.a. 6/9.
   (iii) 27th Brigade as ordered by O.C. 27th Brigade R.F.A.

   No moves to take place before 9.30 p.m.

9. Lieut-Colonel HAWKES, D.S.O., R.F.A. will take over command of Right Group during afternoon 15th instant.
10. O.C. Right Group will arrange that 80th Battery takes over 120th Battery battle positions.
11. O.C. 15th Brigade will arrange to keep guards on 37th and 80th Battery positions.
    O.C. 27th Brigade will arrange to keep guards on 119th and 121st Battery positions.
12. ACKNOWLEDGE by wire.

                                              Major R.A.
15th July, 1918.   Brigade Major, 5th Divisional Artillery.

Copies to :- Right Group   15th Inf.Bde.
             Left Group   95th Inf.Bde
             15th Bde   5th Divn. 'G'
             5th M.G. Bn.   R.A. XI Corps   59th Div.Arty.

Army Form C. 2118.

WAR DIARY
or
INTELLIGENCE SUMMARY.

(Erase heading not required.)

JULY 1918.

Map Sheet 36 A 1/40,000.

Place	Date	Hour	Summary of Events and Information	Remarks and references to Appendices
CROIX MARAISSE	13/14	8am to 8am	Lieut W.M. CRAIG. 130 Battery, medically boarded in England, relinquish of the Brigade strength.	
"	14/15	"		
"	15/16	"		
"	16/17	"	Reorganisation of defences of front in process. 27th Brigade is withdrawn from defences of Gn. Divison front, and comes under 74th (Yeomanry) Divisional Artillery on the ST FLORIS Sector immediately south of the Lys Canal. 24th Brigade relieves 330th and 331st Brigades R.F.A., 66th Divisional Artillery, and with "A", "B" and "C" and "D" Batteries 119th Bde R.F.A. forms Left Group, 74th D.A. covering 231st Infantry Brigade. Brigade disposition:- H.Q. at P.1.b.35.20. Farmhouse, still in civilian occupation. 119 Battery.— J.33.d.9/2. Hedge position– orchard with bullets in front. Building. 121st Battery.— P.3.d.1/7.– Hedge position, ready ST FEMONT; no good cover at present, personnel, and the position has been badly given away from the air, by track in the cornfield. 130 Battery.— P.1.d.4/1.– Hedge position with good cover in orchard by STIENANT– GUARDECOUR Road. 37 Battery.— P.9.c.9/8.– Position in garden of the Asile d'ALIENEES	
P.1.C.3/2 HARTE VEND.	17/18	"	Nothing to report. No hostile activity.	

Signed [signatures]

Officer Commanding

........Battery RFA.   Left Group No. BM/518

Reference attached A.A./7/30.

The 119th and 121st Batteries are detailed for this barrage.

Zones allotted as follows :-

Zero to Zero plus 1

119th Bty. RFA.)   Superimposed on
)   K.31.b 95/60 to K.32.a 30/78.
121st Bty. RFA.)

Zero plus 1 to Zero plus 20

119th Bty. RFA :- K.32.a 7/2 to K.32.a 70/35.

121st Bty. RFA :- K.32.a 70/25 to K.32.a 70/55.

Captain R.F.A.

19th July 1918.   Adjutant Left Group.

SECRET.   RIGHT Group, 5th Div. Artillery No. A.A. 7/30.

O.C. 52nd Battery.
     80th   "
     A/15   "
     D/15   "
     Left Group, 74th Div. Artillery (3 Copies.)
Brigade Major, 5th Div. Artillery.
Brigade Major, 74th Div. Artillery.
Brigade Major, 13th Infantry Brigade.

1. 15th R/Warwicks Regt. will carry out a Raid tonight, July, 19th/20th at about K.32.a.0.7.

2. 18-Pdrs will barrage from K.31.b.95.60 along Trench to K.26.c.7.0, lifting after one Minute to Line from K.32.a.7.2 to K.26.c.7.0.
   The Barrage is allotted as under :-
   Zero to Zero plus 1.
        2 Batteries, 74th Div. Arty, K.31.b.95.60 – K.32.a.30.78.
        A/15 Battery,   K.32.a.30.78 – K.32.a.5.9.
        80th Battery,   K.32.a.5.9 – K.26.c.7.0.
        52nd Battery,   One Gun, K.32.a.5.9,–
                        One Gun, K.26.c.7.0.

   Zero plus 1 to Zero plus 20.
        2 Batteries, 74th Div. Arty, K.32.a.7.2 – K.32.a.70.55.
        A/15 Battery,   K.32.a.70.55 – K.32.a.7.8.
        80th Battery,   K.32.a.7.8 – K.26.c.7.0.
        52nd Battery,   ~~One~~ Both Guns, on TOLL CROSS Cross Roads.

3. D/15 Battery, will bombard the following points :-
        K.32.a.65.20.
        K.32.b.0.1.
        K.26.d.6.0.
        K.26.d.4.7.
        K.26.c.7.4.

4. RATES OF FIRE :-
   18-Pdrs. Zero to Zero plus 3,   INTENSE.
            Zero plus 3 to Zero plus 8,   RAPID.
            Zero plus 8 to Zero plus 15,   NORMAL.
            Zero plus 15 to Zero plus 20, SLOW.
            Zero plus 20,   STOP.

   4.5" Hows.
            Zero to Zero plus 10,   RAPID.
            Zero plus 10 to Zero plus 20, NORMAL.
            Zero plus 20,   STOP.

5. AMMUNITION.   50%, Shrapnel,   50%, H.E.
         106 Fuze will not be used during the first Minute.
6. Zero hour;   1-30 a.m.
7. Correct time will be sent round by Watch this evening.

                                       A.K.Scott,
                                       Capt. R.F.A.
19th July, 1918.   Adjutant, RIGHT Group.

Army Form C. 2118.

WAR DIARY
or
INTELLIGENCE SUMMARY.

(Erase heading not required)

July 1916   [No.] Sheet 36A.

Instructions regarding War Diaries and Intelligence Summaries are contained in F. S. Regs., Part II. and the Staff Manual respectively. Title pages will be prepared in manuscript.

Place	Date	Hour	Summary of Events and Information	Remarks and references to Appendices
HARFLEUR	18/9		110th & 1/120th Batteries cooperate in barrage for raid during night by 5th Division on left.	
	19/20 to 22/23	"	Quiet period. 23rd (Saxon) Division opposite the front is very inoperative.	
	25/26	"	5th Division Horse Show. The following events are won by the Brigade R.F.A. Turnout – 1st, 2nd, 3rd. 119th, 120th, 37th Batteries respectively.	
	26/27			
	27/28		XI Corps Horse Show. R.F.A. Turnout. 1st 119th Battery; 3rd 37th Battery. Driving Competition – 2nd 37th B.g. R.F.A. Individual Mount – 119 Battery. L.D. Horse Chipper – 121 " Officers Jumping – Major Auttenbach, 120 B.g. Wrestling on horseback – 121 R.g. V.C. Race – 121 R.g.	

Herbert
Col. ...

WAR DIARY
or
INTELLIGENCE SUMMARY

(Erase heading not required.)

Army Form C. 2118.

JULY 1915. Trab Sheet 36 M.1/40,000.

Instructions regarding War Diaries and Intelligence Summaries are contained in F.S. Regs., Part II. and the Staff Manual respectively. Title pages will be prepared in manuscript.

Place	Date	Hour	Summary of Events and Information	Remarks and references to Appendices
HARTE VENT	31/7	8a to 6a	119 + 120 Btys. assist 3rd Div troops on left in Rue d'Ouvrage. 119 Bty. position (main & section) heavily gun shelled before & during barrage - both section guns out of action by shell fire. 2nd Lieut H. CUBIE killed.	
			Casualties during July:-	
			Killed { 1 officer (119 Bty) 2 other ranks (120 Bty)	
			Wounded { 5 other ranks (121st Bty.)	

J. Rushton
Lieut. Colonel
Cmdg. 27 Brigade R.F.A.

9

Register No.
Part No 8
Volume No 5

5 Divn

War Diary
of
27th Bde RFA.
for the month August 1918.

N. H. Huttenbach
Major RFA
[signature]
Cmdg 27th Bde RFA

31/8/1.

27 Bde RFA 5

Army Form C. 2118.

WAR DIARY
or
INTELLIGENCE SUMMARY.

(Erase heading not required.)

August 1918
1/40,000 36

Instructions regarding War Diaries and Intelligence Summaries are contained in F. S. Regs., Part II. and the Staff Manual respectively. Title pages will be prepared in manuscript.

Place	Date	Hour	Summary of Events and Information	Remarks and references to Appendices
ST.VENANT	1/2	8.00am	Revd. J.D. Boyd posted to 119 Bty from 120 Bty UK.	
		8am	No 69441. Gr. J. W. Lucas (121) promoted Sgnr. and posted 1574 L. Bde Arty.	
"	2/5	"	Quiet	
"	5/6	"	Relieving Battery Commander of 306 Lt Bde come up to our position.	
"	6/7	"	Rumour of enemy retirement opposite our front; he does retire on the Right flank. Front but not on ours. 1st section of batteries relieved by 1st section of 306 Bde RFA	
"	7/8	"	The enemy still retiring. Most of HB and 2 section of pack batteries in completion of relief move to FONTES	

W. Odlum
Lt. Col.
27 A Bde RFA
Aug 27 A Bde RFA

WAR DIARY
or
INTELLIGENCE SUMMARY.

(Erase heading not required.)

Army Form C. 2118.

August 1918
1/40100 36th

Place	Date	Hour	Summary of Events and Information	Remarks and references to Appendices
FONTES	8/9	8am 10pm	Rest of HQ moved to FONTES. Billets in FONTES very good. General Ponsonby (only 5th Div.) visited the Brigade. Officers arrived to see the officers of the Brigade	
"	9/10	"		
"	10/11	"	The Brigade lined the roads at NORRENT-FONTES at 3.35 pm to cheer the King as he passed through.	
"	11/12	"		
"	12/13	"	Colonel Burkin goes on leave. Major R H Hullenbach commands the Brigade in his absence.	
"	13/14	"	Five N.C.O's from the Brigade sent to England for a Tour of Duty at home.	

Signed
Capt.
& H.C.
Cmg. ? & 36 Bde

Army Form C. 2118.

WAR DIARY
or
INTELLIGENCE SUMMARY.

August 1918

Place	Date	Hour	Summary of Events and Information	Remarks and references to Appendices
FONTES	14/15	8.0 pm / 10.0 pm	The Brigade starts entraining at ARQUES and WIZERNES. Bde H.Q. left FONTES at 8.15 PM (14th) arriving WIZERNES at 8.15 PM entrained with Guards WIZERNES at 11.15 PM arriving DOULENS at about No 2 section DAC. left WIZ 3.21 M left FONG 3.21 M arriving 11.15 PM arriving REGREUVIETTE. REGREUVIETTE DAC. when we detrained and marched to REGREUVIETTE. 7.0 PM (15th) when we detrained and all the small units are there. Very crowded as all the Bgde, D.A H.Q and other small units are there.	
REBREUVIETTE	15/16	" "	We are now 6th Corps, 3rd Army.	
	16/18	" "	—	
	19/19	" "	Brigade left REBREUVIETTE about 6.0 P.M. and marched to AMPLIER through DOULLENS getting into billets at 1.0 AM.	
	19/20	" "	Left AMPLIER at 10.0 PM and marched to AUTHIE WOODS arriving at 6.0 AM (20th) very tedious march as the roads were crowded with troops.	

[signature] Capt.
for H/CB
Brig 71 B ... BDE

WAR DIARY
or
INTELLIGENCE SUMMARY.

(Erase heading not required.)

Army Form C. 2118.

August 1918
1/20,000. 57 C

Instructions regarding War Diaries and Intelligence Summaries are contained in F.S. Regs., Part II. and the Staff Manual respectively. Title pages will be prepared in manuscript.

Place	Date	Hour	Summary of Events and Information	Remarks and references to Appendices
AUTHIES	20/21	3.0 AM to 8.0 AM	Left AUTHIES and went into action during night. a position of assembly E.23 b.57s (ERRART) during darkness	
LONGEAT WOOD	8/22	"	3.00 Hour 4.55 AM. HQ at FATE 4/7 N.W. of BUCQUOY. We are under the 63rd R.N. Divn. at 3.00 hour the Brigade moved up just West of BUCQUOY at 5.30 AM reconnaissance was made through the village and the roads cleared by a Brigade working party. at about 7.0 AM a section of 119 Lt and 121st MG moved to position North of LONGEAT WOOD and East of BUCQUOY respectively. Thick fog prevented observation. at about 10.0 AM the remainder of the 18th Battalion and a section of 37 Lt MG also advanced. By 11.0 AM the whole Brigade was in action in the valley running the WOOD. During the night the enemy reached the valley causing the following casualties. 7 officers wounded (3 at duty) 2 OR killed, 23 OR wounded.	

10 enemy Major E Moreton (at duty) (119)
Lieut O.V.e Meyer Thompson (119)
Lieut N.W. Gort (121)
Lieut E.R. Nunn (at duty) (120)
Lieut J.S. Williams (37)
Lieut R.G. Anderson (119)
Major J. D'Arcy (121)

Army Form C. 2118.

WAR DIARY
or
INTELLIGENCE SUMMARY.
(Erase heading not required.)

Place	Date	Hour	Summary of Events and Information	Remarks and references to Appendices
LONGEAU WOOD	22/25	1.0 AM / 1.0 AM	HQ - F 21 c 4/7 119 - F 29 b 8/4 120 - L 6 a 5/8 just behind ABLAINZEVILLE. 121 - F 30 e 6/3 37 - F 30 a 0/8	
	23/11		at 10.50 am 119 & 115 moved forward to A 25 c 35/35. Barrum many targets engaged by batteries during retiring.	
BUCQUOY	23/11		The attack was continued at 11.0 AM. at 6.30 PM we came into line with 115 & Division and batteries moved to positions between BUCQUOY and ADINFER LE MET, & HQ - H 6 a 9/1, 119 - G 20 a 4/4, 120 - G 14 d 6/4, 121 - G 20 a 5/0, 37 - G 20 a 3/2, 372 - new wire under orders of 37th Divn. [illegible] HQ of Divn. at [illegible] front 4 pm. 37 The Brigade was found fair during the greater [illegible] quiet day.	
BIHUCOURT	24/25			

[signature] Capt.
A. W. O. C.
Bmy 23 LTDn R.F.A.

Army Form C. 2118.

WAR DIARY
or
INTELLIGENCE SUMMARY.
(Erase heading not required.)

Place	Date	Hour	Summary of Events and Information	Remarks and references to Appendices
BIHUCOURT	25/26	1am to 10am	HQ - G.18.a.5/0. 119 - G.18.d.4/4 120 - B.24.a.2/8 121 - G.6.b.2/2 37 - G.18.a.5/0 Attack on SAPIGNIES. As soon as the village was captured the Brigade moved forward, [crossed out] to get into position [crossed out] To East of BIHUCOURT. [crossed out] During the afternoon the batteries got very heavily [crossed out] shelled. Major E. Martin (120), Lieut J.D. Boyd (119) Lieut J Reed (118) were killed during the day. Batteries also had very heavy casualties. In the evening the Brigade advanced to positions North of BAPAUME, under orders from 191st Bde RFA (37th DA). HQ - G.18.a.5/8 119 - H.20.a.19/8 120 - H.20.a.15/70 121 - H.20.a.65/60 37 - H.14.d.15/70.	
BIHUCOURT	26/27	"		

[signatures]
Omay 23rd October 1918

Army Form C. 2118.

WAR DIARY
or
INTELLIGENCE SUMMARY.
(Erase heading not required.)

Instructions regarding War Diaries and Intelligence Summaries are contained in F. S. Regs, Part II. and the Staff Manual respectively. Title pages will be prepared in manuscript.

Place	Date	Hour	Summary of Events and Information	Remarks and references to Appendices
BIEFVILLERS	27/28		Quiet day.	
"	28/29	9am & 10am	At 2 pm we came under shrap of 15th Bde RFA. Sent F.A.R Rayner (?) into BC's reconnoitre positions in front of SAPIGNIES. Bde HQ to other officers ready for the next advance.	
"	29/30	"	At 12 noon 119 and 121 mm found Bd positions in HQ and H.10. NNW of FAVREUIL, and at 2 pm 57th and 120th Btys also moved there HQ 90 to BEUGNY. Battns moved forwards SAPIGNIES.	
"	30/31	"	3.0 am our barrage covers BEUGNY. BEAUGNATRE continuing the barrage attack. 9.0 am our barrage to positions in H.11. N W of BEAUGNATRE. during the barrage the Battns moved to H.D.C.7/9. so soon as they got into action, at 12 noon HQ moved to new position. The Brigade were congratulated by its Bde Commander for the move.	

[signature]
Brig. Gen. C.R.A. RMD

Army Form C. 2118.

WAR DIARY
or
INTELLIGENCE SUMMARY.

(Erase heading not required.)

Instructions regarding War Diaries and Intelligence Summaries are contained in F. S. Regs., Part II. and the Staff Manual respectively. Title pages will be prepared in manuscript.

Place	Date	Hour	Summary of Events and Information	Remarks and references to Appendices
FREMICOURT	3/1	7.0 AM to 9.0 AM	Counter-attack on FREMICOURT at 5.10 am repulsed by new gun barrage. 119 & 120 Bdes. HQ got shelled. Capt. E.R. Bunn joined the Brigade D command unit. Gas shell and hot D leave and man into dug-outs in FAVREUIL. During the advance the Brigade had many casualties at last above 80 & 90 men. Only one gun was transited put out of action by shell fire, one belonging to the 37th Bde receiving a direct hit whilst on the march through BIHUCOURT.	

Casualties

Killed
Major E. Moulton (119) —
Lieut J.D. Boyd (118) —
2 Lieut G. Reid (114.B) —

119 A — 1. OR
120 H — 2. OR
121 H — 3. OR
122 M — 2. OR
37 M —

Wounded
Major E. Moulton (114)
Lieut J.P. Williams (37)
Lieut E.R. Nunn (120) (at duty)
Lieut O.V.P. Mynors-Thompson (119)
Lieut R.J. Andrews (119)
Major J.G. McCoy (121)
Lieut M.W. Guest (121)
Lieut B.W. Brereton (120)
Lieut R.L. Treton (121)
2 Lieut A.J.W. Parson (120)
Sgt R. Whoatle (119) (accident)
2 Lieut K.J. Stafford (37)

119 — 14. OR
120 — 22. OR
121 — 14. OR
37 — 6. OR

Signed
Lt Colonel
Cmdg 2) 12 Bde RFA

Army Form C. 2118.

WAR DIARY
or
INTELLIGENCE SUMMARY.   August 1918.
(Erase heading not required.)

Place	Date	Hour	Summary of Events and Information	Remarks and references to Appendices
			Officers Served during the Month	
			2/Lieut D.H. Workman (37)	
			2/Lieut. A.J.W. Fenwick (120)	
			Lieut. A.D. Wintle (119)	
			2/Lieut. J.H.D. Gell (119)	
			2/Lieut. F. Bailey (114)	
			2/Lieut S.N. Hickman (120)	
			2/Lieut. W.E. Crompton (114)	
			2/Lieut. C.H. Hedges (37)	
			Captain C.R. Bruun (119)	
			2/Lieut. T.H. Tillman (120)	
			Captain P.G. Bowes to Command 121st AT from 23/8/18	
			Lieut. J.A.P.C. Stewart on M in Command 121st AT from 23/8/18	
			No. 41074 Pte. J.W. Culpritt (114) granted Ribbon Bronze Medal for Military	
			Valour. 21/8/18	

SECRET.   5th Divn No. C.C./639/1.

ADMINISTRATIVE INSTRUCTIONS, ETC.

In continuation of 5th Division No. C.C./639 of today.

1.   The Division moves to Third Army. Detraining Stations –
FREVENT, BOUQUEMAISON and DOULLENS.

2.   Timings are given on table issued to –

     Camp Commandant................. Camp Commdt. will entrain
                                      all Div. H.Q. Train.

     Infantry Brigades............... to each Bde.
     C.R.A..........................
Entraining Stations................. Issued to 13th Inf. Bde. to
                                      be handed over.
Detraining Stations................. Issued to 13th Inf. Bde. to
                                      be handed over.

     Divisional Train...............

     The Infantry Entraining and Detraining Officers will be
responsible that they hand over the Time Tables to R.A. Officers
entraining and detraining the Artillery.

3.   Supply Railhead moves to FREVENT on 14th.

4.   Lieut. C.M. DOUGLAS, 2nd K.O.S.B. will remain at ST. OMER
until the whole Division is entrained and will forward all necessary
reports to Corps and Army "Q".
     He will keep in touch, by telephone, with the other
Entraining Stations.

5.   Billets. All Unit Commanders will be responsible that all
billets are left clean and in proper order and clearance
certificates obtained from Area Commandants.

                                              Lt.Colonel,
12th August, 1918.   A.A. & Q.M.G., 5th Division.

Distribution :– To all recipients of C.C./639.

SECRET. 5th Divn No. G.C./639.

ADMINISTRATIVE INSTRUCTIONS FOR ENTRAINMENT OF 5th DIVISION.

Reference Sheet 36.A. - 1/40,000.   12th August, 1918.

1. The Division will entrain in accordance with the attached Tables.

2. **Entraining Stations.**

   (A). ARQUES. Side and endloading ramps. Water trough in Station Yard, 5 horses at a time.
   Drinking water in Station.
   In case of necessity, the yard and small square in front of Station can be used for concentration purposes.

   (B). ST. OMER. Side loading ramps (2). Water trough in Station yard - good supply.
   Drinking water in yard.
   Concentration on ST. OMER Canal bank.

   (C). WIZERNES. Side and endloading ramps.
   Water from River South of concentration field.
   Drinking water in Station.
   Concentration Area - Field immediately South of Station.

   There are Latrines at each Station.

3. **Detraining Stations** and date and time of entrainment will be notified later.

4. **General Instructions.** Attention is directed to the General Instructions which accompanied this office No. G.G./639 dated 8th August, 1918.
   With reference to para. 6, the parties for duty at each Entraining Station will be detailed as follows :-

   ARQUES. By 1/6th A. & S. Highlrs. Headquarters.
   ST. OMER. By 1/6th A. & S. Highlrs. Headquarters.
   WIZERNES. By 15th Infantry Brigade.

   The Trench Mortar Batteries (Medium) will supply any parties required by the Divisional Artillery.
   In addition to the Officers detailed in para. 7, each Brigade will detail an Officer for duty at each Detraining Station. These will proceed by the trains taking the first units of the Brigade in each case.

5. **Police.** The A.P.M. will detail 1 N.C.O. and 6 men for Traffic Control at each of the Entraining Stations.
   Brigades will be responsible for Police and Traffic Control arrangements at Detraining Stations.

6. **Motor Transport.** The Motor Ambulances of the 3 Field Ambulances (less 6) will proceed by road as 1 convoy. Destination and time of departure will be notified later. Two Motor Ambulances, with necessary personnel will be on duty at each Entraining Station until the departure of the last train, when they also will proceed by road as one convoy.
   All other Motor Transport will proceed by road.

P.T.O.

- 2 -

7. **Lorries.** Lorries for the conveyance of baggage and stores to Entraining Stations will be detailed as follows :-

At 10. 0 a.m. 13th August.

    Headquarters, 13th Infantry Brigade, HEURINGHEM (for Bde. H.Q.
                                        and L.T.M. Battery).....2   1.

    Headquarters, 2nd K.O.S.B. (A.25.a.4.6.)................1
          "   1st R.W. Kents (A.......5.0.)................1
          "   14th R. Warwicks (TAMPAGNE)................1
          "   15th R. Warwicks (A.22.b.1.6.)............1

At 1.0 p.m. 13th August.

    Divisional Headquarters..6

At 2.0 p.m. 13th August.

    Headquarters, 95th Infantry Brigade, RACQUINGHEM (for
        Bde. H.Q., and L.T.M. Battery)........................2

    Headquarters, 1st Devons, RACQUINGHEM..................1
          "   1st E. Surreys, " 1
          "   1st D.C.L.I.   " 1
          "   12th Gloucesters " 1

At 8. 0 p.m. 13th August.

    Headquarters, 15th Infantry Brigade, SERCUS (for
        Bde. H.Q., and L.T.M. Battery)........................2

    Headquarters, 1st Norfolks (B.6.d.8.5.)................1
          "   1st Bedfords (B.18.b.9.0.)................1
          "   1st Cheshires (C.9.a.1.2.)................1
          "   16th R. Warwicks (B.12.c.6.2.)............1

    The lorries for 15th Infantry Brigade will load up and park with Units until time to proceed to Entraining Stations.

On 14th August. (Time lorries are required to report will be
                notified direct to O.C., 5th M.T. Coy. by O.R.A.).

    Headquarters, 5th Divl. Artillery, MORBECQ FONTES........1
          "   15th Brigade, R.F.A. WITTERNESSE..........2
          "   27th Brigade, R.F.A. FONTES..............2

    In all cases lorries will deliver their loads at Entraining Stations one hour before time fixed for the departure of the train.

8. Y.M.C.A. have been asked to arrange Coffee Bars at Entraining Stations.

9. **Supplies.** On entrainment, situation as regards supplies will be :-

    <u>On the man.</u>   Unexpired portion of days rations. Following
                   days rations. The Iron Ration.

    <u>On supply vehicles, of Divl. Train.</u> 1 days rations.

        To allow of this, a double re-fill has been made.

A C K N O W L E D G E.
                                                Lt.Colonel,
                                  A.A. & Q.M.G., 5th Division.

Copies to:- 13th. Inf.Bde. 95th Inf.Bde. 15th Inf.Bde. C.R.A.
        C.R.E. 1/8th A.S.S.Bn. 5th M.G. Bn. A.D.M.S. A.D.V.S.
        D.A.D.O.S. Camp Cmdt. F.Amb. (My. Men) D.A.D.T.S.
        5th Sig. Coy. 5th Divl. Train. Base Reception Camp.
        5th M.T. Coy. VI Corps H.Q.

Officer Commanding

Office 119
130
131
37

..............Battery R.A   27th Bde. No. BM/43

Reference attached Operation Order No. 193
herewith. Battery Commanders will reconnoitre these
positions at once and plant some distinguishing mark on
the platform of the gun emplacement, so that it can be
resected by the Topo. Section. B.C's on completion of
their reconnaissance will report to Lt.-Col. C.B.J HAWES,
at present Right Group H.Q.

BC's 360 Bde have been told to are up at once,
in case Left group batteries have to move forward.

[signature]
Captain R.F.A.

7th Aug., 1918.   Adjutant 27th Bde. R.F.A.

SECRET.

5TH DIVISIONAL ARTILLERY OPERATION ORDER NO. 193

B Y

Brig. General. A. H. HUSSEY. C.B., C.M.G.

---------------------------o---------------------------

7TH AUG. 1918.

1. Move of 5th Divisional Ammunition Column is cancelled.

2. The 15th and 27th Brigades R.F.A. will be required to take part in an Operation to be carried out by the 61st Division.

3. The Batteries will form one Group under Lieut. Colonel HAWKES. D.S.O. whose Head Quarters will be at J.27.c 6/7.
   Position of Batteries will be as under. :-

52nd Bty RFA.	old position at	J.28.a 4/4.
80th	"	J.22.c 4/3.
A/15	area around	J.22.d 4/1.
D/15		J.28.c 7/2.
119th	position in	J.28.b.
120th	"	J.22.b.
121st	old position at	P.4.a 9/1.
37th		J.24.a 7/6.

4. Batteries will reconnoitre these positions before moving to new area.

5. 350 rounds per gun will be dumped. 5th D.A.C. are remaining behind to carry this. Batteries will send 1 Officer and 3 O.R's to D.A.C. at BOESEGHEM on morning of 8th instant to superintend carrying and storing of ammunition for their own batteries. D.A.C. will arrange for rations, etc.

6. Batteries will probably move into position on 10th instant.

7. Communications. :-
   Group will furnish to 61st Divisional Artillery, an estimate of wire required to link up batteries.
   This wire will be supplied by 61st Division.
   Permanent establishment of wire must not be touched.

8. Location of wagon lines will be notified later.

9. ACKNOWLEDGE.

Major R.F.A.

a/Brigade Major Royal Art'y 5th Division.

DISTRIBUTION.:-
15th Brigade RFA.) Copies issued
27th   "   ) for Battery Commanders.
5th Div. Ammn Col.)
61st Div. Arty.
5th Div. 'G'.   59th Div. Arty.
No. 1 Coy, Train.   R.A. XI Corps.
S.C.R.A.   C.B.S.O. XI Corps.
S.O.R.A.   H.A. XI Corps.

Distribution.   8th Div. Arty.   1.
                     29th Inf. Bde.   2.
                     74th Div. Arty.   3.
                     ... Bde. RFA.
                     ...th Bde. RFA.

                     57th Bty. RFA.
                     121st "   "
                     ...   "   "
                     110th "   "

Office 119
         130
         131
         37

Extracts from 8th Division Order No. 249

1. The Divisional Artillery will be concentrated in billets/bivouacs with Divisional Artillery on night of [illegible]

2. BILLETS, CAMP AREAS, BIVOUACS. The greatest care will be taken to leave all billets, bivouacs etc. in clean [illegible]

3. TRENCH AND SIEGE STORES. All trench warfare stores will be handed over and receipts obtained. Particular care must be taken to ensure that [illegible]
Sanderson [illegible] clothing be [illegible] will be handed over under no circumstances [illegible]

Extracts from 8th Divisional Artillery Orders No. 191

4. The 51st Divisional Artillery will relieve the 8th Divisional Artillery in the line on the night 6th/7th August 1916. Aug. [illegible]

5. The 27th Brigade RFA will be relieved under the [illegible] of the C.R.A. 7th Division.

6. Officers and NCOs parties of the 51st Divisional Artillery are arriving at the batteries tomorrow and will be attached to them.

7. All Trench Stores, Maps, Photographs and Trench Diaries will be handed over in [illegible] both sides.

8. Command of the First Group will pass on completion of relief. Command of the Artillery covering the 51st Division front will pass to the C.R.A. 51st Division at 1600 hrs on the 8th inst.

10. Separate orders for Supplies will be issued.

11. Three Motor Ambulances, under an O.A.M.C. Officer, will join the 8th Divisional Artillery on the 7th inst, and will be attached to the Divisional Ammunition Column.

                                                    [signature]
                                                    Captain & [illegible]
8th Aug 1916.   Adjutant 8th Div. D.A.

Ref. 5 DA O O No 191

SECRET.

5th Division, No. C.C./637.

HEADQUARTERS,
5th DIVISIONAL
ARTILLERY

ADMINISTRATIVE INSTRUCTIONS TO ACCOMPANY 5TH DIVISION ORDER, NO. 243. REFERENCE SHEETS 36.a. (N.E.) and 36.a. (N.W.) 1/20,000.

1. The Division, on move, will be accommodated in WARDRECQUES Area with Divisional Artillery at first in NORRENT FONTES Area.

2. SUPPLIES. The 13th Infantry Brigade will draw from Railhead (AIRE) to-morrow by motor-transport.
Change of Railheads for Division will be notified later.

3. TRANSPORT. Ammunition echelons will move full. The grenade limber to be packed half with grenades and half with S.A.A.

4. TENTAGE. All units will, as far as time permits, strike all tentage not taken over by 61st Division and deliver it to Area Commandant, BOESEGHEM, or Town Major, TANNAY. Where this cannot be done units will leave a note with the Area Commandant, BOESEGHEM or Town Major, TANNAY saying where the tentage is and numbers.

5. BILLETS, CAMPS, HORSE-LINES, ETC. The greatest care will be taken to leave all billets, camps and horse-lines scrupulously clean.

6. Camp Commandant will arrange for D.A.D.O.S., "Whizzbangs" and Canteen to be accommodated at Divisional Headquarters on move.

7. BATHS. Baths, together with un-issued under-clothing, will be handed over and receipts taken.

8. HARVESTING. All agricultural implements issued to units for the harvesting of crops will be handed over to the relieving units of the 61st Division and a receipt obtained.
Divisional Agricultural Officer will inform the D.A.O., 61st Division the location of ricks and any crops cut in the Area and not carried, in order that the harvest may be completed by the in-coming Division. Also the general scheme for harvesting the area.

9. TRENCH AND AREA STORES. All trench and area stores will be handed over and receipts obtained. Particular care must be taken to ensure the 1,000 petrol-tins for each brigade in line are handed over.
The anti-gas clothing recently issued and also stocks of S.D. Clothing to replace "gassed" clothing will be treated as trench or area stores.

10. DUMPS. Ammunition dumps will be handed over by the unit in whose area the dump is situated. The dumps in the Corps Line will be handed over as follows :-

  At J.26.b.2/3, at present looked after by the Traffic Control at that place, by A.P.M. to A.P.M., 61st Division.

  Dumps near JACKSON Siding (J.13.b.9/2) and in the trench at J.1.d. and J.7.b., together with the ration dumps at VISNADELLO CAMP, will be handed over by the 1/6th Bn., A. & S. Highlanders to the Battalion of in-coming Division taking over VISNADELLO CAMP.

  Dump at Town Major's Camp, NIEPPE FOREST (J.15.c.3/5) will be handed over by Area Commandant to Area Commandant, 61st Division.

P.T.O.

(2)

11. RECEPTION CAMP.- Will close and be handed over at date to be notified later.

12. CANTEEN. Billets and sheds will be handed over direct between the Canteen Officers.
No Canteen Stores will be handed over.

13. SALVAGE. Salvage Officer will hand over all dumps to Salvage Officer, 61st Division.

14. LORRIES. Lorries will be detailed to assist Brigades and Units moving. Detail will be published separately.

15. RECONNAISSANCE LORRIES. One lorry for each R.F.A. Brigade, 13th and 95th Infantry Brigades will report at Headquarters, 5th Divl. Artillery and Rear Headquarters of Infantry Brigades at 10 a.m., to-morrow, to take Staff Captains and parties to the new area to arrange billeting.

16. ACKNOWLEDGE on slip.

Headquarters,
4th August, 1918.

O.W. White
Lieutenant-Colonel,
A. A. & Q. M. G., 5th Division.

Copies to :-

13th Infantry Brigade.	95th Infantry Brigade.
15th Infantry Brigade.	5th Divisional Artillery.
5th Divisional Engineers.	1/6th Bn., A. & S. Highlanders.
No. 5 Bn., M.G. Corps.	5th Div. Train. S. S. O.
A. D. M. S.	5th Sig. Co., R. E.
Camp Commandant.	D. A. D. O. S.
D. A. D. V. S.	Claims and Canteen Officer.
Div. Agric. Officer.	General Staff.
Area Commdt., BOESEGHEM.	Town Major, TANNAY.
Div. Area Commandant.	Town Major, NIEPPE FOREST.
No. 208 D. E. C.	A. P. M.
Baths Officer.	Salvage Officer.
Burial Officer.	61st Division "Q".
XI Corps "Q".	War Diary.

SECRET.

5TH DIVISIONAL ARTILLERY OPERATION ORDER 191

B Y

BRIG. GENERAL A. H. HUSSEY. C.B., C.M.G.

=========X-X-X-X-X-X-X-X-X-X-X-X=========

4TH AUG. 1918.

1. The 61st Divisional Artillery will relieve the 5th Divisional Artillery in the line on the nights 6th/7th Aug. and 7th/8th Aug. 1918, in accordance with the attached Table.

2. The 27th Brigade R.F.A. will be relieved under Orders of the C.R.A. 74th Division.

3. Relief of Trench Mortars will be arranged by respective D.T.M.O's.

4. Officers and Telephonists of the 61st Divisional Artillery are arriving at the Batteries tomorrow, and will be attached to them.

5. All Defence Schemes, Maps, Photographs and Trench Stores will be handed over to incoming Batteries.

6. Groups will arrange handing over of Liaison duties.

7. Command of the Right Group will pass on completion of relief. Command of the Artillery covering the 61st Division front will pass to the C.R.A. 61st Division at 10.0 a.m. on the 8th instant.

8. Two Lorries are reporting at 5th Divisional Artillery Head Quarters at 10 A.M. tomorrow to convey Billeting Parties to the new area.
   Brigades and D.A.C. Billeting Officers, and 1 Officer and 1 O.R. for each battery and D.A.C. Section will report to the Staff Captain, at 9.45 a.m., at 5th Divisional Artillery Headquarters.

9. The A.R.P. will be handed over on the 6th instant.

10. Separate Orders for Supplies will be issued.

11. Three Motor Ambulances, under an R.A.M.C. Officer, will join the 5th Divisional Artillery on the 7th instant, and will be attached to the Divisional Ammunition Column.

12. ACKNOWLEDGE. (Right Group, 27th Bde RFA, 5th D.A.C., 74 Div.A. and 61st D.A.)

Issued from
Headquarters.
R.A. 5th Divn.

9-15 P.M.

Major R.F.A.
d/Brigade Major Royal Art'y 5th Division.

DISTRIBUTION OF COPIES.
Right Group. (5).
27th Brigade RFA.
Left Group.
59th Div. Arty.
5th Div. 'G'.
XI Corps R.A.
74th Div. Arty.
61st ---"-----
31st ---"-----
5th Div. Ammn Col.
Staff Capt. R.A.
Signal Ofr 5th D.A.
D.T.M.O.

RELIEF TABLE

TO ACCOMPANY 5TH DIVISIONAL ARTILLERY OPERATION ORDER NO.191
DATED 4TH AUGUST, 1918.

DATE.	UNIT.	FROM.	TO.	REMARKS.
Night 6th/7th.	1 Section per battery, Right Group, 5th D.A.	Action.	Wagon lines.	All advanced sections to be relieved night 6th/7th.
7th.	5th Div.Arty. less 4 guns per battery.	Wagon lines.	New area.	Details will be issued later.
Night 7th/8th.	Remaining 2 sections per Bty Right Group, 5th D.A.	Action.	New area.	No moves before 8.30 p.m.

Office 119 120 121 37

Officer Commanding

..............Battery 27th D.A. No. [illegible]

Reference 27th Division Operation Order No. [illegible].

1. [illegible]

The [illegible] during the [illegible]

2. The [illegible] lines of [illegible] will be [illegible] the following [illegible].

[illegible]

Completion of each [illegible] will be reported to this Office by code word "WAP".

Captain R.F.A.

[illegible] Aug. 1915. Adjutant 27th. Div. R.F.A.

Office 119 120 121 37

Officer Commanding

..............Battery RFA 27th Div. No. 542.

Reference para. 4 of the Division C.O. 437 of yesterday, guards must be left in charge of all [illegible] till handed over to proper authority.

ACKNOWLEDGE.

Captain R.F.A.

6th Aug. 1915. Adjutant 27th. Div. R.F.A.

SECRET.   COPY NO 1

ARTILLERY ORDER No. 34.
by
BRIGADIER GENERAL L.J.HEXT,C.M.G.
COMMANDING ROYAL ARTILLERY 74th(YEOMANRY) DIVISION.

Ref: Map 36 A, 1/40,000.   5th August,1918.

1. The 306th Brigade,R.F.A. will relieve the 27th Brigade, R.F.A. on the nights 6/7th August and 7/8th August.
One Section from each Battery will be relieved on the first night. The remainder on the second.

2. There will be no movement East of a line GUARBECQUE - BUSNES before 9.pm.

3. All details of the relief will be arranged between Brigade Commanders concerned.

4. All documents, trench maps, photos etc., will be handed over by outgoing units and receipts obtained.

5. Rope ladders and climbing irons will be considered as trench stores and will be handed over by 27th Brigade,R.F.A. to 306th Brigade,R.F.A.

6. Route for 306th Brigade,R.F.A. will be via FONTES - squares O,19,& 20 - BERGUETTE.
Route for 27th Brigade,R.F.A. via MOLINGHEM and MAZINGHEM.

7. Command of Units will pass on completion of a Units relief.

8. Completion of relief will be wired to this office by the Code word ANT. BOOTS

ACKNOWLEDGE.

                                                    Major. R.A.
                                                Brigade Major. R.A.
Issued at 5.30.pm.   74th(Yeomanry) Division.

Copy No.1-5. O.C. 27th Bde.R.F.A.   No. 6. O.C. 44th Bde.R.F.A.
        7.   O.C. 117th Bde.R.F.A.   8 & 9. O.C. 74th D.A.C.
       10.   H.Q.74th Div."G"   11. H.Q. 74th Div. "Q"
       12.   A.P.M. 74th Divn.   13. R.A. XI Corps.
       14.   R.A. 5th Divn.   15. R.A. 61st Divn.
   16 & 17. War Diary.   18. File.

SECRET.

5TH DIVISIONAL ARTILLERY OPERATION ORDER NO. 192

BY

BRIG. GENERAL. A. H. HUSSEY. C.B., C.M.G.

o-o-o-o-o-o-o-X-X-X-X-X-o-o-o-o-o-o-o-o-oo-o-o-o

6TH AUG. 1918.

1. 5th Divisional Artillery, less Divisional Artillery Headquarters and 4 guns per battery, will move to new area on 7th instant, in accordance with attached March Table.

2. Batteries will leave not more than 4 teams and necessary transport on vacating Wagon Lines on 7th instant.

3. Headquarters 5th Divisional Artillery will move to NORRENT FONTES on 8th instant.

4. Trench Mortar Batteries will move to QUERNES Area, under Orders from D.T.M.O., on 7th instant. On arrival in new area, they will be attached to 5th Div. Ammn Column.

5. One Lorry will be at disposal of each Brigade Headquarters and will report at 8.0 a.m., 7th instant, at H.Q. Wagon Lines.

6. 15th and 27th Brigade Headquarters and 4 guns per battery will march independently to new area on relief.

7. Baggage wagons will march with units. Baggage wagon horses will report to units in evening of 6th instant.

8. All units (including 27th Brigade R.F.A.) will hand over tents on charge, to incoming units and get receipts.

9. ACKNOWLEDGE.

ISSUED FROM
Headquarters,
R.A. 5 Division.

9-55 A.M.

Major R.F.A.
a/Brigade Major Royal Artillery 5 Division.

DISTRIBUTION OF COPIES.
15th Brigade RFA. (5).
27th ----"-----
5th Div. Ammn Col.
D.T.M.O.
S.C.R.A.
No. 1 Coy, Train.
61st Div. Arty.
74th ----"-----
59th ----"-----
Left Group.
5th Division 'G'.
XI Corps R.A.

----------------X-X-X-X-X-X----------------

SECRET.

MARCH TABLE.

REFERENCE SHEET 1/40,000 36.A.

To accompany 5th Divisional Artillery Operation Order No. 192 dated 6 Aug. '18.

Unit.	Starting Point.	Time.	Route.	Remarks.
5th Divisional Ammunition Column.	Forked Roads at PECQUER. (I.20.c 3/1).	12 Noon	PONTE DE THIENNES – STARTING POINT – Railway Crossing H.29.d 9/9 – Cross roads H.35.a 9/8 – BOITOIS Farm N.4.c 9/6 – Billets at GUERNES.	
15th Brigade RFA less Headquarters & 4 guns per bty.	---ditto---	1.50 P.M.	STARTING POINT – Then as above – Billets at WITTERNESSE.	
No. 1 Coy 5th Div. Train.	---ditto---	2.30 P.M.	STARTING POINT – Then as above – Billets at LAMBRES.	Billets will be allotted by Area Commandant, LAMBRES.
27th Brigade R.F.A. less Headquarters and 4 guns per battery.	Under orders of Officer Commanding 27th Brigade R.F.A.		Billets at FONTES.	

DISTANCES: 100 yards between Batteries, D.A.C. Sections, etc.
500 yards between Brigades.

War Diary

27th Brigade R.F.A

Volume 5
Part 9

September 1918

2/10/18

J Berkley Lieut-Colonel
Cmdg 27th Bde RFA

WAR DIARY or INTELLIGENCE SUMMARY

Army Form C. 2118.

Place	Date	Hour	Summary of Events and Information	Remarks and references to Appendices
	23rd		10.14th Fire So rds hr Battery, 37ʳᵈ 200 [?] on the 24 hours. Hostile artillery inactive. No S.A.11 fire L Inaiz (120) awarded the M.M. At 8.0 now pointed Captain of 37ᵗʰ Battery. 20th CMD the Major Corr the Brigade hr 6ᵗʰ DAC and is posted to the 37ᵗʰ Battery. Major transport instructed me to proceed to Provoste. No 915958 Gnr R Maylor (Pr) awarded the MM.	
	24ᵗʰ		5hrs Batterie fire 50 rds Each harassing fire 4.55 60 rds 2.0. pm 120ᵗʰ Battery Capt. Fare Killed 1 Driver killed two wounded. 13 horses Killed and 3 wounded.	
	25ᵗʰ		Bosch quiet during the day and night. Resumed a usual harassing fire during the day and night. Quiet day.	
	26ᵗʰ		Battery [?] harassment for the Bange on the following days. Both St.Clair, Netter Tour across	

Army Form C. 2118.

WAR DIARY
or
INTELLIGENCE SUMMARY.
(Erase heading not required.)

Sept. 1918.

Instructions regarding War Diaries and Intelligence Summaries are contained in F.S. Regs., Part II. and the Staff Manual respectively. Title pages will be prepared in manuscript.

Place	Date	Hour	Summary of Events and Information	Remarks and references to Appendices
Inchuil	1st	4:55am	27th Brigade helped the New Zealanders in a barrage in which they took all objectives. The Batteries move to #13, 2010' N of B Framicourt. HQ to area 7/6 North East of Bouquemaise. 2nd Lt Tillman joined the Brigade and was posted to 120th Battery from I Bde.	
	2nd	5:15am	Bergues Wo attacked. Attack not very successful. Batteries remained in same position though the New Clare Lithem had got right back. The Brigade was ordered to act as advance Guard. The Batteries moved to 119X I33d 9/9, 120X—I13d 95/30, 12th—I13d 95/30, 37X—I13C 75/75.	
	3rd	7:15am	Brigade was ordered to advance to 119X I33a 6/3, 120X I36b 25/45, 12th—I36b 3/4, 37X—I23d 2/8. HQ to I38b 7/0. These positions were behind Bois Colonel Lebucquière.	
Velu	4th		2nd Lt Bratton 94th Battery wounded while reconnoitering and Lts Clive. 2nd Lt Lewis also 119th 94th Bttys Detailed at required at date. Relieved the 15th Inf Bde. Information we got nothing to advance Guard. In the afternoon we the Infantry BDe to 32nd Bde 27th Bde RFA.	

WAR DIARY
or
INTELLIGENCE SUMMARY
(Erase heading not required.)

Army Form C. 2118.

Place	Date	Hour	Summary of Events and Information	Remarks and references to Appendices
Harcourt Wood	5th		The Batteries to J.34. The Huns put up stubborn resistance in Harcourt Wood. The Batteries return for teas and Major Hallenbach return to 126 Battery. Col. Berkeley returns from leave and H.Q. moved to J.34.c.5.1. The Battries have a quiet day. No 67444 Gr. J. Richardson (121st) and No 69059 Gnr. M. Shield are awarded the M.M. 17/5/18	
	6th	11AM	Very heavy rain on the enemy. Other reported to be retiring No move. The Huns still retiring in the latter	
	7th		We expect to be withdrawn but orders were cancelled at 6.0 P.M	
	8th		A quiet day. No change	
	9th		We started to prepare for the Stunt on the 12th our Batteries had a very hard time fit up ammo to tracks one very much and teen compliments were to her gun	
	10th		In the Evening Batteries were forward to J.33.d. South of Havrincourt along the Canal. Capt Warburton returns to the 37th Battery. 2nd Lt Stafford and 2nd Lt Larsen Report	

WAR DIARY or INTELLIGENCE SUMMARY

Army Form C. 2118.

Place	Date	Hour	Summary of Events and Information	Remarks and references to Appendices
Armaries	11th		HQ move to Q.28c 1/1. having been moved out of Q.62nd Advanced Div HQ	
		6:15 PM	Batteries fired barrage to help 2nd Div. who attack on our right. 2nd Div. capture Eastside of Canal. Afforte Harrencourt.	
	12th		2nd Lt Bell joined the Brigade and was posted to 14th Battery. 2nd Lt Hobson also joined and was posted to 21st Battery.	
		5:25 AM	Two hour Brigade fired a barrage, Company of some smoke operations very successful and Harrencourt and Rocauelt were captured.	
	13th	10 PM	HQ and Batteries march to the Sart into the New Zealand Div's area. HQ at P29a 6/15, Batteries to Q 26c these positions are south of Harrencourt. Did not for want of M.T. order for two more M.T. received before 6 PM. Batteries in favour very little.	
	14th		A very quiet day.	
	15th		5th Div. Infantry take over from the New Zealanders from the 10 hr. Brigade comes under L.D.A. {2nd AFA Bdo. 2nd AFA Bdo. RFA}	27

Army Form C. 2118.

WAR DIARY
or
INTELLIGENCE SUMMARY.
(Erase heading not required.)

Instructions regarding War Diaries and Intelligence Summaries are contained in F. S. Regs., Part II. and the Staff Manual respectively. Title pages will be prepared in manuscript.

Place	Date	Hour	Summary of Events and Information	Remarks and references to Appendices
METZ	16th		Heavy bombing all round the area though at the Bosches right. A quiet day. No 200632 Gnr A H Bemis (120) No 172893 Gnr J Graham (37) } awarded the M.M. No 775262 Gnr J Ferrell (37) 2nd Lt J.E. Hutton is posted from 121st Batt to 37th Batt 2nd Lt M.A. Mason and 2nd Lt R.H. Mansfield join the Brigade and are posted to 121st Battery	
	17th		A very heavy thunderstorm during the previous night. A quiet day.	
	18th		121st Battery regn shoots. Shelled with H.V's. Cement coordinates to 14 horses. Batteries carry at harness fairs all day. Enemy Trench System.	
	19th		121st Battery regn shoot shelled Cement casualties 16 horses wounded Battery Fonkes Left Cardesse. 12 N.T.L. horses to Schelles	Lieut Colonel D.U. P.R.F.A 27th Bde R.F.A

WAR DIARY or INTELLIGENCE SUMMARY

Army Form C. 2118.

Place	Date	Hour	Summary of Events and Information	Remarks and references to Appendices
	20th		The following were awarded the Military Cross also the Military Medal. Lt J.S. Williams (37) Lt E.W. Gossett (120) Awarded the M.C. Lt H.V. Ford (121) No. 38051 Dr Sandercombe (119) Awarded the D.C.M. No. 63877 BSm J Barton (37) Batteries continued to harass hostile trenches by day. Batteries carried out harassing fire. 1st Arthurine area a quiet day. News came through that Lt Grainger had died of wounds. Capt Dunbarton handed over to Lt Oscarmorney for O.P. in N.S.E. corner of salt of Gonzeaucourt.	
	21st		A very quiet day	
	22nd		The Batteries carried out a 2 minute area shoots. 37th Battery fired 150 rounds of S.A.A. Very little shelling. Strong rain in the afternoon.	

M.M.Forsyth Major RFA
2 i/c 2nd Bde, RFA

Army Form C. 2118.

WAR DIARY
or
INTELLIGENCE SUMMARY.
(Erase heading not required.)

Instructions regarding War Diaries and Intelligence Summaries are contained in F. S. Regs., Part II. and the Staff Manual respectively. Title pages will be prepared in manuscript.

Place	Date	Hour	Summary of Events and Information	Remarks and references to Appendices
27 MDZ	27	7.52 am	Barrage opens for 13th Infantry Bde who are attacking. Advanced HQ are at 120th Battery position. Col Barkly of 13 Inf Bde at P21 Central. Our Infantry are held up and Batteries did not move forward. At 6.45 pm the SOS went up but the Bde did not attack on our front.	
	28	2.40 am	Barrage opens for 95th Inf Bde who both attack across 2.30 pm	
			HQ move forward to Dead Man's Cross. Surge event. The Brigade is not working with the 15th Infantry Bde. During the afternoon the Batteries move up to Q 22 d. where they opened harassing fire on Jood Inn Ridge.	
		10 pm	The Battery Commanders received orders to reconnoitre forward positions on 29b and to get their Batteries into action by 4.30 am and to be ready to fire a barrage at 5.30 am. The one Battery ... action ...	
	29		...	

WAR DIARY or INTELLIGENCE SUMMARY

Army Form C. 2118.

Place	Date	Hour	Summary of Events and Information	Remarks and references to Appendices
		5.50 1.30	Carried out on Prut destroyed. The Bde went with 40th the Mor. The Beorge fired for 15th Inf Bde the 1st all thrown after the Bange the Batteries came under heavy machine gun fire and were unable to hoe about the day. 2nd Lt Duke (RA) Wounded Wilson 37th Wounded.	
	30th	9.20 am	Bange fired with them a lower Mean a Rept, move up to Bd'd entrance. Infantry Bde Rifle Hd Quaoooq now they are about Muddy the Batteries moved forward to Red and 21c not taking positions and Rd R 25b Songolean and Hd Qrs (39th Divn) where 1st Bde The Column form the 11th Inf Bde and Artillery is not taken over by 223m Bde Rft. Major Evans and Major Satterleewent. From Russe to Paso.	
		6 PM	2nd Lt Moran (RA) to Gambuscatta. Pack Battery.	

5th Division.

War Diary.

27th Bde. R.F.A.

October 1918.

Her Maj. Atty.
2) Brigade

October 1918.

Army Form C. 2118.

WAR DIARY
or
INTELLIGENCE SUMMARY.
(Erase heading not required.)

October 1918.

Instructions regarding War Diaries and Intelligence Summaries are contained in F.S. Regs., Part II. and the Staff Manual respectively. Title pages will be prepared in manuscript.

Place	Date	Hour	Summary of Events and Information	Remarks and references to Appendices
Joncourt	1st		A Quiet day. Major Bowman awarded the M.C. No 141163 Gnr (Now) R.F. Trussler (121st) awarded the M.M. No 147400 Sgt K. McLean (37th) No 71599 Bgr T. Slater (37th)	
	2nd		119th Battery moved forward to R22d	
Le Vacquerie	3rd	5 p.m.	The Batteries moved forward to 120th R.17.c. 121st R.15.b. 37th R.17.c. HQ to 37th old position at R20.d.	
	4th		2nd/Lt Sims joined the Brigade and was posted to 121st Battery RFA. A quiet day.	
	5th		The Huns evidently and our Infantry crossed the Canal. The Battery could not cross till the Bridges were completed. Pushed two at 6 p.m. The Brigade moved after the 223 Bde R.F.A. Pushed one at about midnight. The Batteries had a very trayful crossing, although the Bont had previously done much shelling round the Bridges. The Batteries took up positions— 119th— M.29.c.4.2., 120th— M.35.b. 121st— M22.a. 37th— M22.e. HQ Pont F. M24.c. 2nd/Lt Archibald (120th) awarded the M.C.	

(A7291) Wt. W3891/M1273. 75,000. 1/17. D.D. & L. Ltd. Forms/C.2118/11.

WAR DIARY
INTELLIGENCE SUMMARY

Army Form C. 2118.

Place	Date	Hour	Summary of Events and Information	Remarks and references to Appendices
Rupelle	5th		HQ moved this afternoon to M.27.c.6/3. The Batteries had to leave they being out of Range. Otherwise it was a quiet day.	
	6th		No more firing. Quite a quiet day. Batteries fired on barrage on the early morning and about Midday advanced as to the Masnières Beaurevoir line. 3000 yds S.E. of JESDAIN. HQ moved to near Bel Aise farm. C.RHO to M7c1 5/5. Capt Mawson (mo) returned from leave. Major MP. Burns (37) branched.	
	9th	5.50am	D) C.F. Holmes (119) advanced to MM during the night and early morning Batteries are ordered to move only a few hundred yds in order to gain range. Orders for the Range came in very late and the Batteries had to kick in the Range. During the morning they moved to M.4 a.9 and fire till about 7.30 p.m. and to a farm M.07a the Devil about 12a P.M.	

Army Form W. 3121.

Schedule No. (To be left blank)	Unit	Regtl. No.	Rank and Name	Action for which commended	Recommended by	Honour or Reward	(To be left blank)
	at 7 P.m.			Battery went into action just behind LIGNY into a house in LIGNY		HQ moved	
10th				Battery fires a barrage about 6 a.m. In the moment Col Beatley went forward and established his HQ at Chateau CLARMONT and Batteries moved up to J.15. 4 P.m. two orgs became and Batteries only fired on things they could see. This position overlooked first BETHENCOURT			
11th				Oho moz. Batteries camped at Mony Kaassin 1.10.c.8. Splus somg Ays hour. hours 30 hm hour. This was a fine scene over to the other of Artillery approx at and away to the order on the absolute and to the house of origional.			
12th				The Battery Commander recoiled position on G.M South B View but only the hot broke up there. at 4 P.m. the HQ moved to the Boon oran released to have attacked but it came to nothing			
13th				The 375 Battery moved up to G.M lentig freely by the enemy at 4 P.m. the HQ moved			

John Giffin
2 cols Art

Army Form C. 2118.

WAR DIARY
or
INTELLIGENCE SUMMARY.
(Erase heading not required.)

Instructions regarding War Diaries and Intelligence Summaries are contained in F. S. Regs., Part II. and the Staff Manual respectively. Title pages will be prepared in manuscript.

Place	Date	Hour	Summary of Events and Information	Remarks and references to Appendices
Chateau	14th		A quiet day. Captain Whistler (120th) wanted Major to command the 37th. It shows 119th wanted second in command of the 120th	
"	15th		A normal day	
"	16th		During the night the 37th were heavily shelled	
"	17th		6th Sess. Nothing special took place. Major Logan (119th) went on leave	
"	18th	4.45 a.m.	the Batteries fired a barrage which r/g Lieut Wolfmarker into Matterwith. Major Rutherford (120th) accorded the DSO	
			the Batteries fired a shot barrage in the enemy moving up to the enemy line 11.10 and 12.15 start at 11.10 to wait of our [...] 5 minutes later of midnight	
			One hour 5 minutes barrage on our target 5 minutes after midnight	
	19th		37th Battery came up in one section. Otherwise a quiet day	
			2nd Lt Rockland (120th) went on leave	
	20th	2 am	The Brigade on the fork to more forward Wilkhoek are established at about 7.30 am	

(A7092) Wt. W13898N1293. 750,000. 1/17. D.D. & L., Ltd. Forms/C011/14

Army Form C. 2118.

WAR DIARY
or
INTELLIGENCE SUMMARY.
(Erase heading not required.)

Place	Date	Hour	Summary of Events and Information	Remarks and references to Appendices
			The Batteries continued to shell MONT QUENTIN & ESSE. The 121st Battery was the first to move when they had moved two guns which it was thought undesirable to move and the remainder stood fast. At 4 p.m. a barrage was fired and the Infantry took the streets E of they day. Callow Lawn (120 d) advanced the M.C.	
	2 pm		During the 24 hours advanced Brigade H.Q. was at J 11. During the support Batteries moved up to ESSE and the H.Q. BALASTRE. During these movements the Brigade was working in close support to the 95th Infantry Brigade.	
	22.0		The divisional liaison with Infantry was handed over to the 15th Bde who both with 15th Infantry Bde at ODEREN reopened and was hosted to 119th Battery. The 27th Bde was again ordered to move	
	23.0		and moved at 2 am	

J.M. [signature] 28/9/18

WAR DIARY
or
INTELLIGENCE SUMMARY

Army Form C. 2118.

Instructions regarding War Diaries and Intelligence Summaries are contained in F.S. Regs., Part II. and the Staff Manual respectively. Title pages will be prepared in manuscript.

Place	Date	Hour	Summary of Events and Information	Remarks and references to Appendices
			4pm. The Brigade started to advance at some 600 yds it reached E20 returns had not got in. Those positions were on the Infantry had not got in. Those positions were only 600 behind the Infantry - a retirn of the road being practically in the front line. From here they fired a barrage and practised the Infantry to take the 2nd position. The Brigade then advanced 600 yds and came into action at E21 there they carried out harassing fire they thenreturned about 600 yds and came into action at E17a just behind Benvann Yrss the advanced into position in E12a just in front of Benvann 3½ the am forward 600 yds at the standard rate	

Army Form C. 2118.

WAR DIARY
or
INTELLIGENCE SUMMARY.
(Erase heading not required.)

Place	Date	Hour	Summary of Events and Information	Remarks and references to Appendices
	24th		The Bde Stays Informance may be carried as one of the utmost solemnity and intt in the history of the Brigade. At the enemy HQ moved nt to BEAURAIN. Two Coys 2nd [ ] at about 6:30 am the Brigade advanced into positions on W29b and a few behind these positions. 12th [Inf?] 42 hours took cat by aerothal. In the grout Battens took up to D19 tanks and HQ to M9d 1.3 to NEUVILLE.	
	25th	11:30 am	Prime Comd Trough that the Brigade was moving back to at about 4pm Batteries started from back to [ ] Beaurain [ ] the 12th the [ ] the Brigade had been artyielding the up 21st Batteries kept a good day cleaning up [ ]	
BEAURAIN.	26th		CM Odlum went on leave and 2nd It Chumley 121st [ ] acting adjutant	

Army Form C. 2118.

WAR DIARY
or
INTELLIGENCE SUMMARY.

(Erase heading not required.)

Instructions regarding War Diaries and Intelligence
Summaries are contained in F. S. Regs., Part II.
and the Staff Manual respectively. Title pages
will be prepared in manuscript.

Place	Date	Hour	Summary of Events and Information	Remarks and references to Appendices
BEAURAINS	27/6		The Brigade had a quiet day, having the men billets used for Church or Beaurains	
	28th		The Bosch Shells came and fell two paces at Beaurains	
	29th		Nothing unusual happened. The Brigade fell in at a point to put on the afternoon at Pick Were some refreshments from all the units turned about Colonel Date D.S.O. Came to Command the Brigade	
	30th		Captain Dixon (120th) Dxxx in charge	
	31st.		Nothing of special importance occurred.	

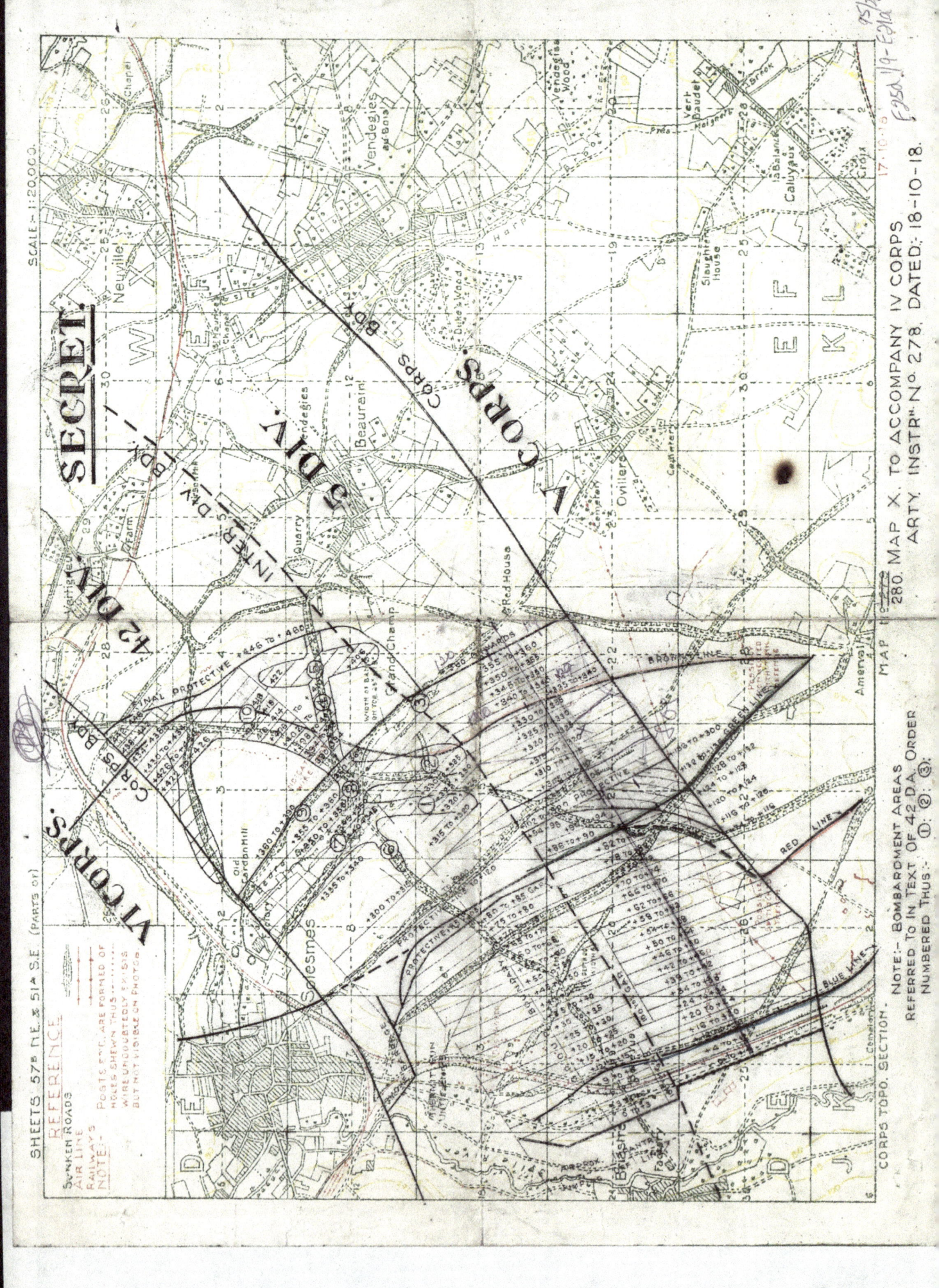

Officer Commanding

    _____ Battery RFA.

    Lieut. Colonel BERKLEY, on leaving the Brigade, has asked that the following farewell message may be read out to all the men of the Brigade.

> "Officers, N.C.O's. and Men of the 27th. Brigade - I am now nearly 56 years old and the time has come when it is for the good of all that I should give place to a younger and more active man. It was my ambition to go through with you to the end -
>
> I want to thank you all, Officers, N.C.O's. Gunners and Drivers, and the Signal Sub-Section, for your loyal support of the honour and good name of the Brigade.
>
> I am very very proud to have had the honour of commanding for nearly three years, four Batteries, whose gallantry and cheerful endurance of hardships has been splendid, and whose turnout at this year's Horse Show testified to their sense of Soldierly smartness.
>
> I wish you all good luck - May God grant all of you a happy return home.

                            J. BERKLEY, Lieut. Colonel.

                                    Captain R.F.A.

19-10-18.   Adjutant 27th. Bde. R.F.A.

SECRET & URGENT.

OPERATION ORDER NO. 217.
by
BRIG. GENERAL A. H. HUSSEY. C.B. C.M.G.
Commanding 5th Divisional Artillery.

22ND OCT '18.

1. The advance is being resumed on October 23rd.

2. ZERO HOUR will be 02.00 hours Oct. 23rd.

3. IV Corps Objectives and Divisional Boundaries are shewn on the attached barrage map.

4. The 5th Division are capturing the RED and the BLUE Objectives with the 15th Infantry Brigade — 1st BEDFORDS on right, 1st CHESHIRES on left, 1st NORFOLKS in support.
   The 37th Division pass the 111th Infantry Brigade through the 15th Infantry Brigade on the BLUE LINE to capture the GREEN and BROWN Objectives.
   The G.O.C. 37th Division takes over Command of the Divisional Sector on the BLUE LINE and the C.R.A. 37th Division takes over Command of the covering Field Artillery at the same time.
   The 17th Division are attacking on our right and the 42nd Division on our left. The NEW ZEALAND Division passes through the 42nd Division on the BLUE LINE.

5. The attack by the 5th Division starts at ZERO plus 20 minutes, and **not** at ZERO.

6. Position of H.Q., etc., will be
   5th Division H.Q. ... ... CAUDRY.
   5th Div. Adv. Report Centre... BRIASTRE.
   5th Div. Art'y H.Q. ... CAUDRY.
   _____"_____ Forward Exchange E.21.b 5/1.
   _____"_____ A.R.P. ...
   37th Division H.Q. ... CAUDRY.
   37th Div Adv H.Q. ... ... BRIASTRE D.24.c 8/6.
   37th Div. Art'y H.Q. ... CAUDRY, moving to BRIASTRE.

   15th Inf. Brigade H.Q. ... BRIASTRE D.30.b 2/3.
   _____"_____ Adv Report Centre E.21.b 6/2.
   1st BEDFORDS H.Q.)
   1st CHESHIRE H.Q.) ... E.21.b central.

   5th D.A. Cable Dump D.30.b 1/6, where cable can be obtained on application to Signal Officer 5th Divnl Art'y.

7. WHITE Very Lights will be fired on the capture of each Objective.

8. Contact Aeroplanes will call for Flares at

   07.00 hours,
   09.45 ---"---,
   11.00 ---"---, and 14.30 hours.

Page 2.

9. There will be a pause of 2 hours on the GREEN LINE, after which 111th Infantry Brigade are exploiting the success up to the BROWN LINE.

10. Watches will be synchronised at 22.00 hours. Oct. 22nd.

11. ACKNOWLEDGE. (Brigades R.F.A.)
                      only

Major R.A.

Brigade Major Royal Artillery 5th Division.

DISTRIBUTION OF COPIES.

    15th Brigade R.F.A.   5.
    27th   "   5.
    123rd   "   5.
    124th   "   5.
    317th   "   6.
    5th Division 'G'.   1.
    IV Corps R.A.   1.
    15th Inf. Brigade.   4.
    56th Heavy Arty Group.   4.
    37th Division 'G'   1.
    37th Divisional Art'y.   1.
    -------x-x-x-x-x-x-x-x-x-------

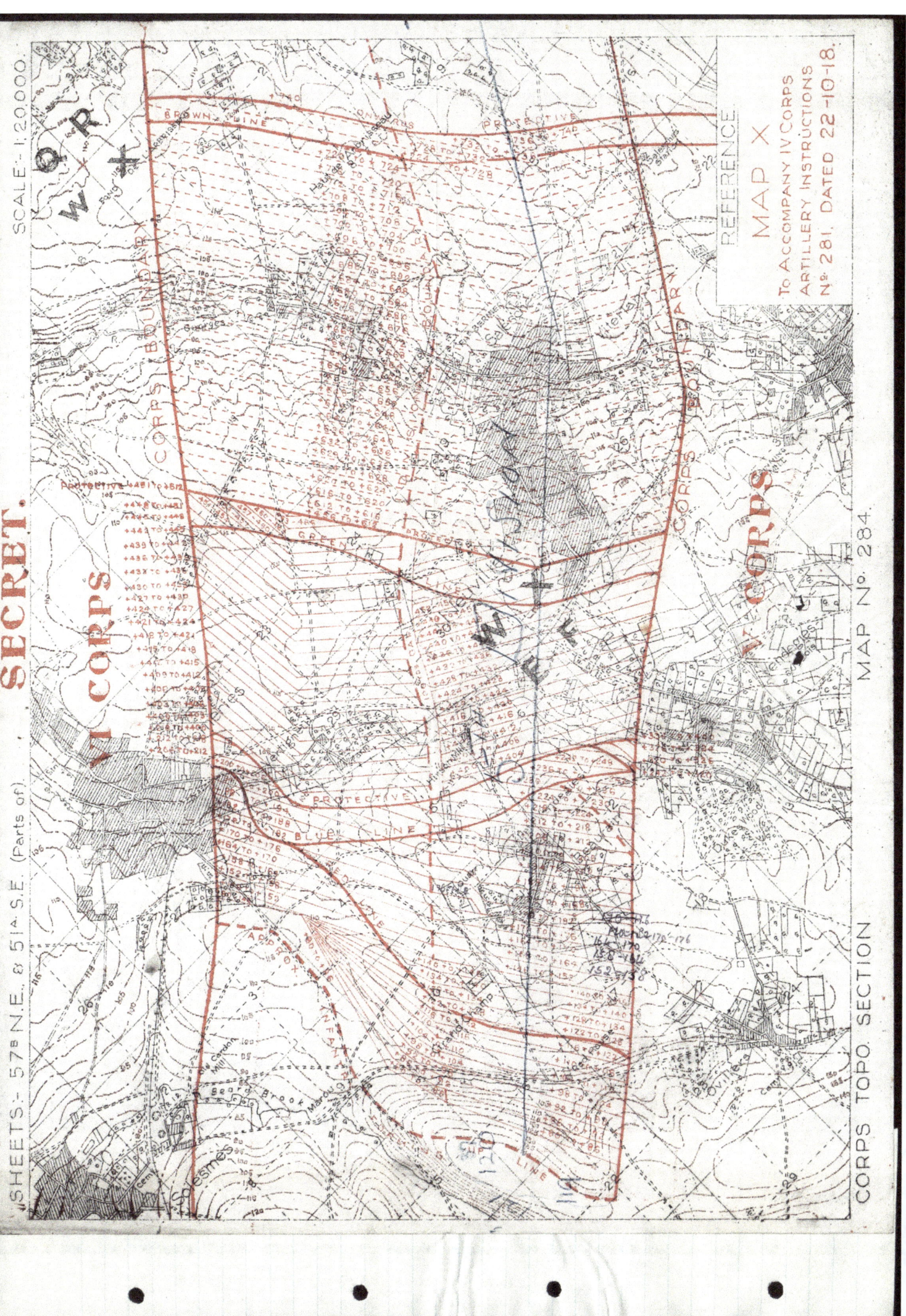

SECRET.

5TH DIVISIONAL ARTILLERY INSTRUCTIONS.

22ND OCT. 1918.

Reference Operation Order No. 217 dated 22/10/18.

1. **GROUPING.** The Field Artillery covering 5th (& 37th) Div. will be grouped as follows :-

HARVEY'S GROUP.	) 15th Brigade R.F.A.
(Lt. Col. HARVEY D.S.O.)	) 27th " "
CROFTON'S GROUP.	) 123rd Brigade R.F.A.
(Lt. Col. CROFTON. D.S.O.)	) 124th " "
	) 317th " "

Each Group will cover the whole Divisional front.
~~The attention of Officer Commanding CROFTON'S GROUP is drawn to para. 7 sub-para. (c).~~
This Grouping will come into force at mid-night 22/23 Oct.

2. **LIAISON.** HARVEY'S GROUP will be responsible for Liaison with the 15th Infantry Brigade.
CROFTON'S GROUP will be responsible for Liaison with the 111th Infantry Brigade of the 37th Division.

3. **MOVES OF BRIGADES.**
(a) At ZERO plus 80, 123rd Brigade R.F.A. will be limbered up near BELLE VUE E.19.central ready to move and will move to positions in E.10.c. to support the advance from the BLUE LINE.
During the pause on the BLUE LINE -
317th Brigade R.F.A. will move to positions in E.16.b.
27th   "   "   "   "   "   " E.17.a.
These three Brigades will open fire on the BLUE LINE Protective Barrage from their new positions at ZERO plus 395.

(b) During the pause on the GREEN LINE
15th Brigade RFA will move to positions about E.12.central.
124th   "   "   "   "   " the QUARRY in E.11.a
These two Brigades to be in action ready to fire by ZERO plus 600 mins.

4. **RATES OF FIRE, ETC.** The barrage will be put down as shown on the attached map.
The barrage will commence at ZERO plus 80 mins.

18-Pounders. Z. plus 80 to Z. plus 90.   ... INTENSE.
Z. plus 90 " Z. plus 254.   ... NORMAL.
Z. plus 254 " Z. plus 400.   ... SLOW.
Z. plus 400 " Z. plus 460.   ... NORMAL.

4.5" Hows. As for 18-Pdrs., except rate from Z. plus 80 to Z. plus 81 will be GUN FIRE.

5. AMMUNITION. ....

PARA. E.

5. AMMUNITION. 18-pdrs.) H.E. 106 Fuze as far as possible, except
Z. plus 80 to Z. plus 385.) on the village-areas shewn shaded on the
Z. " " 400 " Z. " " 400.) barrage map on which shrap. only will be
fired. During daylight 1 rd. in $_6$ will be
Z. plus 385 to Z. plus 400. ... SMOKE. smoke.
4.5" Hows. H.E. 106 fuze throughout.

6. TASKS FOR 4.5" HOWS. All 4.5" Hows. will open on the Sunken Rd.
running through E.16.a., b. & d. at Z. plus 80 lifting off as the 18-
pdr. barrage gets within 200 yards of them, after which they will lift
200 yards ahead of the 18-pdr barrage paying particular attention to
all Sunken Roads and avoiding the areas shewn shaded on the barrage
map on which shrapnel only is to be fired.

7. 6" TRENCH MORTARS. The targets for the two mobile T.M's will be -
    Road Junction E.16.d.3/8   - 1 T.M.
    RED HOUSE E.16.d.6/6.   - 1 T.M.
Lifting when the 18-pdr barrage gets within 300 yards and keeping that
distance ahead of it up to limit of range, then Stop.

8. SPECIAL TASKS.
(a) 317th Brigade R.F.A. will detail one section of 18-pdrs, to
enfilade the Sunken Road in E.16.a, b, & d, from a position near the
FACTORY in E.2.c.
    This section to open on this road and lift 100 yards ahead of the
rest of the 18-pdr barrage when the latter reaches this road.
    This section will rejoin its Brigade as the latter changes position.
(b) 15th Brigade, R.F.A. will site one How. to enfilade exactly the
Sunken Road E.16.b. - E.10.d, and later the Sunken Road E.11.b.6/7 -
E.6.c.0/7, keeping 200 yards in advance of the 18-pdr barrage.
    This how. will rejoin its Brigade as the latter moves forward.
(c) 124th Brigade, R.F.A. will put a smoke screen on the high ground
on W.30.c. and d. and X.25.c. from Z. plus 330 till Z. plus 400.

9. All Brigades moving forward will take full echelons and also
their D.A.C.Sections. Ammunition will be dumped at new positions
and echelons refilled at old positions.
    When vacated positions have been cleared of ammunition refilling
will be carried out at the A.R.P. in ~~E.8.a.~~ D300

10. 12 rds. per gun smoke will always be carried, -
    6 rds per gun in battery echelons.
    6 ------"--------- D.A.C.
In addition 12 rds. per gun smoke will be held at the A.R.P.

11. In all cases of moves Wireless Masts must move with a specially
detailed battery.
12. Each Bde. will superimpose 1 battery to answer aeroplane calls.
13. ACKNOWLEDGE.

                                             Major R.A.
22-10-1918.   Brigade Major, 5th Divisional Artillery.

ADDENDUM NO. 1 TO 5TH DIVISIONAL ARTILLERY OPERATION ORDER NO. 217
DATED 22/10/18.

1. Reference ARTILLERY INSTRUCTIONS issued with 5th Divisional Artillery Operation Order No. 217.

   Para. 2. : Grouping will come into force at 6.0 p.m., 22nd October.

   Para. 3(a). : 27th, 123rd and 317th Brigades R.F.A. will open fire from their new positions at Z. plus 385 on the BLUE LINE Protective Barrage.

   Para. 5. : Each battery on reaching the BLUE LINE Protective Barrage will fire one round per gun Smoke.

2. Reference Operation Order No. 217.

   4 Tanks have been detailed to assist 15th Infantry Brigade in BEAURAIN.

                                          Wallace
                                          Major R.F.
               Brigade Major Royal Artillery 5th Division.

COPIES TO :- Recipients of O.O. 217.

SECRET.   Copy No. 13

Ref Map.   37th Divisional Artillery
Sheets.   Operation Order No 191.
57 b N.E. A.
51 a S.E. 1/20,000.

1.   These orders are to be read in conjunction with and in
continuation of 5th Divisional Artillery Order No 217.

2.   37th Division in the Right Sector & New Zealand Divn
in the Left Sector are to pass through the 5th and 42nd Divisions
respectively on the BLUE Line and capture the GREEN LINE &
subsequently the DOTTED GREEN & BROWN LINES.

3.   The 21st Division will be attacking on the right of the
37th Division.
    (N.B. The colouring of their objectives does not correspond
        throughout with the colouring of the objectives on 37th Div
        front.)

4.(a)   The attack on the GREEN, DOTTED GREEN and BROWN LINES will
be carried out by 111th Inf Brigade with one Battn 112th Inf Bde
(1st ESSEX) attached.

  (b)   112th Inf Bde (less one Battn) will be in support.

  (c)   63rd Inf Bde will be in reserve.

5.   The attack from the BLUE to the GREEN LINE will be carried
out under an artillery barrage creeping forward at the rate of
100 yards in 4 minutes.

6.   After the capture of the GREEN Line the success will be
exploited by 111th Inf Bde to the DOTTED GREEN & BROWN LINES for
which operation the 123rd Brigade R.F.A. will come under the
orders of G.O.C., 111th Inf Bde.

7.   There will be a pause of approximately 2 hours on the
GREEN LINE.
        There will be a pause of one hour on the DOTTED GREEN Line
on the front of the N.Z. Division.
        If strong enemy resistance is encountered and the DOTTED
GREEN & BROWN LINES are consequently attacked under a barrage,
there will be a similar pause on the front of the 37th Division.
If only slight opposition is encountered in NEUVILLE and SALECHES
there will be no pause on the DOTTED GREEN Line on 37th Div front.

8.   The forward moves of the artillery will be so regulated
that all batteries can take part in the barrage from the BLUE to
the GREEN Lines.

9.   The D.T.M.O.,37th Divl Artillery will arrange for the
Mobile 6" T.Ms and their ammunition wagons to move forward with
the 123rd Bde.RFA. at Zero plus 80, and for liaison with the
111th Inf Bde. Their chief role will be to destroy any post
holding up our Infantry advance.

(2)

10. Owing to the difficulty in getting ammunition forward from railhead, there must be no reckless shooting on the part of batteries.

11. F.O.Os must always ensure they have means of communicating with their guns - if no wire, then by visual signalling & orderlies.
There must be no risk of delay in bringing immediate fire to bear on any objective.

12. If in the advance from the "BLUE" to the "GREEN LINE" the 21st Division are held up, "GROFTON" Group must be prepared to switch the fire of one battery to cover the right flank of the 111th Inf Bde advance.

13. Four Tanks have been allotted to 5th Division for mopping up BEAURAIN at dawn in case the enemy may be still holding out. They will then come under the orders of G.O.C.,111th Inf Bde to assist in the capture of the GREEN LINE.

14. Contact aeroplanes will call for flares at the following hours:-
0700.   1100.
0945.   1430.
A counter attack aeroplane will be in the air from daylight.

15. The BRIASTRE - MAROU - BEAURAIN Road is allotted to the 5th and 37th Divisions. As far as possible cross-country tracks should be used.

16.(a) Advanced 37th D.A.H.Q. will close at HAUCOURT at 2100 hrs on 22nd Oct, re-opening at the same hour at CAUDRY (I 24 a 93) (adjoining 5th D.A.H.Q).

(b) Advanced 37th D.A.H.Q. will close at I 24 a 93 at 0800 hrs on 23rd Oct and re-open at the same hour at BRIASTRE D 24 c 86.

(c) An Advanced Divl Report Centre will be established at D 24 c 06 from 1700 hrs on 22nd Oct.

17. ACKNOWLEDGE. (Bdes RFA and D.T.M.O by wire)

G.L.Ingestone
Lieut. R.A.

22nd Oct.1918.   for Brigade Major.,37th Divisional Artillery.

Copies to:-
RA.IV Corps,	21 D.A.	112 I.B.	123 Bde.RFA.	L.O.111 I.B.
HA. -do-	42 D.A.	15 Bde.RFA.	124 -do-	Staff Capt.
CBSO.-do-	N.Z.D.A.	27 -do-	37 D.A.C.	Sigs. DA.
37 Divn.	63 Inf Bde.	317 -do-	37 DTMO.	Diary.
5 D.A.	111 -do-	56 Bde.RGA.	D.M.G.C.	File.

Office   119   120
          121   37

Officer Commanding
----+++++++++Battery RFA

Reference attached Operation Order No. 217.

1. All batteries of this Brigade must be ready to move forward at 6.0 a.m.

2. Batteries are reminded that from their present positions they only barrage up to the Blue line. The barrage from the Blue line Protective onwards will be fired from the new positions in E.17.a and Barrage Table for this should be worked out before the move forward.

3. 37th Battery will fire on lively points in the left half of the Divisional Zone.

4. The 119th Battery will take Southern half of Divisional Zone and 120th Battery the Northern half. The 121st Battery will cover the whole Divisional front and will be prepared to answer all aeroplane calls. The 37th Battery will arrange for informing the 121st Battery of all aeroplane calls.

5. 1st Line Wagons will use BELLE VUE - MAROU Road.

(signed)
Captain R.F.A.

22-10-18.   Adjutant 27th. Bde. R.F.A.

WIRELESS PRESS.

24th Oct. 16.30 hours.

The AMERICAN Secretary of State has made public the following from the Secretary of State to Charge D'Affaires of SWITZERLAND ad Interim in charge of GERMAN interests in UNITED STATES :-

Department of State.
October 23rd, 18.

Sir,
I have the honour to acknowledge receipt of your Note of 22nd, transmitting a communication under date of 20th from GERMAN Government, and to advise you that President has instructed me to reply thereto as follows :-

Having received the solemn and explicit assurance of GERMAN Government that it unreservedly accepts the terms of PEACE laid down in his address to Congress of UNITED STATES on 8th Jan. '18 and the principles of settlement enumerated in his subsequent addresses, particularly the address of 27th Sept. and that it desires to discuss the details of their application and that this wish and purpose emanates, not from those who have hitherto dictated GERMAN Policy and conducted the present war on GERMANY'S behalf but from ministers who speak for the majority of the REICHSTAG and for an overwhelming majority of the GERMAN people and having received also the explicit promise of the present GERMAN Government that the humane rules of civilised warfare will be observed both on land and sea by the GERMAN armed forces the President of the UNITED STATES feels that he cannot decline to take up with Governments with which the Government of the UNITED STATES is associated the question of an ARMISTICE. He deems it his duty to say again, however, that the only ARMISTICE he would feel justified in submitting for consideration would be one which should leave the UNITED STATES and Powers associated with her in a position to enforce any arrangement that may be entered into and to make a renewal of hostilities on the part of GERMANY impossible. The President has, therefore transmitted his correspondence with the present GERMAN authorities to the GOVERNMENTS with which the UNITED STATES is associated as a belligerent with the suggestion that if those Governments are disposed to effect PEACE upon the terms and principles indicated, the Military Advisors and the Military Advisors of the UNITED STATES be asked to submit to the Governments associated against GERMANY the necessary terms of such an ARMISTICE as will fully protect the interests of the Peoples involved and ensure to the associated Governments the unrestricted power of safeguard and to enforce the details of the PEACE to which the German Government has agreed provided they deem such an ARMISTICE possible from a military point of view.

123.Brigade.R.F.A. 15.Brigade.R.F.A.
124.Brigade.R.F.A. 27.Brigade.R.F.A.   SC/8504.
37th D.A.C.   317.Brigade.R.F.A.
                    1/1.Kent.H.Battery.

The following reconnaisssance report is forwarded for your information.

ROADS. are numerous and in good order.
The following roads have been examined and are reasonably free from land and other mines:-

E.9.c.6.9. to E.11.b.8.6.	10' pave, well drained, good surface, suitable for double lorry.
E.6.a.7.6. to E.11.b.6.6.	12' metalled 4" thick, fairly well drained, horse transport or single lorry in good weather.
E.6.a.7.9. to F.7.a.6.9.	12' metalled 4" thick, and well drained. A shell has broken culvert at E.6.d.7.3. and a hole has been sunk at E.6.d.5.8. ready for blowing, but this would not interfere with single lorry traffic.
E.11.b.6.3. to E.16.d.4.8.	10' lightly metalled, metalling very patchy and only good for H.T.
E.23.d.9.9. to E.b.c.5.7.	12' metalled 3" thick, farily well drained, suitable for H.T. or emergency single lorry.
E.9.c.4.8. to E.23.b.6.3.	8' pave, 3' metalled berm each side, well drained. Suitable for single or double in good weather. Has crater at at E.23.b.8.3. about 15' diameter and 7' deep.

Railway. has been examined from W.25.d.9.2. to F.2.a.1.9. All rails are broken. Crater about 25' diam and 12' deep at E.6.b.3.8.- E.6.b.6.7. F.1.b.6.9. and F.1.d.90.95. No mines were found.

Villages. of BEAURAIN and PETIT VENDEGIES were carefully examined for mines and booby traps and can be considered free. Also RED HOUSE MILL and NEUVILLE Station.

24.10.1918.

Captain.R.A.
Staff Captain.37th Div Artillery.

Officer Commanding

_____ Battery RFA.

119
120
131
37

1. A short barrage will be put down at 21.00 hours as under :-

2. At Zero hour open on line from R.35.c 0/7 to X.5.b 3/7 remaining on this line for 1 minute then left to R.35.a 0/1 to X.5.b 8/8 for 1 minute.

3. All 18-pdr. Batteries superimposed on the same line.

4. Rates of Fire

   Zero to Zero plus 1 1/2 mins.   -   INTENSE.

   Zero plus 1 1/2 - Zero plus 2   -   3 guns per Battery fire 1 round each.

   Zero plus 2   -   STOP.

5. After operation S.O.S. lines will be

   18-pdrs. - X.12.a 2/4 - X.6.c 0/6 all superimposed.

   37th Bty. will lay on line X.6.a 5/4 - X.6.c 5/8 but will not fire S.O.S. without orders from this Office.

6. AMMUNITION.

   As available. No No. 106 Fuze.

7. ACKNOWLEDGE. by Wire.

Captain R.F.A.

24-10-18.   Adjutant 27th. Bde. R.F.A.

Operation Order No 3,
by
Lieut. Colonel M. CROFTON, D.S.O., R.F.A,
Commanding.................................GROUP.

24th October 1918

S.O.S. Lines as under will come into force forthwith :-

15th Bde. R 34 b 0.8 to R 35 c 2.5.

317th Bde. "A" Bty. Along Railway R 35 c 2.5 to X 5 a 3.7.
      "D" "   "   "   X 5 a 3.7 to X 5 a 8.1
      "B" "   "   "   X 5 a 8.1 to X 5 d 0.3

124th Bde. X 5 d 0.2 to X 11 d 0.0

27th Bde. Superimposed over whole front and to be prepared to concentrate particularly from X 5 Central to X 11 Central.

Howitzers.

15th Bde. Railway R 35 a and 29 c.

317th Bde. Road in R 35 d and 36 a.

124 Bde. Road in X 5 d and 6 c.

27th Bde. High Ground X 5 b and 6 a.

Copies to :-

D.A.
112th Inf.Bde.
124th Bde R.F.A.
 15th   "   "
 27th   "   "
A,B,C, & D/317.

Captain,
Adjutant,
G R O U P" R.F.A.

WIRELESS PRESS.   Oct. 25th   00.30 hours.

Third and Fourth Armies made another splendid advance yesterday
between SCHELDT and LE CATEAU front of about 20 miles. The advance
which had reached of when from 3 to 4 miles last night and was still
continuing was through very difficult country. Knowing that the
attack was imminent enemy had crowed many Divisions into line and
before and during early part of battle sent over great quantities of
High Explosives and Gas Shells. They fought stoutly but were
unable to resist our progress on any part of the front. Sir
DOUGLAS HAIG describes Operation as "Highly Successful" and adds
that several thousand prisoners and M.G. have been captured.
By advance to SAMBRE E. of LE CATEAU Fourth Army has reached
the edge of the battle-field of LANDRECIES which saw heavy fighting
in 1914. Further N. between VALENCIENNES and TOURNAI
First Army pushing through RAISMES Forest has taken BRUAY. Towards
TOURNAI, BELEHARIES and ESPAIN have been captured. Fighting is
now heavier on this front. There was stubborn fighting yesterday
on line of the SERRE and SOUCHE behind which Germans have now
retired. FRENCH succeeded in crossing the SOUCHE and maintaining
themselves on E. bank. AMERICAN forces between ARGONNE to the
MEUSE are faced by 30 Divisions on this narrow front. METZ was
again bombarded yesterday.

Italian destroyers have attacked ST GIOVANNI DI PALUA
on ALBANIAN Coast. BRITISH troops are on their way to KRASNOYARSK
in western SIBERIA. Japanese troops have reached IRKUTSK on
trans-siberian railway W. of Lake BAIKAL. BERLIN wireless message
say Karl LIEBKNECHT has been released from confinement. Tonnage
of ships sunk by enemy in Sept. was lower than any month since
Aug. 1916. Corpl DAVID HUNTER, Highland Light Infantry, one of
"Seven Heroes of MOEUVRES" cited by HAIG in his recent Communique
has been awarded the Victoria Cross. Without food or water
surrounded by Germans and constantly attacked he held important
post for 48 hours. King and Queen of Belgians yesterday flew
to BRUGES in two aeroplanes. After violent fighting
SERBIANS have captured BUKOVIK mountain Group N.E. of ALLEKENSIS
E. of SERBIA. N.W. of ZAPECAR Allied Forces have reached the BOR
Coppermines which Germans have used extensively for munitions.
British House of Commons decided by 275 votes to 25 that it was
desirable Bills should be passed forthwith making women eligible as
Members of Parliament. It was stated in Commons that in Scheme
for Demobilisation priority will be given to those troops
who had had longest service in the Field.   Daily Mail understands
that the Head of the AMERICAN Diplomatic Mission in EUROPE in
connection with Establishment of an Inter-Allied Diplomatic Council
will be Colonel Edwd HOUSE, Confidential Advisor of President WILSON.
He visited billigerent States, including GERMANY, during the war.

REPORT ON PRISONERS CAPTURED DURING RECENT OPERATIONS.

In our attack on October 20th, 3 Officers and 338 O.Rs. were captured. The enemy Divisions holding the Sector opposite us were the 25th and 1st Guard Reserve divisions. The 25th Division, which was chiefly involved in the attack, was classed as a "counter-attack division" and had been out of the line for 6 weeks. It was strong and fresh and had been put in the line with definite orders to hold the RAILWAY EMBANKMENT at all costs. They had been told that this position was of vital importance and that support and reserve troops were to move forward and counter-attack in the event of the BRITISH gaining a footing there. All 3 Regiments of this Division were in the line, each with one battalion forward, one in support and one in reserve. Our attack in the early morning accounted for the forward battalions of each Regt., the survivors of which retired to the positions of the support battalions. When our attack was continued in the afternoon the support battalions were similarly disposed and there remained only the reserve battalions of each Regiment which hurriedly put up a defensive position West of BEAURAIN. Meanwhile a battalion of the 4th Division was hurriedly pushed forward in the evening of the 20th instant, and took up a position in the outskirts of BEAURAIN, with orders to hold the Village.

Meanwhile the 1st Guard Reserve Division, which had come into the line in a very weak state, had suffered heavily and was unable to hold its sector. Consequently the 30th Division, which was resting after heavy engagements on this front, was brought forward and put in the line between the 25th and the 1st Guard Res. Divns. At the same time the enemy's artillery was reinforced, so that the enemy was prepared to offer strong resistance to us when we continued our attack on the morning of October 23rd. His orders were again to the effect that no retirement was to take place.

In our attack on October 23rd we captured 3 Officers and 88 O.R's., among the Officers was a battalion commander and his adjutant.

It has already been stated that the enemy's intentions were to hold his positions at all costs. In no case did it appear that we outnumbered the enemy, and prisoners themselves attributed our successes first to the superior morale of our troops and secondly to our preponderance of artillery. Prisoners of the Field Artillery of the 25th Division declared that a comparison between BRITISH and GERMAN artillery would be absurd and that they had never seen such a concentration of Heavy Arty. as that through which they had passed on their way to the Cage. Infantrymen stated that GERMAN artillery continually fires short and that Gunners have told them that complaints are useless as the guns are worn out and unreliable, they added that the heavy counter-preparation which the enemy put down on our front on the night October 22nd/23rd inflicted severe casualties on their own troops. High tributes were paid to the intensity and accuracy of our artillery fire and to the demoralising effect of the concentrations to which we subjected the enemy's positions from time to time. Several prisoners testified to the effect of our Machine Guns and to the speed with which they took up

/advanced

advanced positions and engaged fresh targets. One prisoner, the survivor of M.G. team, stated that his gun engaged a BRITISH M.G. team which they saw coming into action without success, whilst the BRITISH Gun got into action and knocked out the gun and team with the exception of himself. The enemy's horses are in a very bad condition, artillery prisoners expressed astonishment that our horses had stood the advance so well.

The morale of the prisoners generally was very low. Many had been told that an armistice was assured within a fortnight, if they would hold out so long; and in several cases they asked on arrival at the Cage if it were true that the Entente Powers were going to accept the KAISER'S peace offer. Leave had recently been stopped till October 28th and the current rumour was that this step had been taken to facilitate the evacuation of occupied territory. It appears that the enemy is doing his utmost to raise the dejected spirit of his troops by the promise of an early peace and that the more intelligent are beginning to doubt whether there is much foundation for these promises. A Battalion Commander, when invited to express his opinion on the final issue, said that he feared GERMANY would retain nothing that she had won but her fame. Other Officers affirmed that GERMANY'S only Reserves now are exhausted troops who are constantly being disturbed from a much-needed rest and sent back to the line. Men of the 1st Guard Res. Division related with bitterness that, as a punishment for retiring at CAMBRAI, they had been put back in the line in this Sector, their Divl. Commander having assured them that they would stay there till the whole Division could be fed from one Cooker.

In conclusion, it can be confidently stated that whereas prisoners taken by us a month ago were of opinion that final victory for GERMANY was impossible, those taken within the last few days regarded her defeat as certain.

INTELLIGENCE.
25th October 1918.   5th Division.

5th DIVISION SUMMARY OF INFORMATION.
25th October 1918.

OPERATIONS:
Third Army.

During the night 23rd/24th October BEAUDIGNIES was captured and a bridgehead formed East of it. The attack was resumed on the 24th in conjunction with the Armies on each flank. Considerable opposition was again experienced on the right, but in spite of it POIX DU NORD, WAGONVILLE, ENGLEFONTAINE, and CHISSIGNIES were captured. East of BEAUDIGNIES resistance stiffened but to the North RUESNES was taken.

From G.H.Q. timed 09.45 hrs. today :-
S. of the OISE the FRENCH attacked on front CHEVRIES - LUCY and took 350 prisoners. S. of DEYNZE FRENCH have reached COURTRAI - DEYNZE Road E. of OLSEN.
In FLANDERS the FRENCH have taken WAEREGHEM with 200 prisoners.

INTELLIGENCE.
AERIAL. to 16 hrs. 24th. - Nearly 2 tons of bombs were dropped of which ½ ton was dropped on LE QUESNOY Station on the evening of the 23rd, and nearly 1½ tons on various ground targets during the 24th. 190 rounds were fired.

ENEMY DEFENCES. Photographs taken on 23rd. show no defences dug in the following squares :- R.19.c. and d., 11.c. & d., 15.b. and d. 16, 17, 21.b. 22.a. and b. 23.a.

DISTRIBUTION OF ENEMY'S FORCES.
111th Div.
76th I.R..(1st Bn.) SALESCHES. Oct 24th.
A prisoner of the 76th I.R. was found hiding at SALESCHES. He stated that his divisional train was at JOLIMETZ. It is possible that the 76th I.R. is on this front but this prisoner was probably a straggler and the presence of the Regt. is doubtful.

4th Division.
140th I.R.(all Bns) S. of CHISSIGNIES. Oct.24th - Prisoner.
14th I.R. (1st & 3rd Bns.) near RUESNES.

185th Division.
28th R.I.R. near CHISSIGNIES. October 24th. Prisoner.
65th I.R.   do.   do.

58th Division.
106.I.R. (3rd Bn.) S.W. of CHISSIGNIES. Oct. 24th. Prisoner.

25th Division.
45th Bearer Coy. - VENDEGIES area. Oct. 23rd. Prisoner.
I Pnr. Bn.3rd Coy.   do.   do.

Miscellaneous.
The 25th and 1st Gd. Res. Divn. are considered to have been withdrawn also elements of the 9th Res. Divn.

Disbanding of the 25th Res. Division.

Later prisoners of the 168th I.R. taken yesterday afternoon state that the other two Regts. of the 25th Res. Divn., the 83rd and 118th R.I.Rs. were broken up last week.

2.

INTENTIONS.

On this front the only orders prisoners had received were to hold on, and they know nothing of any retirement.

The Army on our left reports that the Canal line near ST AMAND is to be held for a few days only, and then a withdrawal will take place to a line near MONS.

Civilians report that the banks of the ESCAUT near VALENCIENNES are mined for flooding the country. Civilians were evacuated from W. of this line to NIVELLES owing to the proposed inundations, and also to work on defences near NAMUR and LIEGE. The defences at CONDE and MAULDE are confirmed.

A Platoon Commander of the 87th R.I.R., 21st Res. Divn, states that the enemy is endeavouring to hold on until the system RETHEL - MAUBEUGE - MONS is completed. Pioneers of the 21st Res. Divn., after our attack on the line LE CATEAU - ST QUENTIN were sent to the vicinity of MAUBEUGE to help to complete this system.

SUMMARY.

The presence of one Regt. of the 58th Divn. is significant, considering that the other two Regts. are in line near VALENCIENNES, in that it shows that the enemy has few reserves available and is forced to move a Regt. from one Army Sector to that of another.

The 4th Divn, which was in Army Reserve, appears to have been put in peacemeal to reinforce weak sectors.

The enemy's forces seem to be considerably disorganised.

The only orders which appear to have been issued, are to hold on. Prisoners state that a defensive line is in course of construction about RETHEL - MAUBEUGE - MONS; but that it is not yet completed, and that our advance is consequently to be delayed as long as possible.

EXTRACTS FROM CAPTURED DOCUMENT.

(a) Div. Order of 25th Divn. dated 15/10/18. "The D.C. is expecting a renewal of the attack by the enemy from NEUVILLY North through SOLESMES. The task of the Division is to hold the railway as the main line of resistance and deny to the enemy crossings of the River SELLE.

(b) Garrison of South Tank Fort on Road in E.8.a.3/0.:-

    2 L.T.M's, with 100 rounds each.
    1 M.T.M.
    1 Field Gun. 180 rounds.
    2 Heavy M.G. 4,000 rounds armour piercing.

Personnel - 1 Officer, 3 Sgt. Majors, 7 N.C.O's, 33 O.R. The Fort was connected by telephone with H.Q.

PRISONERS.

18.00 hrs. 23rd to 18.00 hrs. 24th :-

	Officers.	O.R.
Unwounded.	22	2,000
Wounded.	7	334
		2,334
Since Oct. 1st.	404	14,811
Since Aug. 21st.	1,515	65,988

The total number of Guns captured by the Army from the 21st Aug. to the 19th October is 485.

25th October 1918.

INTELLIGENCE.
5th Division.

No 52

War Diary
27th Brigade R.F.A.

November 1915

SECRET.

5th DIVISION.
****

REPORT ON OPERATIONS.

From 1st November to 11th November 1918.

1. **1st to 3rd November.**

    During this period the Division remained in Corps Reserve, with the exception of 15th Brigade R.F.A., under Lieut-Colonel HARVEY, D.S.O., which had relieved 317th Bde. R.F.A. in the line near SALESCHES on night 27/28th October.

2. **OPERATIONS OF 5th NOVEMBER.**

    A. **PLAN OF ATTACK.**

    On November 2nd information was received from IV Corps that the general advance was to be resumed on November 4th. The First, Third and Fourth British Armies and the First French Army were all taking part in this advance, and as far as the Third Army was concerned the final objective allotted was the general line St. REMY CHAUSEE - PONT-SUR-SAMBRE - BAVAI - MONTIGNIES-sur-ROC Road. The line from the high ground between LANDRECIES and LOCQUIGNOL, thence East of JOLIMETZ to the high ground N.W. of GOMMEGNIES, and along the spur running N.N.W. from WARGNIES-le-GRAND to ETH was given as an intermediate objective.

    On the IV Corps front the 37th and N.Z. Divisions were to carry out the initial attack, making good the portion of the Army intermediate objective on the Corps front. After this had been gained success was to be exploited as far as the Eastern outskirts of that portion of the FORET DE MORMAL still standing (i.e. an approx. line N. and S. through LE GODELOT).

    The 5th and 42nd Divisions were to be prepared to pass through the 37th and N.Z. Divisions respectively, to continue the advance, the 5th Division on night 4/5th November, the 42nd Division on night 5/6th November.

    After the intermediate objective of the Army had been gained and success exploited the advance on the IV Corps front was to be continued to the final objective by the 5th Division and N.Z. Division, the latter being replaced by the 42nd Divn. on the night 5/6th November.

    Five Brigades of Field Artillery were allotted to the 5th Division and it was arranged that the barrage should be adopted to the nature of the ground over which it passed. That is to say over scrub and where trees were sparse an H.E. and Shrapnel barrage would be employed with 4.5" Hows. ahead of the 18-pdrs. Where the Forest was thick the Infantry would not close up to the barrage which was to consist of 4.5" Hows. firing 250 yds. ahead of the Infantry, with 18-pdrs. being directed 150 yds. ahead of the 4.5" Hows.

    For the first stages of the attack 5th Divisional Artillery was placed under orders of 37th Division.

    The G.O.C. 5th Division decided to carry out the allotted task on a two-brigade front, the 95th Infantry Brigade on the right, on a two-battalion front; the 15th Infantry Bde. on the left on a one-battalion front, the 13th Infantry Brigade being held in Divisional reserve.

2.

B. THE ASSEMBLY.

On the night of the 3/4th November the 15th and 95th Infantry Brigades moved to the NEUVILLE - SALESCHES - BEHURAIN area. At the same time the 13th Infantry Brigade moved to BEAURAIN - BRIASTRE area. On the 4th November Divisional H.Q. moved to NEUVILLE. The attack of the 37th Division and N.Z. Division which started at 05.30 hours on 4th November and by 11.00 hours it was reported that on the 37th Division front the line PONT-A-VACHE - Fme. de L'HOPITAL - L'ETANG had been captured.

ACTION OF ARTILLERY.

The Divisional Artillery moved into positions selected after dark on November 3rd. 15th Brigade R.F.A. between BEAUDIGNIES and GHISSIGNIES, 27th Brigade R.F.A. E. of BEAUDIGNIES. During the night 3/4th November these positions were shelled by the enemy.

Four mobile 6" T.M"s. were brought into action in GHISSIGNIES.

Orders were then issued for the three Infantry Bdes. to move forward. The 15th and 95th Infantry Brigades moved to the LOUVIGNIES - GHISSIGNIES area and the 13th Infantry Brigade to the NEUVILLE - SALESCHES area.

Information was now received that the 37th Division had established a line along the Western outskirts of the FORET DE MORMAL and was exploiting the success gained towards the Eastern edge of the uncut portion of the Forest, S. of the LE GODELOT Cross Roads. At the same time orders were received from the Corps that the 5th Division was to pass through the 37th Divn. as soon after daylight as possible on 5th November. Instructions were issued to the 15th and 95th Infantry Brigades accordingly.

Brigadier-General OLDMAN (Commanding 15th Inf. Bde.), decided that, having regard to the state of the Roads and the distance to the final objective, it would be better to pass the 1st BEDFORDS through the 1st NORFOLKS and keep the 1st CHESHIRES in reserve to exploit any success gained, and further, that in view of the difficulty which would naturally be experienced in passing through the Forest and keeping any sort of organisation, it would be advisable to leap-frog battalions as often as possible.

Brigadier-General NORTON (Commanding 95th Inf. Bde) decided to attack with the 1st E. SURREYS on the right and the 1st D.C.L.I. on the left, keeping the 1st DEVONS in reserve.

ACTION OF ARTILLERY. Nov. 4th.

The barrage opened at 05.30 hours on Nov. 4th. From 06.00 hours to 06.15 hours enemy carried out a heavy area shoot and 27th Brigade R.F.A. suffered some casualties.

Up to 07.30 hours 15th Brigade R.F.A. were heavily shelled and machine gunned, but suffered few casualties.

At 11.00 hours Brigades began to move forward, but owing to the Infantry being held up at the Chapel S.E. of BEAUDIGNIES the move was delayed. By 15.30 hours all batteries were in action in JOLIMETZ.

THE ASSEMBLY.

At 21.00 hours the 15th Infantry Brigade began moving forward to an assembly position about LE ROND QUESNE Road with one battalion - the 1st CHESHIRES - at JOLIMETZ. Brigade H.Q. moved to Fme. De L'HOPITAL, with an advanced Report Centre at COULON (S.5.c.)

At 01.15 hours the 5th November the 95th Infantry Bde moved forward to an assembly position about LE RU DU BOIS AUB (S.12.c.) with one battalion - the 1st DEVONS - in JOLIMETZ.

ARTILLERY PLAN.

To assist the advance of the 5th Division, artillery was affiliated as follows :-

15th Bde.R.F.A.)
D/123rd Bty.R.F.A.) under Lieut-Colonel HARVEY, D.S.O.
Two mobile T.M's.) to 95th Infantry Brigade.
of 5th D.A.)

27th Bde. R.F.A.)
D/124th Bty.R.F.A.) under Lieut-Colonel WHITE, D.S.O.
1 mobile T.M.) to 15th Infantry Brigade.
of 37th D.A.)

155th Army Bde. R.F.A., 123rd Bde. R.F.A. (less D/123) and 124th Bde. R.F.A. (less D/124) 37th D.A. were in Divisional reserve at LOUVIGNIES as also 127th Heavy Battery R.G.A. and 106th Siege Battery R.G.A.

155th Bde. R.F.A. was ordered to move as soon as the situation would permit to positions immediately west of the FORET DE MORMAL, to cover the whole Divisional front, and to keep touch with the 95th Infantry Brigade, but not to move further East without orders from Div. H.Q. 15th and 27th Brigades R.F.A. were each to send forward an 18-pdr. battery with one of its sections advanced in close support of the Infantry. Remainder of each Brigade to follow one battery at a time, after the Infantry were one mile East of LE GODELOT - LOCQUIGNOL Road.

The How. Batteries of 37th Division Artillery were to revert to their own Brigades as soon as the 15th and 27th Bdes. R.F.A. were in action East of the above mentioned Road.

The M.T.M's. were to follow the leading section of each Brigade.

C. **OPERATIONS OF 15th & 95th Inf. Bdes. on 5th & 6th Nov.**

At 05.30 hours on 5th Nov. the 15th and 95th Inf. Bdes. began their advance, passing through the 112th Inf. Bde. 37th Division just West of the LE GODELOT - CARREFOUR DE LA ROUILLE AUX EQUETTES Road. The line of this Road had been gained by both Brigades by 08.00 hours, the 95th Infantry Brigade reaching it slightly in advance of the 15th Infantry Brigade. Up to this point the enemy had not been encountered. The advance was continued without any pause, and by 09.30 hours the 1st D.C.L.I. and 1st E. SURREYS (95th Inf. Bde.) and the 1st BEDFORDS (15th Inf. Bde.) had captured the first objective (the LA GRANDE CARRIERE - FORESTERS HOUSE (N.36.a.) Road), meeting with practically no resistance. The 1st NORFOLKS (15th Infantry Brigade) were drawn into reserve at LE GODELOT. On the 95th Infantry Brigade front the 1st E. SURREYS captured 2 prisoners and a wagon and team, loaded with Machine Guns.

At 10.15 hours the advance was resumed towards the second objective (EMBU FARM - W. of LA PORQUERIE - LA CORNE - LAIE DE LA HAUTE RUE). Considerable opposition was encountered and it was not until two mobile trench mortars had been brought up and the area in the Forest, immediately W. of LA PORQUERIE, bombarded by artillery, that the attack could be driven home. On the 95th Infantry Brigade front patrols had located the enemy and a section of the 52nd Battery R.F.A. opened fire on them, eventually driving them off about 14.30 hours. In spite of the fact that the enemy then opened fire with artillery on the front and support lines, the 95th Infantry Brigade were able to make a little ground, but their left flank was exposed to enfilade Machine Gun fire owing to the fact that the 1st BEDFORDS (15th Infantry Bde.) were still held up on their front. Up to this time the 15th Infantry Brigade had been unable to gain touch on their left with the N.Z. Division, who had been experiencing considerable resistance at this juncture, information was received from patrols of the 3rd KING'S OWN HUSSARS, however, that the N.Z. Division had passed on beyond the first objective on their front. On receiving this information Brigadier-Genl. OLDMAN decided to push the 1st CHESHIRES through on the left of the 1st BEDFORDS in order to turn the enemy's flank. The 1st CHESHIRES, who had already been ordered to march on FORESTERS HOUSE after the capture of the first objective, were in position there by 14.45 hours, in spite of the fact that the march to this point had been exceedingly arduous, the roads being very heavy through continuous rain, and having been very cleverly demolished, at the brook-crossing places, especially near LE GODELOT and FORESTERS HOUSE. The advance along the Divisional front was then continued and by 16.00 hours the whole of the second objective had been captured, and patrols pushed forward by the 1st E. SURREYS secured 17 prisoners in HURTEBISE FARM. In the course of the attack by the 1st BEDFORDS considerable casualties were inflicted on the enemy, 30 dead being counted in one place.

By 22.00 hours the third objective, the line of the BACHANT - PONT-SUR-SAMBRE - BAVAI Road, had been captured on the front of the 15th Infantry Brigade, who reported that they were in touch with the 1st D.C.L.I. on their right, but not yet in touch on the left. Little opposition was met with during this advance, but the hostile artillery fire was considerable. Brigadier-General OLDMAN decided, therefore, to consolidate the position already gained, pushing patrols down the river SAMBRE. A further advance, until the situation on the left had been cleared up, was not possible and the darkness of the night and the state of the roads, made any chance of getting up bridging material impossible. The G.O.C. 5th Division, therefore, approved of the postponement of the attempt to establish a bridgehead over the River SAMBRE until the next day.

In the meanwhile, the 1st D.C.L.I. in spite of a steady Machine Gun and artillery fire, entered the village of PONT - SUR - SAMBRE capturing 16 prisoners and one Machine Gun. At 06.00 hrs. Nov. 6th the 1st E. SURREYS moved forward to the line of the BACHANT - BAVAI Road, gaining touch there with the 1st D.C.L.I.

Both Brigades pushed patrols towards the River SAMBRE, but these were met with heavy Machine Gun and Artillery fire from the right bank of the River and the high ground beyond. These patrols, however, were able to ascertain that the PONT-SUR-SAMBRE - AYMERIES Bridge had been completely demolished. The Machine Gun and Artillery fire was maintained throughout the day, and it was obvious that any bridging of the river would have to be done during the night 6/7th November.

At 14.00 hours the 42nd Division who had relieved the N.Z. Division on the night 5/6th November reported that they were held up at HOISES FARM and LES CINQ CHEMINS, which made it clear that they, too, would not be able to effect a crossing of the river until the next day. Touch was gained with the right battalion of the 42nd Division N.E. of LA HAUTE RUE.

Brigadier-General OLDMAN decided to cross the river with the 1st NORFOLKS W. of LA BLANCHE BORNE by a Pontoon bridge, considering it probable that all existing bridges would have been destroyed. For this purpose the 1st NORFOLKS were ordered up to LA HAUTE RUE early on the morning of the 6th.

The G.O.C., 5th Division having visited both Brigade Commanders, approved their plans for bridging the river after dusk on 6th November and instructions were issued accordingly to the C.R.E. and to the R.E. Companies attached to the 15th and 95th Infantry Brigades.

At 15.15 hours Major R.M. CLOUTMAN. R.E., Commanding the 59th Field Coy. R.E. reported that he had visited the QUARTES Bridge and had found it intact. This reconnaissance was carried out in a most gallant manner. Major CLOUTMAN, seeing that the bridge had been prepared for demolition by the enemy rolled over the tow-path, and after swimming the river cut the leads of the charge. An enemy M.G. situated in the FACTORY swept the bridge during the whole of this plucky action. Major CLOUTMAN also reported that the lock sluices appeared to be intact and offered facilities for crossing the river in single file. For this gallant action Major CLOUTMAN was recommended for and received the V.C.

On receipt of this important information, General OLDMAN ordered the 1st CHESHIRES to send forward a Platoon to the QUARTES Bridge to prevent the enemy repairing the leads of the demolition charges. Two 6" T.M's. were also ordered up to shell the approaches to the bridge, which, as subsequent examination showed, they did with great accuracy.

The Platoon of the 1st CHESHIRES got into position about 17.30 hours, but unfortunately arrived just too late to prevent the enemy repairing the leads and blowing up the bridge, which he appears to have done about 17.15 hours.

In the meantime the 59th Field Company R.E. had got to work on bridging the river at a point immediately W. of LA BLANCHE BORNE as already planned, the officer commanding the 27th Brigade R.F.A. being requested to put down a light artillery bombardment on the right bank of the river to cover the preliminary operations of building the bridges. The difficulties in the way of getting material up to this point were immense owing to the mud and the cratered roads, but were successfully overcome.

A patrol report was then received to the effect that the LOCK was also impassable. This necessitated alteration in the plan previously formed. Brigadier-General OLDMAN went at once to the Officer Commanding the 1st CHESHIRES and ordered him to send two Companies to cross the Pontoon Bridge West of LA BLANCHE BORNE directly it was finished, and establish a bridgehead in that vicinity. Together with the Officer Commanding the 1st NORFOLKS Brigadier-General OLDMAN then proceeded to reconnoitre the LOCK to see what could be done about bridging it. At the sametime two Companies of the 1st NORFOLKS were ordered to be sent there at once. These Companies started bridging with telegraph poles, but, owing to heavy M.G. fire, were unable to complete bridge. In the meantime information had been received that the V Corps had effected crossings over the river SAMBRE and were endeavouring to occupy AULNOYE from the South and East.

The G.O.C. therefore decided to issue orders for the attack to be resumed the next day.

ACTION OF ARTILLERY 5th & 6th NOVEMBER.

Nov. 5th. 121st Battery R.F.A., 27th Brigade R.F.A. was detailed as advanced guard battery under orders of O.C. 1st NORFOLKS and moved in rear of 1st BEDFORDS. The remainder of the Brigade followed in rear. On arrival at LE GODELOT 37th and 119th Batteries moved into action 1,000 yards S.W. of FORESTERS HOUSE, 120th and 121st Batteries being kept in reserve.

At 16.00 hours 120th and 121st Batteries were ordered into action near LE GRANDE CARRIERE to cover PONT-SUR-SAMBRE. 52nd Battery R.F.A. was detailed as advanced guard battery to 95th Infantry Brigade and moved forward with 1st D.C.L.I. and the advanced guard section several times came into action to give temporary support to the Infantry. The remainder of the Batteries left JOLIMETZ at 08.00 hours and at about 16.00 hours came into action as follows :-

D/123 Battery — about 1200 yds. S. of LE GODELOT covering the high ground W. & S.W. of LA PORQUERIE.

A/15 & 80th Btys.— Just N. of LE GRANDE CARRIERE.

D/15 Battery. — in LE GRANDE CARRIERE.

The Batteries fired harassing fire throughout the night on PONT-SUR-SAMBRE.

155th Brigade R.F.A. was kept in support and at 14.15 hours moved forward, a battery at a time, to positions between the Wood South of LE GODELOT and the LE GRANDE CARRIERE - FORESTERS HOUSE Road.

72nd Army Bde. R.F.A. (now affiliated to the Division) moved to LOUVIGNIES.

6th Nov. At dawn 37th and 119th Batteries of 27th Bde. R.F.A. moved to position just W. of LA PORQUERIE and 08.00 hrs. the 120th and 121st Batteries moved to the same area. From 20.00 hours to 22.00 hours these Batteries carried out an area shoot to assist the crossing of the river.

At 16.00 hours 80th and A/15 Batteries of the 15th Bde. R.F.A. came into action at LA PASSE ZEBELIN, D/15 Battery East of LE GRANDE CARRIERE, 52nd Battery at EMBU FARM. The mist rendered observation very difficult, but a few rounds were fired at M.G's. on ridge N. of PANTIGNY.

3. OPERATIONS OF 7th NOVEMBER.

A. PLAN OF ATTACK.

In view of the situation which has been described in the preceding paragraph, the G.O.C. 5th Division decided to push forward the 15th Infantry Brigade by all available crossings over the river SAMBRE to make good the high ground East of the River from BOUSSIERES (exclusive to 5th Divn) to the line of the railway East of BOISGEORGES and then along the East of the Railway to the Divisional boundary. The 95th Infantry Brigade were ordered to pass through the 15th Inf. Brigade after this line had been made good continuing the attack on the whole divisional front as far as the MAUBEUGE - AVESNES Road.

B. THE ASSEMBLY.

By 06.00 hours, the Pontoon Bridge over the River was complete, and the two Companies of the 1st CHESHIRES went across followed by the 1st NORFOLKS. In the meantime the 95th Inf. Brigade assembled in the village of PONT-SUR-SAMBRE in readiness to cross the river in rear of the 15th Inf. Brigade.

C. OPERATIONS BY 15th & 95th INF. BDES. on 7th NOVEMBER.

Immediately after crossing the river the two Companies of the 1st CHESHIRES and the 1st NORFOLKS pushed ahead and made good the line of the Railway East of BOIS GEORGES with a flank thrown back on the left, since the 42nd Division had not yet been able to get up into line.

By 10.50 hours this Division had occupied HARGNIES and by 11.45 hours had made good the line of the Road running S. from this village, with Cavalry patrols pushing on towards the river SAMBRE, but the bend of the River at BOUSSIERES was occupied by the enemy during the remainder of the day.

At 12.35 hours the 1st DEVONS (95th Inf. Bde) had crossed the River SAMBRE and now passed through the 15th Infantry Bde. with orders to gain the line of the Road from the Southern edge of HAUTMONT to FONTAINE and the village of FONTAINE (inclusive). This Battalion moved forward in advanced guard formation under heavy Field Artillery fire, considerable difficulty being experienced in taking up the line of the Railway (E. of BOIS GEORGES) owing to intense M.G. fire from the direction of BOUSSIERES.

At 13.00 hours the advance of the 1st DEVONS was held up by heavy M.G. fire and T.M. fire from the direction of ST REMY-MAL-BATI. The right Company of this Battalion, however, managed to get forward, and meeting with no resistance advanced and captured the village of FONTAINE, taking one 5.9" How. and gaining touch there with the left of the 21st Division who had reached the West outskirts of LIMONT FONTAINE at mid-day. A gap of about 1,000 yds. had now been formed between the right Company of the 1st DEVONS and the remainder of the Battalion,

and later this Company was withdrawn to a position S.W. of
ST. REMY-MAL-BATI in order to maintain touch between the 21st
Division and the remainder of the 1st DEVONS.

During their advance the 1st DEVONS had encountered
stern resistance and had suffered a considerable number of
casualties, including 6 Officers.

The 1st NORFOLKS of the 15th Infantry Brigade maintained
their position on the line of the Railway until the whole of
the 95th Infantry Brigade had passed through during the night
7/8th, when they were withdrawn into billets in PANTIGNY. The
1st BEDFORDS remained in LA PEAQUERIE and the 1st CHESHIRES
billeted in PONT-SUR-SAMBRE and PANTIGNY. During the night
the 95th Infantry Brigade re-organised, preparatory to carrying
out a fresh attack the following day.

ACTION OF ARTILLERY NOVEMBER 7th.

No bridge across the SAMBRE was available till 15.30
hours. A/15 and D/15 Batteries crossed the River and came
into action at PANTIGNY. 52nd Battery came into action West
of the River. 80th and A/15 Batteries and 27th Bde. R.F.A.
remained in readiness West of the River.

4. OPERATIONS ON 8th NOVEMBER.

A. PLAN OF ATTACK.

On instructions received from Corps, the G.O.C. 5th Divn.
ordered the 95th Infantry Brigade to continue the advance on
the 8th November and the 13th Infantry Brigade to be prepared
to relieve or pass through the 95th Infantry Brigade when the
line of the MAUBEUGE - AVESNES Road had been made good.

Brigadier-General NORTON (95th Inf. Bde.) ordered the
1st DEVONS to advance with a protective screen of Cavalry and
Cyclists and capture a line from the Road Junction just South
of the FM. DE BOIS DES DAMES to the Road Junction South of
LE PAYE, thence S.E. to the Northern outskirts of BEAUFORT (excl).
The 1st E. SURREYS were ordered to advance N.E. and capture
ST. REMY-MAL-BATI. This Battalion was then to form a flank
facing North. The 1st D.O.L.I. were to advance to the line
of the HAUTMONT - FONTAINE Road, pivot on their left flank and
then attack Northwards in order to outflank HAUTMONT. The 42nd
Division having been unable to effect a crossing on its front
during the night passed a Brigade of Infantry over the bridge
at PONT-SUR-SAMBRE to threaten the Southern flank of the enemy
at HAUTMONT by an attack on the BOIS DU QUESNOY.

B. THE ASSEMBLY.

Battalions who were re-organising after the attack of
7th November assembled without any unusual incident occurring.

C. OPERATIONS BY 95th & 13th INF. BDES. from 8th to 10th Nov.

At 06.30 hours on 8th November the infantry moved forward.
At 06.45 hours the Cavalry and Cyclists crossed the Railway
East of BOIS GEORGES and passed through the Infantry meeting
no opposition from the enemy. On the left the Cavalry patrols
reached the outskirts of HAUTMONT. On the right, the line of
the HAUTMONT - FONTAINE Road was made good, but it was not found
possible to go beyond this Road owing to heavy Artillery and
M.G. fire. In the meantime the 1st E. SURREYS had passed through
the village of ST. REMY-MAL-BATI without opposition, taking up
a line on the high ground N.E. of the village, but both this
line and the village were heavily bombarded by the enemy until

16.00 hours. On the left the 1st D.C.L.I. reached a line about 300 yds. S. of BOIS DU QUESNOY and gained touch with the Units on either flank. The casualties had so far been comparatively heavy, 1st E. SURREYS losing about 50, including 2 Officers, and the 1st DEVONS 90, including 9 Officers.

At 10.30 hours troops of the 42nd Division were observed moving up on the left apparently meeting little or no resistance. Although the resistance on the part of the enemy on the front of the 95th Infantry Brigade had not been of a determined nature, isolated M.G. posts had given considerable trouble, and the enemy artillery had shewn great activity. The spirit of the troops remained excellent considering the inclemency of the weather and the fact that for 3 days they had been wet through and covered with mud.

In the meantime the 13th Infantry Brigade had moved from LA PORQUERIE at 10.15 hours and had crossed the River SAMBRE. Considerable difficulty was experienced by this Brigade in getting forward beyond the River owing to the persistent shelling of all Roads in the vicinity of PANTIGNY and ST. REMY-MAL-BATI. At 19.00 hours, however, the 2/K.O.S.B's. on the right and the 1st R.W. KENTS on the left, each with one section of "A" Coy., 5th Battalion M.G.C., moved to pass through the 1st DEVONS (95th Infantry Brigade). The night was pitch dark and it was raining hard, but by about 01.00 hours on 9th November a connected line had been formed from about LES QUARTRE CHEMINS (W.13.a.) where the 2/K.O.S.B's. were in touch with the 51st Infantry Brigade (17th Division), thence E. of FONTAINE to the high ground about 1,500 yds. N.E. of this village, whence the left of the 1st R.W. KENTS was thrown back to join with the 125th Infantry Brigade (42nd Division), at the S.E. corner of the BOIS DU QUESNOY. At 03.00 hours, 9th November, Brigadier-General BECKWITH (Commanding 13th Inf. Bde) ordered the 16th R. WARWICKS to move to ST. REMY-MAL-BATI. Instructions having been issued by Division that the advance was to be continued and information received from the 17th Division that they intended advancing on and through BEAUFORT at 05.30 hours, the 2/K.O.S.B's. and 1st R.W. KENTS were ordered by Brigadier-General BECKWITH to co-operate, the latter being told to refuse their left flank until the 125th Infantry Brigade secured the high ground N. of LE PAYE. At 03.30 hours the 42nd Division reported that they were in possession of the OLD MILL and FORT HAUTMONT, though some M.G. fire had still been coming from just West of LE PAYE up to about 03.00 hours. By 05.00 hours the 2/K.O.S.B's. reported that they had a post on the AVESNES - MAUBEUGE Road about 1,000 yds. South of LE PAYE and the 1st R.W. KENTS a post about LE PAYE itself.

It seemed quite obvious that the enemy was withdrawing and orders were sent out to keep on advancing, maintaining touch with Units on the flanks. By 06.05 hours the 13th Infantry Brigade front had been advanced to the line of the BEAUFORT - LE PAYE Road and was being pushed forward in conjunction with the 52nd Infantry Brigade on the right and the 125th Infantry Brigade on the left. One Squadron (less two Troops) of the 3rd KING'S OWN HUSSARS, and three Platoons of the IV Corps Cyclists had been ordered up at 07.00 hours to push on in bounds, the Cyclists occupying each line as the Cavalry advanced from it.

The first bound was to be the ridge West and N.W. of
DAMOUSIES. The second, the Railway line just West of the
river SOLRE, and the third, the high ground N. and N.W. of
BOIS DU CARNOY. At 09.00 hours 13th Infantry Brigade H.Q.
moved to FONTAINE, and Brigadier-General BECKWITH ordered the
16th R. WARWICKS to move there from ST. REMY-MAL-BATI. On
instructions received from Corps orders were now issued from
the Division that the Infantry of the 13th Infantry Brigade
were to stop on a line just East of the AVESNES - MAUBEUGE Rd.,
forming a line of resistance there whilst the Cyclists were to
stop on the line of the River SOLRE and hold the crossings
there, the Cavalry coming back into DAMOUSIES for the night.
Before these orders could reach the front line the 2/K.O.S.B's.,
however, were in DAMOUSIES, and the 1st R. W. KENTS had crossed
the River SOLRE and gained touch with the enemy on the South
and West outskirts of FERRIERE LA PETITE, where some enemy
snipers were shot and transport fired on. One Section of the
119th Battery R.F.A. working with the 1st R. W. KENTS
asforward guns also actually crossed the River, constructing
a bridge for themselves and remaining there in rear of the
1st R. W. KENTS posts until after dusk when they and the
Infantry posts withdrew by order. The 2/K.O.S.B's. and the
1st R. W. KENTS were then withdrawn on a line covering
MARLIERE with the left of the 1st R. W. KENTS in FORT BORDIAU.
Touch was gained with the 52nd Infantry Brigade (17th Division)
just East of BEAUFORT and with 125th Infantry Brigade (42nd Div)
about 800 yards N. of LE PAYE. The Cavalry had reported all
ground clear of the enemy as far as the high ground East of
BOIS DU CARNOY.

On November 10th the Cavalry were ordered to reconnoitre
first, the line BERELLES - AIBES, and if that were found clear
to send out patrols as follows :-

One along the AIBES - LA RATIENE - COUSOLRE Road to
report on its condition.

One to MARBLE WORKS just S.W. of COUSOLRE, to report if
the enemy held that village, and also on the condition of the
Railway leading to the MARBLE WORKS and the AIBES - COUSOLRE Rd.

In the afternoon of the 9th orders were received that
the VI Corps would take over the pursuit on the Army front, the
IV Corps holding its present front with the 42nd Division.
Accordingly at 09.00 hours on the 10th November the 13th Inf.
Brigade was ordered to hand over its front to the 42nd Divn.
This was completed by 14.30 hours, 13th Infantry Brigade moving
back into billets in PANTIGNY - LA PUISSANCE - PONT-SUR-SAMBRE.

Cavalry and Cyclists were handed over to the 42nd Divn.
at 11.00 hours.

5. ACTION OF ARTILLERY 8th to 10th NOVEMBER.

8th November. Batteries of 15th Brigade R.F.A. remained
in action in PANTIGNY where they were joined by 52nd Battery. On
13th Infantry Brigade taking over Divisional front, 27th and
155th Brigades R.F.A. were formed into a group under Lieut-Col.
WHITE. D.S.O., and affiliated to the 13th Infantry Brigade. 27th
Brigade R.F.A. took up positions South East of ST. REMY-MAL-BATI,
and 155th Brigade R.F.A. moved to position of readiness South of

11.

same village.

15th Brigade R.F.A. came into Divisional reserve.

Harassing fire was carried out throughout the night.

November 9th. One Section from 119th Battery moved up with the Cavalry to DAMOUSIES. The bridges across the SOLRE river had been destroyed, but Lieut. WINTLE with the assistance of some of the 3rd HUSSARS and some civilians repaired the bridge and the Section crossed the River in support of the Cavalry.

On receipt of orders that the 13th Infantry Brigade were to hold a line of resistance on the line MARLIERE - PONT-SUR-SAMBRE the Section was withdrawn West of the River and ordered to rejoin the Battery.

The 72nd Army Brigade R.F.A. moved to LE GRANDE CARRIERE.

November 10th. 72nd Army Brigade R.F.A. marched to LE ROND QUESNE, 15th Brigade R.F.A. to LE GRANDE CARRIERE, 27th Brigade R.F.A. to PONT-SUR-SAMBRE

November 11th. 72nd Army Bde. R.F.A. marched to GHISSIGNIES, 15th and 27th Brigades R.F.A. to LOUVIGNIES.

6. NOVEMBER 10th & 11th.

The Division was withdrawn from the line and proceeded to the JOLIMETZ - LE QUESNOY area, the Artillery moving to LOUVIGNIES and GHISSIGNIES.

7. GENERAL SUMMARY.

The difficulties encountered during the advance through the FORET DE MORMAL can justly be described as stupendous, especially for the artillery who were constantly being bogged up to the axles. The 52nd and 121st Batteries, who were in close support, never failed to be up in time when they were required. Roads were few and indifferent, and the persistent rain soon reduced them to seas of mud. The enemy had blown up numerous bridges and had also blown craters in many places, with the result that Motor Transport was practically impossible and Horse Transport alone had to be employed to get forward supplies of all kinds.

The R.E. and Pioneer Battalion did admirable work in repairing Roads, the former especially deserve the fullest praise for their efforts in getting forward material to the River SAMBRE and building bridges over that River.

****

WAR DIARY
INTELLIGENCE SUMMARY

Army Form C. 2118.

November 1917

Place	Date	Hour	Summary of Events and Information	Remarks and references to Appendices
BEAUMONT	1st		Orders came through that the Batteries were to select positions on about R.33 C and D. Col Pate and the Battery Commanders went forward and selected their positions Such one. Lost. South East of BENDIGNIES. In the enemy batteries started.	
"	2nd		returning up guns to these positions Batteries commenced taking up ammo	
"	3rd		During the morning HQ moved up to R.33.c.6.5 later. Rear of Battery positions.	
"	4th		Gun fire near 5:30 am. During the night previous the Bosh put down a very heavy concentration at intervals. Enemy casualties to the 121st Battery. From the Ranges Moved the Battery Position was heavily shelled Lt Stafford 37 O.R. 2nd Lt Mann 2 Other Wounded and the 120th lost 14 men. Lt. O'Co, the Clerk and Corporal wounded. ill [?] ROONEY at his the station the Battery Commander Moved to JOLIMETZ	

WAR DIARY or INTELLIGENCE SUMMARY

Place	Date	Hour	Summary of Events and Information	Remarks and references to Appendices
JOLIMETZ			Enemy had only two Men Captured quite a short while. Position was selected for the Batteries as follows:— 119th — S.9.b.69 120th — M.33.c.87 121st — S.3.d.85.20 37th — S.3.d.82.63 These positions were just outside JOLIMETZ. Batteries received orders to move forward to these positions at 3.30 and were in action at 5.30 pm. The Batteries had considerable trouble on the roads owing to these positions being to [illegible] etc on horse lines.	
	5th		AQ 860 established during the morning in JOLIMETZ. It was believed that they + Booth only held the Forêt de MORMAL very thinly. Orders were sent out that the 27th Bde were to follow the 15th Infantry Bde in Column of Route through the Forest under instructions from the 121st Battery front on close support to the Wharton Bde Met [illegible]	Div Arty [illegible]

Army Form C. 2118.

WAR DIARY
or
INTELLIGENCE SUMMARY.
(Erase heading not required.)

Place	Date	Hour	Summary of Events and Information	Remarks and references to Appendices
			1st Norfolks who were the advanced guard. The 121st met the Infantry at 55c 82 but were delayed in moving forward owing to the roads having two plans up. The orders were for the rest of the Brigade to cross the Church at Jouemets at 5.30 am. The Infantry were late and did not pass the Church till about 7am. HQ moved up about 7am to the Brigadier who was a Jouemets at 55c 61. HQ sent through that the Batteries were not to advance at once. About 9.30 am HQ moved at to Le Cadelot at 3a 72. The Batteries passed thro Mont zbar 11.30 am and the 27th came straight into action at T.36 and the 119th at T.51. The rest later up a position at T.5c and rear at T.76. The latter two and us? fell into action about 6 pm. Although the 87 and 119 received orders to advance and take up positions in C2D and O2C at dawn the 119 Div.	

6th

WAR DIARY
or
INTELLIGENCE SUMMARY.

Army Form C. 2118.

(Erase heading not required.)

On return by 8am and the 37th by 8.30 am. The B.G.C. on
returning gave information on they had to advance N.E. &
that the noise which had been heard was
came into action at 12 noon at U24 and the 121st at U410 at U23.
H.Q. moved at about during the morning to La Corne la Ba..
2nd R.F.A. Bde killed while proceeding to H.Q.
to report the arrival of his Battery.
Batteries after a great march after lunch they crossed
orders to move forward all the Battrs into action by
5 p.m., the 37th Brig. at V5 to 9592, 119th at U11 to 9560,
120th at U11 and 121st Set U11-27. Three battries are that
but of the River Sambre on that is) the village of Pont sur
Sambre. H.Q. moved to Pont sur Sambre.
The 15th Infy Bde have been ordered the Bridges over the

Army Form C. 2118.

WAR DIARY
or
INTELLIGENCE SUMMARY.
(Erase heading not required.)

Place	Date	Hour	Summary of Events and Information	Remarks and references to Appendices
	8th		Convoy the 95th Inf Bde. During the morning position was blocked on the outskirts of Frans. at midday the 13th Infantry Bde relieved the 95th and the Division rite the Infantry was taken over by the Brigade, the 15th Bde Armoured Wheeled at Division Brigade HQ moved to Shring ordering the sphere the Battalion's took into the reserve Position. The 120th at Notres. 121st at Vadar. 37th at Vivaer. A section of the 119th too at Notres in elaboration to the KOSB's. There found measures cry to the difficulty of petrol armoured and employment to land and to war time	

WAR DIARY or INTELLIGENCE SUMMARY

Army Form C. 2118.

Place	Date	Hour	Summary of Events and Information	Remarks and references to Appendices
	12th		Roads burnt in a very bad condition. The Brigade did not reach Avion till about 3.30 P.M.	
	13th		During the morning news came through that an ARMISTICE had been signed with Germany to take effect from 11 AM the 11th November.	
	14th		Major Brown (Adjt) evacuated from here, also 2nd Lt Lockhead. The Battery then spent a busy day cleaning up. Attention was then to cleaning up. 2nd Lt Braham (37th) sent on leave. Major Brown returned and took command of the B/126. Major Philitt apt to command the 37th Battalion having some time a leave. A conference was held at these HQ at 12 noon, by Col Harvey. News came that 2nd Lt Evans (Sur.)

Mch Hurley
2nd Lt RA

WAR DIARY or INTELLIGENCE SUMMARY

Army Form C. 2118.

Place	Date	Hour	Summary of Events and Information	Remarks and references to Appendices
	9th		On have the same 4 guns of the 119th mobile and of to take a station of action. Two these 4 batteries of the 119th were drawn Reinforcements to the early the Brigade. In the moment it was found that the Bde had gone over back. It was impossible to follow him, owing to the difficulty of traffic etc. The Infantry was ordered not to advance and so the Battery Commander held himself in available as far house.	
	10th		AQ moved up to FONTAINE at Mielbeg, orders came in that the Brigade Division was being withdrawn and that the 4th Division Arty take over our front. The Batteries passed the Stations at our own point. Marched to PONT-SUR-SAMBRE to Billets just meanly of the 15th Bde RFA.	
	11th		the march was renewed at 9am. The Clem had great difficulty in getting through the forest of MORMAL owing to the	

Army Form C. 2118.

WAR DIARY
or
INTELLIGENCE SUMMARY.
(Erase heading not required.)

Instructions regarding War Diaries and Intelligence Summaries are contained in F.S. Regs., Part II. and the Staff Manual respectively. Title pages will be prepared in manuscript.

Place	Date	Hour	Summary of Events and Information	Remarks and references to Appendices
LAVENTIES	16th		had Club of Sports.	
	17th		An ordinary day's routine	
	18th		" "	
			An inspection of a selection of Fat. Battery took place to decide which was the best gun	
			team of march	
	19th		A Gen. D.A. Sports Committee assembled at Div. H.Q. to arrange a sports programme.	
	20th		A Battalion Sports Committee assembled to decide the management of the Brigade Sports	
			An Battalion football	
			a football match v James started	
	21st		News was received that It Stafford was killed by the D.A. amongst the machine gun Battalion. News was received that It Stafford 37th Battery	

WHR/Rifle
2nd/5th Regt

WAR DIARY
or
INTELLIGENCE SUMMARY.

(Erase heading not required.)

Army Form C. 2118.

Place	Date	Hour	Summary of Events and Information	Remarks and references to Appendices
	22nd		Had area of Courcelles had area of Courcelles Chaze. A usual days routine. Capt Davies (20th) returned from leave. Capt Odlum (adjutant) returned from leave.	
	23rd		A Church Parade was held at 10.30 am. a the 57th Battery's football ground, for the whole of the Army DA. This was the first photograph? the DA had had of holding a thanksgiving service.	
	24th		A normal days work.	
	25th		An inspection by the Brigade by the C.R.A at 10.30 am.	
	26th		Lt Col White D.S.O sent on leave to Paris	
	27th		Nothing unusual occurred. Ext orders marked to Ret. In	

Army Form C. 2118.

WAR DIARY
or
INTELLIGENCE SUMMARY.
(Erase heading not required.)

Place	Date	Hour	Summary of Events and Information	Remarks and references to Appendices
	28th		A usual days nature.	
	29th		In the evening the Brigade entertained the Nurses of the Canadian CCS at Ol Quoeny to a dance	
	30th		The Divisional Point to Point was held. Major Chidson (RO) Won the Race between the 4 best Officers Horses. A Race took place between the foun Battery the 15th Bde, 2nd, & 5th Armies of the 27th Bde against the Brigade for the Brigade on which the	

2nd Bde RAH

WAR DIARY
or
INTELLIGENCE SUMMARY.

Army Form C. 2118.

(Erase heading not required.)

Honours and Awards for the Month of NOVEMBER

99757	Sjt T Franjer	121st
105276	Sjt AM Dufto	121st
171003	Sjt J Patterson	121st
102960	Dr EJ Jones	121st
5265	Pte J Wolff J Donsen A/C	119th
64053	Dr A Pritchard	119th
830783	Sjt H Phinny	119th
42323	Dvr (A/Cpl) E.R. Hall	119th
73626	Ptn E McCormach	120th
69915	Dr W Cox	120th
120483	Bdr DJ Ranger	37th
20440	Dr E Smith	37th
4116	Dr D Yeomery	37th
710164	Dr TB Webb	37th

M M's

CONFIDENTIAL

Register No. 72
Part No.
Volume No. 5

WAR DIARY

of

27th Brigade Royal Field Artillery

for the month of

6%/1919

[signature] Capr
for   Lieut-Colonel

Cmdg. 27th Brigade R.F.A.

Army Form C. 2118.

WAR DIARY
or
INTELLIGENCE SUMMARY.

(Erase heading not required.)

December 1918
Aut 57. 1/40000

Instructions regarding War Diaries and Intelligence Summaries are contained in F. S. Regs., Part II. and the Staff Manual respectively. Title pages will be prepared in manuscript.

Place	Date	Hour	Summary of Events and Information	Remarks and references to Appendices
LOUVIGNIES	1st		A Church Service was held in the Brigade Recreation Room	
"	2nd		Lt. C.H. Bitton joined the Brigade and was posted to the 12nd Battery	
"	3rd 4th 5th		Nothing of any special importance occurred	
	6th		Col Dute DSO went to D.A., the Hounds having gone a chase. The thirty sports, the East-Jersey's concert party came and for a two shows, one at 5pm, one at 7pm. Major Moon (149) took Command of the Brigade, in the absence of the Colonel.	
	7th 8th 9th 10th		158th Bde R.F.A Point to Point meeting	

[signature] Capt.
Adjt 57 Bde RFA

Army Form C. 2118.

WAR DIARY
or
INTELLIGENCE SUMMARY.
(Erase heading not required.)

December 1918
Sheet 57

Place	Date	Hour	Summary of Events and Information	Remarks and references to Appendices
LOUVIGNIES	18.11		Lieut S.H. Marks posted to 37 H Bty 2/A on joining the Brigade.	
"	12.11			
"	13.11		The Brigade left LOUVIGNIES at 10.10 am and marched to BAVISTAIN just South of BAVAY, good billets	
"	14.11		Marched to FEIGNIES	
"	15.11		Marched to MAUBERGE only a 6 mile march	
"	16.11		Marched to ESTINNE-AU-MONT, into civilization again - electric light and tramways	
"	17.11		No march. Major N.A. Hutchinson DSO rejoined from leave.	

Capt 25 D Bn R.F.A

Army Form C. 2118.

WAR DIARY
or
INTELLIGENCE SUMMARY.

(Erase heading not required.)

Map — BRUSSELS 1/100,000

Decem. 1918

Place	Date	Hour	Summary of Events and Information	Remarks and references to Appendices
	18th		Marched to HOUDENG-GOEGNIES. Excellent billets, but a very wet and cold march.	
	19th		Marched to SENEFFE.	
	20th		Marched to LONGSEE. Very cold and rained the whole march. Very bad billets.	
	21st		No march.	
	22nd		Marched to find are HQ — VINCINETTE CHATEAU. 37th — BOSSIERES 10th — BOTHY 11th — MAZY 12th — ISNES. Billets on the whole are fairly good but not so good as was expected. No room in VINCINETTE Chateau for the men. Rapid put-in-action billets in MAZY. 120 & 85 are very comfortable; 119th and 120th fairly comfortable but very crowded; 37th Bty uncomfortable. All the villages except ISNES have electric light. Offrs. mess trouble all divisn. were got with cart and a large percentage of the men have got bedsincept in BOSSIERES.	

Army Form C. 2118.

WAR DIARY
or
INTELLIGENCE SUMMARY.
(Erase heading not required.)

Army: GHQ – BRUSSELS 1/12000

Month and year: December 1918

Instructions regarding War Diaries and Intelligence Summaries are contained in F.S. Regs., Part II. and the Staff Manual respectively. Title pages will be prepared in manuscript.

Place	Date	Hour	Summary of Events and Information	Remarks and references to Appendices
MARTINETTE	2/12		It was impossible to give the men a really good Christmas dinner owing to the late arrival of supplies etc. owing to lack of railway trucks and the state of the permanent way. Field Cooking spent about 10 days in Paris trying to get Christmas fare that was only able to get Rum and a few extras owing to transport difficulties, & has to pay exorbitant prices for any local produce. It's not all over. So there existed dinner very imperfectly got up to a very good standard with the civilians.	
	3/12		A list of awards since December 1st is attached.	

[signature]
Capt ?? M.Gen CRA

Honours and Awards during November - December, 1918. - 7-11-1919.

47221	Corpl.	H.I.REYNOLDS	37th.Bty.	M.M.
20440	Dvr.	E.SNAITH.	do	M.M.
41116	Dvr.	D.TOOMEY.	do	M.M.
710164	Dvr.	T.B.HOLT.	do	M.M.
120483	Bdr.	D.J.RAINGER.	do	M.M.
77077	Gnr.	P.FITZPATRICK.	do	M.M.
	Lieut.	G.W.MORRIS.	do	Mention.
74233	Bdr.	W.ALEXANDER.	119th.Bty.	M.M.
64053	Dvr.	A.GOODHAND.	do	M.M.
830783	Gnr.	H.PHEASY.	do	M.M.
5265	Pte. (A/Sgt)	J.WARDER. (A.V.C.)		M.M.
42323	Bdr. (A/Cpl)	E.R.HALL.	do	M.M.
173367	aBdr.	A.H.ABBOTT.	120th.Bty.	M.M.
3498	Sgt.	G.LAY.	do	M.M.
73626	Bdr.	E.McCORMACK.	do	M.M.
69965	Dvr.	H.S.COX.	do	M.M.
	Major	N.R.HUTTENBACH.	do	Mention.
33892	Far.Sgt.	H.ROBERTS.	do	Mention.
6568	Gnr.	F.KIRKPATRICK.	121st.Bty.	M.M.
99757	Gnr.	F.GRAINGER.	do	M.M.
105276	Gnr.	A.M.LEPTS.	do	M.M.
171003	Gnr.	J.PATTERSON.	do	M.M.
102960	Dvr.	S.G.JAMES.	do	M.M.
64840	Cpl.(A.SGT)	C.TOZER.	do	M.M.
76728	Cpl.	W.E.CORNELIOUS.	do	M.M.
65199	Dvr.	W.J.PORTER.	do	M.M.
67771	Gnr.	A.C.GORDON.	do	M.M.
8166	L.Bdr.	G.SHAW.	do	M.M.
170631	Ftr.	F.HOLFORD.	do	M.M.
60182	Sgt.	P.POOLE.	do	M.M.
200437	Dnr.	G.TAYLOR.	do	Mention.

---------------- xxx ------------------

WAR DIARY
INTELLIGENCE SUMMARY

Army Form C. 2118.

Place	Date	Hour	Summary of Events and Information	Remarks and references to Appendices
Hargicourt			Honours and awards for the month of Jan.	
	1.1.19		Capt Morris (57th) M.C. mentioned 2nd Lt Thirsk (120th) M.C. No 279153 Com Sgt Ethersdge (114th) D.C.M. No 200437 Pte J. Taylor 12.U.M mentioned Major N.M. Stratton bar D.S.O. M.C (120th) mentioned	
	During		Fm Sgt H. Roberts (120th) mentioned No 47277 Com Sgt Pitson (37th) D.C.M No 40763 Sgt Wilson (37th) D.C.M No 32963 A/Bdr McDonald 114th D.C.M Capt Odlum (A/A) M.C.	
	2.1.19			

J.W. Naylor 2nd Lt RKA

Brig '27 Btte RKA

CONFIDENTIAL

Register No.....................
Part No......813..............
Volume No......6..............

WAR DIARY

of

27th. BRIGADE ROYAL FIELD ARTILLERY

for the month of February, 1919.

for Lieut.- Colonel

1/3/1919.   Commanding 27th. Brigade R.F.A.

Army Form C. 2118.

WAR DIARY
or
INTELLIGENCE SUMMARY.
(Erase heading not required.)

Feb 1919

Instructions regarding War Diaries and Intelligence Summaries are contained in F.S. Regs., Part II. and the Staff Manual respectively. Title pages will be prepared in manuscript.

Place	Date	Hour	Summary of Events and Information	Remarks and references to Appendices
GOUZUNE CHATEAU	1st		At Chorney, 121st Battery, went to be Section of this 5th Don Canteen.	
"	2nd		At Supper, H.Q. went to hospital.	
"	3rd to 5th		Everything very quiet. Heavy snow during the night.	
"	6th		14 men demobilized.	
"	7th		39 men demobilized.	
"	8th		9 men leave for demobilization. Very cold weather set in.	
"	9th		A quiet day.	
"	10th		Major Huttenbach (120th), 2nd Lt Fitz (114th), Capt Megovan (119th) returned 3.50. MC	
"	11th		from leave. Nothing unusual. 9 men from the Brigade demobilized.	
"	12th		Major Huttenbach DSO, MC leaves the Brigade and proceeds to England.	

A.H.H. Triplex
Lt R.F.A.

Army Form C. 2118.

WAR DIARY
or
INTELLIGENCE SUMMARY.
(Erase heading not required.)

Instructions regarding War Diaries and Intelligence Summaries are contained in F. S. Regs., Part II and the Staff Manual respectively. Title pages will be prepared in manuscript.

Place	Date	Hour	Summary of Events and Information	Remarks and references to Appendices
COZINNE CHATEAU	13th		Captain Dhiolies (119th) posto to command the 120th Battery R.F.A.	
"	14th		Colonel White D.S.O. rejoined the Brigade from leave. A day's cleaning party is held at Brigade H.Q.	
"	15th		The Thaw begins to set in	
"	16th		Atony Thaw & firevents off the snow.	
"	17th		Capt. Morison Mc (Mol) and Capt. Odlum Mc (cy) went off to Brussels, and Capt. McGovern Mc came to H.Q. to do adjutant.	
"	18th		A football match was played against the 72nd Bde R.F.A. at the 120th Battery's ground at M.23. Ending in a draw, 1 all. 2nd Lt Anderson, 2nd Lt Jenson Mc returned from leave.	
"	19th		2nd Lt H.W. Richards (87th) leaves for demobilization. 250 horses leave the Brigade	

John Fisher
Lt R.F.A.

Army Form C. 2118.

WAR DIARY
or
INTELLIGENCE SUMMARY.
(Erase heading not required.)

Instructions regarding War Diaries and Intelligence Summaries are contained in F. S. Regs., Part II. and the Staff Manual respectively. Title pages will be prepared in manuscript.

Place	Date	Hour	Summary of Events and Information	Remarks and references to Appendices
COLZINNE CHATEAU.	20th		2nd Lt Lockhead MC (120th) rejoins the Brigade from leave.	
"	21st		Captain Morison MC (116) leaves the Brigade for demobilization.	
"	22nd–24th		At Seneffe. Went on leave.	
"	25th		Very very quiet.	
"	26th		A football match against the 72nd Bde R.F.A., on their ground at Seneffe. Ending in a win for them 4–2 3–2.	
"	27th		Col White DSO and Capt Odlum MC leave for Brussels.	
"	28th		Nothing unusual.	

AW Ryan
Lt R.F.A.

Jan - Mar

CONFIDENTIAL

Register No..................
Part No........12.............
Volume No......5.............

WAR DIARY

of

27th. BRIGADE ROYAL FIELD ARTILLERY

for the month of

January 1919

2/2/1919.

Capt
for Lieut.-Colonel

Commanding 27th. Brigade R.F.A.

Army Form C. 2118.

Map - Brussels 1/100,000

WAR DIARY
or
INTELLIGENCE SUMMARY.
(Erase heading not required.)

Jan 1916.

Instructions regarding War Diaries and Intelligence Summaries are contained in F. S. Regs., Part II. and the Staff Manual respectively. Title pages will be prepared in manuscript.

Place	Date	Hour	Summary of Events and Information	Remarks and references to Appendices
VICHMETTE CHAPEL	1st		Demobilization started. 15 men sent away	
"	2nd		2nd line not wanted to MC. Nothing of importance happened.	
"	3rd			
"	4th			
"	5th			
"	6th		Colonel White D.S.O sent a Cross. Captain Odlum (a/s) awarded the M.C.	
"	7th			
"	8th		Captain Marion (b/o) received the MC	
"	9th		Nothing unusual occurred.	
"	10th			

Army Form C. 2118.

WAR DIARY
or
INTELLIGENCE SUMMARY.

(Erase heading not required.)

Instructions regarding War Diaries and Intelligence Summaries are contained in F. S. Regs., Part II. and the Staff Manual respectively. Title pages will be prepared in manuscript.

Place	Date	Hour	Summary of Events and Information	Remarks and references to Appendices
VIGNIETTE CHATEAU.	11th	11 a.m.	demobilized.	
	12th	6 a.m.	left for demobilization	
	13th			
	14th	16 men demobilized		
	15th		2nd all ranks rejoined the Bn. from leave.	
	16th			
	17th			
	18th		Rugby football match against the 72nd Bn RFA on the 105th Battery's ground at MAZY ending in a win for team in draw for 72nd Bn RFA on their ground at SOMBREFF ending in a draw.	
	19th		Lts Shortis, Rector, Charlton demobilized also 45 men.	

WAR DIARY
or
INTELLIGENCE SUMMARY.

Army Form C. 2118.

Place	Date	Hour	Summary of Events and Information	Remarks and references to Appendices
BOSSIERE	20			
	21st		HQ moved to GOEZINNE Chateau, the property of the Baron De Vynck.	
	22nd			
	23rd		Eisd Battery war offered a motor lorry to go and visit the Battle field of Waterloo 24 men demobilized.	
	24th		120th Battery gave a dance at their Chateau at MN33 Lt Anderson (119th) Dept of Issue. Conducting the arrngmt for demobilization. 25 men demobilized.	
	25th		B 11 men	

Army Form C. 2118.

WAR DIARY
or
INTELLIGENCE SUMMARY.
(Erase heading not required.)

Map BRUSSELS 1/100,000

Instructions regarding War Diaries and Intelligence Summaries are contained in F. S. Regs., Part II and the Staff Manual respectively. Title pages will be prepared in manuscript.

Place	Date	Hour	Summary of Events and Information	Remarks and references to Appendices
BOUSSIÈRE	26th		2nd Lt Lockhead met out on leave.	
"	27th		8 men for demobilisation. Frost and ice set in	
"	28th		7 men for demobilisation. Lieut. P. H. Channing rejoined 121st & 05 RFA from leave	
"	29th		Capt. G.W. Groves rejoined 37th & 05 RFA from R.A. courses in U.K.	
"	30th			
"	31st			

Dobson Capt
for Lt Col
Cmdg 37 HowBde RFA

CONFIDENTIAL

Register No.
Part No.
Volume No. 6

WAR DIARY

of the

27th Brigade Royal Field Artillery

for the month of

March 1919

3758

2/4/19

Capt
for
Lieut-Colonel

Commanding 27th Brigade R.F.A.

WAR DIARY Map- Belgium - Namur   Army Form C. 2118.
or
INTELLIGENCE SUMMARY.   March 1919

(Erase heading not required.)

Instructions regarding War Diaries and Intelligence
Summaries are contained in F. S. Regs, Part II.
and the Staff Manual respectively. Title pages
will be prepared in manuscript.

Place	Date	Hour	Summary of Events and Information	Remarks and references to Appendices
GODINNE Chateau	1st	9am	As usual	
	2nd	9am		
SPY-MAZY	3rd	"		
	4th	"	Major M.P. Evans rejoined 371 Bty RFA from Xth course at WAVRE.	
"	5th	"		
"	6th	"	Major L.J. Browne to hospital sick	
"	7th	"	Brig General Geddes inspects the horses of the Brigade	
"	8th	"		
"	9th	"	Concert by the R.A. Band at SOMBREFFE	
"	10th	"		
"	11th	"	S.A. Dinner dance in Brussels	
	12th 13th 14th			

Bollum Capt
adjt 85 Bde RFA

WAR DIARY
or
INTELLIGENCE SUMMARY.
(Erase heading not required.)

Army Form C. 2118.

Map — Belgium — Namur

March 1919

Place	Date	Hour	Summary of Events and Information	Remarks and references to Appendices
GOZINNES Station	15th	8 am	The troops marched to CIWY (near CHARLEROI) arriving there about 3.0 P.M. It was a long march and tiring owing to all the vehicles being already been taken to Charleroi. CIWY is in the coal-mining area and very bad for billetting especially for units B with horses. Most of our horse-lines were on the slieth	
"	"	8 am	150 horses went to GFM BIOUL for sale to the Belgians.	
CIWY	16th			
"	17th		—	
"	18th		Lieut. J. Demaine and Lieut. E.R. Munn with 50 men with	
"	19th		off by march route for posting to the 2nd Army (Rhine) Lieut. & H.K. Gapon ? Lieut R.N. Forehead and 50 men, with 157 Bde	
"	20th	"	RFA mules left for 2nd Army (Rhine)	

J.B. Ellum Capt
Capt. 87 H. Bde RFA

WAR DIARY or INTELLIGENCE SUMMARY

Army Form C. 2118.

Map Belgium - Namur

March 1919.

Place	Date	Hour	Summary of Events and Information	Remarks and references to Appendices
GILLY	9/3	9am to 8pm	All men not proceeding home with the Cadre are posted to 15th Reo RFA. The Cadre consists of HQ, Lt Col AKG White J and 12. OR, Capt. W.J. Odlum 37th Bty - Major M.P. Browne J and 63 OR 2/Lt G.H. Woodhams 119th Bty - Major R.H. Pludesley J and 63 OR 2/Lt J. Everest Capt J.A.W. McGovern Capt R.H. Lewis J and 63 OR 2/Lt O.J.H. Lawson 121st Bty - Capt. W.J. Morris J and 63 OR Lt R.G. Anderson HQ, 37th Bty and 121st Bty started entraining at Charleroi at 10.0am and left in one train at 7.0pm. All vehicles and equipment accompany the Cadre. 119th Bty and 120th Bty are due to leave on 23rd. Brig Genl A.H. Hussey, his staff and the SA Officers came to the station to see us off and say good-bye.	B/McVeagh Capt Adjt 37th Bde RFA

(46340) Wt W3500/P713 750,000 3/18 — 2688 Forms/C2118/16. D. D. & L. London, E.C.

Army Form C. 2118.

WAR DIARY
or
INTELLIGENCE SUMMARY.
(Erase heading not required.)

Map Belgium - Namur
March 1919

Instructions regarding War Diaries and Intelligence Summaries are contained in F. S. Regs., Part II. and the Staff Manual respectively. Title pages will be prepared in manuscript.

Place	Date	Hour	Summary of Events and Information	Remarks and references to Appendices
ANTWERP	9th Feb	8:00 am	Reached Antwerp at 6:00am (22nd) after a very cold journey - there was only one good coach on the train. We went up to the Bosphor Camp, until our guide died. In the docks we were uncomfortable, everything prepared for us. 9:0 am excellent sent about everything given us for the journey by the kitchen of the boat. All the men were given passes to Antwerp church.	
"	23rd			
"	24th		HQ, 27th Bde, (21st Div), 11th Bde RFA (Col. Drew) and 3 R.H.A. batteries left in the Sicilian at 4:30 p.m. everyone very comfortable on board. We hear that 110th and 120th Bdes was held up at Calais as the authorities were afraid of a strike in England. However we followed no later. We anchored during the night near the mouth of a fine day, but a little windy. The Scheldt seems to hear of mines.	
"	25th			
"	26th		Arrived at Southampton at 11:00 am but did not leave until 8:0 p.m owing to all the stores and vehicles being terribly mixed on the boat and taking a long time to be disembarked. The arrangements at Southampton for the embark of the men was excellent. We arrived at AMESBURY at 6:0 pm and had tea that was excellent. 2d 3d Reserve Brigade, who was only tea this afternoon that we were sent down all the teams that arrived Woolworth, was at fully prepared for us. They sent down all the team that they could to bring up our vehicles to LARKHILL, where we had to walk (5 miles).	

D.D. & L. London, E.C.
(59340) W1 W5500/P713 750,000 3/18 D & L 1588 Forms/C2118/10.

sgd. 27th Bn RFA

Army Form C. 2118.

WAR DIARY
or
INTELLIGENCE SUMMARY.
(Erase heading not required.)

Instructions regarding War Diaries and Intelligence Summaries are contained in F. S. Regs., Part II. and the Staff Manual respectively. Title pages will be prepared in manuscript.

Place	Date	Hour	Summary of Events and Information	Remarks and references to Appendices
LARKHILL	3/8		119 & 120 H.A.G. are attached to 14th Reserve Bty. 37th Bde & allotted to 15th Reserve B.G. Also seem to get been named when 119 & 120 H.A.Bty will arrive.	
LARKHILL	28/8 31/8		119th and 120th H.A. Bty RFA reached Larkhill Camp at 11.30 PM to-day. They left Charleroi on the 26th, left Antwerp on the 28th (5.0 PM) and reached Southampton about 10.0 am 31st. They came out in a very small and crowded boat and had a rather uncomfortable journey. On the way the weapons and equipment sets moved up on the boat all units lost a considerable quantity of their equipment on its journey.	

B. D. & L., London, E.C.
(6030) Wt W5300/P713 750,000 3/18 c.1688 Forms/C2118/16.

B. Allen Capt.
L.H.A.C.
Comg 27 H.A. Bde RFA

FINIS

www.ingramcontent.com/pod-product-compliance
Lightning Source LLC
Chambersburg PA
CBHW080236250426
43670CB00043BA/2563